Program Evaluation and Family Violence Research

Program Evaluation and Family Violence Research has been co-published simultaneously as *Journal of Aggression, Maltreatment & Trauma*, Volume 4, Number 1 (#7) 2000.

T0386137

Program Evaluation and Family Violence Research

Sally K. Ward, PhD
David Finkelhor, PhD
Editors

Program Evaluation and Family Violence Research has been co-published simultaneously as *Journal of Aggression, Maltreatment & Trauma*, Volume 4, Number 1 (#7) 2000.

Routledge
Taylor & Francis Group
New York   London

First published 2000 by
The Haworth Maltreatment & Trauma Press®, 10 Alice Street, Binghamton, NY 13904-1580
USA

This edition published 2013 by Routledge
711 Third Avenue, New York, NY 10017
2 Park Square, Milton Park, Abingdon, Oxon, OX14 4RN

Routledge is an imprint of the Taylor & Francis Group, an informa business

Program Evaluation and Family Violence Research has been co-published simultaneously as *Journal of Aggression, Maltreatment & Trauma* ™, Volume 4, Number 1 (#7) 2000.

The development, preparation, and publication of this work has been undertaken with great care. However, the publisher, employees, editors, and agents of The Haworth Press and all imprints of The Haworth Press, Inc., including The Haworth Medical Press® and Pharmaceutical Products Press®, are not responsible for any errors contained herein or for consequences that may ensue from use of materials or information contained in this work. Opinions expressed by the author(s) are not necessarily those of The Haworth Press, Inc.

Cover design by Thomas J. Mayshock Jr.

Library of Congress Cataloging-in-Publication Data

Program evaluation and family violence research / Sally K. Ward, David Finkelhor, editors.
    p. cm.
    "Co-published simultaneously as Journal of aggression, maltreatment & trauma, volume 4, number 1 (#7) 2000."
    Includes bibliographical references and index.
    ISBN 0-7890-1184-0 (alk. paper)–ISBN 0-7890-1185-9 (alk. paper)
    1. Family violence. 2. Family violence–Treatment–Evaluation. I. Ward, Sally K. II. Finkelhor, David. III. Journal of aggression, maltreatment & trauma.
HV6626 .P76 2000
362.82′92–dc21
                                        00-058208

Program Evaluation and Family Violence Research

CONTENTS

OUTCOMES RESEARCH

EVALUATING INTERVENTIONS IN SPECIFIC INSTITUTIONAL SETTINGS

COLLABORATION AND ACTIVIST ISSUES

ETHICAL ISSUES IN EVALUATING INTERVENTIONS

ABOUT THE EDITORS

Sally K. Ward received her PhD in Sociology from Brown University in 1977. She has been a faculty member at the University of New Hampshire since 1980. She teaches courses in research methodology, urban sociology, social policy, evaluation research, and applied sociology. Her current basic research interests include an analysis of out-of-wedlock childbearing in the U.S.–a longitudinal analysis of trends and correlates of this type of family formation; an analysis of income inequality in large urban communities; and a study of community response to economic decline. She is generally interested in how larger social forces affect local communities. Her applied work includes an evaluation of the Whole Village Family Resource Center in Plymouth, NH; and an evaluation of the International Research Opportunities Program at University of New Hampshire.

David Finkelhor, PhD, is Co-Director of the Family Research Laboratory and Professor of Sociology at the University of New Hampshire. He has been studying the problems of child victimization, child maltreatment and family violence since 1977. He is well known for his conceptual and empirical work on the problem of child sexual abuse, reflected in publications such as *Sourcebook on Child Sexual Abuse* (Sage, 1986) and *Nursery Crimes* (Sage, 1988). He has also written about child homicide, missing and abducted children, children exposed to domestic and peer violence and other forms of family violence. In his recent work, he has tried to unify and integrate knowledge about all the diverse forms of child victimization in a field he has termed Developmental Victimology. He is editor and author of 10 books and over 75 journal articles and book chapters. He has received grants from the National Institute of Mental Health, the National Center on Child Abuse and Neglect, the US Department of Justice, and a variety of other sources. In 1994, he was given the Distinguished Child Abuse Professional Award by the American Professional Society on the Abuse of Children.

ABOUT THE CONTRIBUTORS

Bruce Ambuel, PhD, is Associate Professor of Family and Community Medicine at the Medical College of Wisconsin, Milwaukee, and Director of Behavioral Science at the Waukesha Family Practice Residency Program. For the past nine years, Dr. Ambuel has worked to develop community-based collaborative training and intervention programs for medical students, residents and practicing health care professionals. He developed the Family Peace Project, an award-winning and innovative model program for training health care professionals and trainees to identify and help victims of partner violence in medical settings.

Sue Boney-McCoy, PhD, is Assistant Professor of Psychology at Eastern Connecticut State University. Her research interests include child abuse, sexual revictimization, relationship violence, sexual harassment, violence measurement issues and risky health behavior.

Rosemary Chalk, BA, is a senior program officer within the Institute of Medicine, part of the National Academies organization in Washington, DC. Ms. Chalk joined the IOM staff in 1989 and has directed several studies on family violence during the past decade. She has published in the area of misconduct in science, research ethics, the use of science in public decision-making, and public participation in science. Ms. Chalk received a BA in political science from the University of Cincinnati and was a graduate student in the science and public policy program of the George Washington University.

Deborah Daro, PhD, is Research Fellow, Chapin Hall Center for Children at the University of Chicago. With over 20 years of experience in evaluating child abuse treatment and prevention programs, she has directed some of the largest multi-site program evaluations completed in the field. Dr. Daro holds a PhD in Social Welfare and a master's degree in City and Regional Planning from the University of California at Berkeley.

Barbara Fallon, MSW, is currently Co-Manager of the Canadian Incidence Study of Reported Child Abuse and Neglect, and Project Manager for the Client Outcomes in the Child Welfare Project. She is a PhD candidate at the Faculty of Social Work, University of Toronto. Ms. Fallon has extensive experience in conducting research focusing primarily on women and children and has published in the areas of child maltreatment, child health and outcome measurement.

Joel H. Garner, PhD, is Research Director at the Joint Centers for Justice, Inc. Between 1974 and 1990 Dr. Garner served as a program manager at the National Institute of Justice and between 1990 and 1992 served as Research Director at the U.S. Sentencing Commission. Dr. Garner is currently working on an NIJ sponsored study that is measuring the use of force by police in Montgomery County, MD, and a study assessing the potential impact of the Oklahoma Truth-in-Sentencing Legislation.

Richard J. Gelles, PhD, holds The Joanne and Raymond Welsh Chair of Child Welfare and Family Violence in the School of Social Work at the University of Pennsylvania. He is the author or coauthor of 23 books and more than 100 articles and chapters on family violence. Dr. Gelles received his BA degree from Bates College (1968), an MA in Sociology from the University of Rochester (1971), and a PhD in Sociology at the University of New Hampshire (1973).

Edward W. Gondolf, EdD, MPH, is Associate Director of Research for the Mid-Atlantic Addiction Training Institute (MAATI), where he conducts externally-funded research on the response of the courts, mental health practitioners, alcohol treatment clinicians, and batterer treatment programs to domestic violence. He is also Professor of Sociology at Indiana University of Pennsylvania (IUP). Dr. Gondolf is the author of several books on domestic violence.

Sandra Graham-Bermann, PhD, is Associate Professor of Psychology and Co-Director of the Interdisciplinary Research Program on Violence at the University of Michigan. Her research on the impact of family violence on children's social and emotional adjustment includes studies of children in shelters, in the community, in schools, and in clinical populations. As clinical psychologist and researcher she has been consultant to the Department of Justice, as well as to local shelters, nursery schools, and community programs.

L. Kevin Hamberger, PhD, is Professor of Family and Community Medicine at the Medical College of Wisconsin, Milwaukee, WI, and Director of Behavioral Science at the Racine Family Practice Residency Program. For the past 16 years, he has conducted programs of treatment and research with victims and perpetrators of partner violence. His research interests include characteristics and treatment of abusive men, gender-based motivations for perpetrating partner violence, and identification and intervention with partner violence victims in medical settings.

David Kolko, PhD, is Associate Professor of Child Psychiatry and Psychology at the University of Pittsburgh Medical Center. At Western Psychiatric Institute and Clinic, he directs the Special Services, a treatment research program for youth referred by the Juvenile Court. He is currently involved in a study to evaluate services for juvenile sexual abusers (*PCCD*) and a clinical trial examining the effectiveness of multimodal treatments for young children with disruptive disorders (*NIMH*). He is serving a second term on the Board of Directors of the American Professional Society on the Abuse of Children and is Co-Chair of its Research Committee. His primary clinical-research interests involve the evaluation of treatments directed towards child antisocial behavior, including firesetting, adolescent sexual offending, and child physical abuse/family violence.

Bruce MacLaurin, MSW, has worked as a manager, program evaluator, and researcher for mental health and child welfare services in nonprofit agencies in Ontario and Alberta. He is currently a PhD candidate at the Faculty of Social Work of the University of Toronto, and is employed as Research Associate with the Bell Canada Child Welfare Research Unit. His current research interests are related to child welfare effectiveness, foster care services, and street youth and he has published several journal articles and book chapters on these topics.

Christopher D. Maxwell, PhD, is Assistant Professor in the School of Criminal Justice at Michigan State University. Dr. Maxwell was previously at the University of Michigan and is a graduate of Rutgers University (MA, 1994, PhD, 1998). His research interests include the social control and criminal justice processing of intimate violence and hate-motivated crimes, the efficacy of aggression and delinquency prevention programs, and the impact of social and ecological contexts on patterns of delinquency, crime, and criminal justice decision-making.

Anna-Lee Pittman, MA, is Project Manager for the Youth Relationships Project and is responsible for the coordination and implementation of this program in various communities. She has a Masters degree in Library and Information Science. She is also the author of several papers and chapters about the YRP program and co-author of the *Youth Relationships Manual* (Sage, 1996).

David B. Sugarman, PhD, is Professor of Psychology at Rhode Island College. Although he has conducted research on a variety of domestic violence issues, his primary research interests focus on the risk factors associated with marital and dating violence. He has been a major proponent of the application of meta-analytic techniques to family violence research.

Nico Trocmé, PhD, is Director of the Bell Canada Child Welfare Research Unit, a founding member of the Center for Applied Social Research at the Faculty of Social Work, and Research Affiliate with the Center for Studies of Children at Risk, McMaster University. Dr. Trocmé has played an active role in reviews of child welfare policy and services in Ontario.

Christine Wekerle, PhD, is Associate Professor in the Department of Psychology at York University, Toronto, Ontario. She is a member of clinical (adult) and clinical-developmental (child & family) graduate programs and is currently on a research leave (New Investigator Fellowship, Ontario Mental Health Foundation). Dr. Wekerle has published in the areas of dysfunctional parenting, child abuse and its prevention, in addition to adolescent dating violence and prevention programming.

David A. Wolfe, PhD (University of South Florida), is Professor of Psychology and Psychiatry at the University of Western Ontario in London, Ontario, Canada. He is a founding member of the Centre for Research on Violence Against Women and Children at the University, and past President of Division 37 (Child, Youth and Family Services) of the American Psychological Association. David has broad research and clinical interests in abnormal child psychology, with a special focus on child abuse, domestic violence, and developmental psychopathology.

INTRODUCTION

Program Evaluation
and Family Violence Research

Sally K. Ward
David Finkelhor

This volume grew out of a conference, the Program Evaluation and Family Violence Research Conference, held by the Family Research Laboratory (FRL) at the University of New Hampshire in July, 1998. It was one of a continuing series of family violence research conferences sponsored by the FRL since 1981 to facilitate the growth of the field and advance the family violence research agenda.

The first family violence research conference in 1981 was nearly devoid of evaluation research with one notable exception. Larry Sherman presented findings from the Minneapolis police experiment about batterer arrest policies at a session that was dramatic and controversial in a number of respects. One element of the drama for some was accommodating to the idea that family violence interventions, which

Address correspondence to: Sally K. Ward, PhD, Department of Sociology, University of New Hampshire, 20 College Road, Durham, NH 03824.

[Haworth co-indexing entry note]: "Program Evaluation and Family Violence Research." Ward, Sally K., and David Finkelhor. Co-published simultaneously in *Journal of Aggression, Maltreatment & Trauma* (The Haworth Maltreatment & Trauma Press, an imprint of The Haworth Press, Inc.) Vol. 4, No. 1 (#7), 2000, pp. 1-6; and: *Program Evaluation and Family Violence Research* (ed: Sally K. Ward, and David Finkelhor) The Haworth Maltreatment & Trauma Press, an imprint of The Haworth Press, Inc., 2000, pp. 1-6. Single or multiple copies of this article are available for a fee from The Haworth Document Delivery Service [1-800-342-9678, 9:00 a.m. - 5:00 p.m. (EST). E-mail address: getinfo@haworthpressinc.com].

1

were so young, so exciting and so emblematic of an only recently accepted public policy interest in this topic, could be subjected to the harsh, cold judgment of scientific evaluation. Fortunately, the findings brought good news (relief), because they almost entirely endorsed the policy preferences of the time. Some of the complex questions about what role evaluation has to play in the family violence field were avoided, until now.

The complex questions are no longer being avoided. The field is different, more mature, more ready to deal with those questions. The papers in this volume are both attempts to confront some of these questions and testimonies to many of those changes. What are some of them?

First, an inevitable social problems transformation has occurred in the family violence field. In the early phases of most social problem advocacies on any problem, much of the science seems to be focused on matters of legitimation. How big is the problem? How accurate (or misleading) are the prevailing stereotypes? How bad are the consequences? Once a social problem establishes a certain level of acceptance and institutionalization, other, more practical problems set in. Advocates become practitioners, practitioners need feedback on their practice, and evaluation becomes a useful tool in this quest. This has happened in the family violence field as social innovations like shelters, and batterer treatment, and child advocacy centers have become institutionalized.

Various aspects of this institutionalization have affected the climate and nature of evaluation research in the field of family violence. Funding streams have been established, diversified and increased in some areas. This has made it possible to consider funding for evaluation, not simply for program maintenance and expansion.

Federal agencies have taken an increased initiative for evaluation. A number of the important evaluation efforts reviewed in papers in this volume had a federal inspiration or contribution, including research on batterer treatment, arrest policy, sexual abuse treatment, and home visitation.

The pool of potential evaluation sites has increased enormously with the dissemination of practice innovations to locales all over the country. Traditional disciplines have also accepted family violence research as a legitimate scholarly concern and have infused family violence with more respectability for potential researchers and practitioners. Thus, district attorneys, judges and police departments may view these practice issues as more important and worthy of the sacrifices necessary for research undertaking. Clinical psychology has come to see sexual abuse or batterer treatment as important subspecialties. Some of this practice has taken root in the kinds of practice settings, such as university clinics, where evaluation may be a more accepted part of the practice environment.

Family violence has also developed stronger roots in the public health field. Adoption of the issue by a recent Surgeon General and then the American Medical Association, consideration of the topic by the National Academy of Science as well as the Centers for Disease Control, has marked a migration of the issue into the more mainstream scientific establishment. Of the various disciplines with involvement in family violence, public health perhaps more than others has a strong tradition of evaluation and clinical trials, which may be helping to promote evaluation research in the field.

All these factors have combined to increase the quantity of evaluation efforts now occurring in the family violence field. The contributions to this volume reflect the experience generated by this work as well as the questions raised.

The field of evaluation research has also undergone significant transformation in recent years. Early work in evaluation emphasized the need for rigorous scientific methods, including randomized control group experiments and quantitative analyses of data from evaluation experiments. While the use of randomized designs is still the gold standard of evaluation, alternative designs have proliferated in the face of implementation strategies that rule out the use of randomly assigned control groups, and as a result of resistance among influential stakeholders to random assignment. Qualitative analyses and multifaceted quasi-experimental designs have become more common in the published literature and in the repertoire of evaluation researchers.

In addition to design developments, evaluation research has grown to ask questions not only about what works but why certain programs or program elements work. In particular, evaluations often incorporate analyses of the theory of change implied by programs that are being evaluated. It is not enough to answer the question about whether a program works–important as that question is. In order to be most useful to program staff and policy makers, research must also identify which aspects of a program have which effects and why. Such questions cannot be answered without a clear understanding of the theory underlying the program development.

In addition to design and theory developments, evaluation research has had to respond to program developments that create very challenging research tasks. A good example is the increasing reliance on comprehensive community initiatives to deal with intractable social problems ranging from childhood poverty to child development to violence. Such efforts hold much promise since they are built on the realistic assumption that social problems do not occur in isolation but rather in a social context that is complex. However, the more comprehensive a social intervention, the more challenging the evaluation on the impact of the intervention. The intervention is multi-faceted, its implementation widespread, and the outcomes are numerous. Finding a no-treatment comparison group is challenging in such a situation, and relying on the gold standard of random assignment is, therefore, very difficult.

The papers in this volume illustrate the state of the art evaluation research in the field of domestic violence interventions. They address the challenges of doing such research in ways that maintain scientific validity and practical utility, and they illustrate the various settings in which domestic violence evaluations have been carried out.

The first paper by Gelles argues that the child welfare system is in crisis, in part because of the lack of evaluation of child welfare interventions, and in part because of the lack of measurable effects for those interventions that have been evaluated. The solutions include more researcher collaboration with program staff, more funds for evaluation research, and greater flexibility in the design and implementation of evaluation studies. Rosemary Chalk, in article 2, reports on the National Research Council study of family violence prevention and treatment services referred to throughout the current volume. This study identified 114 evaluation studies conducted from 1980 to 1996 that were rigorous enough to yield valid information about the impact of interventions in the area of child maltreatment, domestic violence, and elder abuse.

The third article by Sugarman and Boney-McCoy and the fourth by Garner and Maxwell examine, in depth, one of the best examples of the use of randomized experimentation in the evaluation of domestic violence interventions–the Spouse Assault Replication Program. The Sugarman and Boney-McCoy paper is a review of the use of meta-analysis for evaluation research, and it uses as an illustrative example data from the police arrest studies. The Garner and Maxwell paper focuses on the police arrest studies to argue for the importance of randomized experimentation and for the importance of replication in evaluation research.

In article 5, Deb Daro discusses the Healthy Families Initiative and the evaluation of its home visitation component. Healthy Families is one of a number of comprehensive community interventions designed to provide a support system for parents. It is also an example of an intervention that was designed partially on the basis of empirical social science research on child development and child abuse. The results of the research on the impact of Healthy Families are mixed and illustrate the challenges of the interaction between research and practice, and Daro reviews several dimensions of these challenges.

Papers 6 and 7 focus on outcomes research in child welfare. Kolko reviews the research on child sexual and physical abuse. His review makes it clear that the research on child abuse has followed the same general progression as evaluation research in general–from small, single-case studies with limited methodological rigor to large studies with more rigorous and valid designs and analytical strategies. Nico Trocmé and his colleagues review an approach to outcomes research under development in the Canadian child welfare system. The approach is explicitly ecological in nature and comprehensive in its design.

Sandra Graham-Bermann (article 8) reviews research on interventions designed to help children exposed to violence in the home, most of which are school-based programs. She argues for the same kind of research rigor (e.g., pre- and post-test measures, adequate comparison groups, a multiplicity of data sources, etc.) called for in all of the articles of this volume which would advance the knowledge base in this relatively new area of domestic violence research.

The increasingly extensive research on dating violence is reviewed by Pittman, Wolfe, and Wekerle in article 9. As with the research on children exposed to violence in the home, many of the interventions described in this paper are school-based programs. Pittman, Wolfe, and Wekerle identify many of the same methodological issues discussed in other articles, including a pre-post design, random assignment, and follow-up measurements over a period of time. Despite the widespread recognition of the importance of these elements of basic research design, their use in the evaluation of teen violence programs is relatively rare. Those studies reviewed in this paper illustrate the state-of-the-art teen violence intervention research.

The final two articles deal specifically with issues of collaboration between researchers and community advocates, and ethical issues in research on batterers. These are issues that are common in social science research but they are especially salient in research on domestic violence interventions. Community advocates are frequently suspicious of "outsiders" who are called in to conduct research on interventions that the advocates have struggled to create and implement. Hamberger and Ambuel in article 10 identify a number of barriers that make the necessary collaborations difficult and they make specific suggestions for greater success in such collaborations.

Finally, in article 11 Gondolf reviews human subjects issues in research on batterer prevention programs. Some of these issues are common to all research with human subjects, but some are unique to research on violence that puts victims and perpetrators at risk in several ways. He reviews the procedures he has developed for a multi-site evaluation of batterer programs.

Together these papers illustrate both how far evaluation research on domestic violence interventions has come and the remaining barriers to high quality, valid research in this field. This research has followed the path of research in other areas that have been subjected to evaluation studies. The good news is that the research is increasingly rigorous, and while the research is not perfect, we need to increase our efforts to improve the quality. The papers in this volume are an attempt to contribute to that important effort.

OVERVIEWS OF RESEARCH
ON FAMILY VIOLENCE INTERVENTIONS

How Evaluation Research
Can Help Reform and Improve
the Child Welfare System

Richard J. Gelles

SUMMARY. The child welfare system in the United States is in crisis. Despite funding and staffing increasing, and despite legislative changes and reforms, the system still cannot meet the mandate to protect children from harm and assist caregivers and families. This paper argues that one of the key factors limiting the effectiveness of the child welfare system is that the system does not carefully and properly evaluate the interventions and programs that are used to protect children and assist families. The paper reviews the available data from evaluation research on child welfare interventions, speculates on why there is so little evaluation of child welfare interventions, and proposes a tentative solu-

---

Address correspondence to: Richard J. Gelles, PhD, School of Social Work, University of Pennsylvania, Philadelphia, PA 19104 (E-mail: Gelles@ssw.upenn.edu).

[Haworth co-indexing entry note]: "How Evaluation Research Can Help Reform and Improve the Child Welfare System." Gelles, Richard J. Co-published simultaneously in *Journal of Aggression, Maltreatment & Trauma* (The Haworth Maltreatment & Trauma Press, an imprint of The Haworth Press, Inc.) Vol. 4, No. 1 (#7), 2000, pp. 7-28; and: *Program Evaluation and Family Violence Research* (ed: Sally K. Ward, and David Finkelhor) The Haworth Maltreatment & Trauma Press, an imprint of The Haworth Press, Inc., 2000, pp. 7-28. Single or multiple copies of this article are available for a fee from The Haworth Document Delivery Service [1-800-342-9678, 9:00 a.m. - 5:00 p.m. (EST). E-mail address: getinfo@haworthpressinc.com].

7

tion to the paucity of research and the child welfare system crisis. *[Article copies available for a fee from The Haworth Document Delivery Service: 1-800-342-9678. E-mail address: getinfo@haworthpressinc.com <Website: http://www.HaworthPress.com>]*

KEYWORDS. Family, children, violence, interventions, child abuse

The child welfare system in the United States is in crisis. The media are quick to report the repeated failures of the child welfare system to protect children; and, they have many opportunities to report on such failures. As many as half of the children who are killed by parents or caretakers are killed after the children and their families have come to the attention of the child welfare system (Gelles, 1996). Children are also killed in foster care, again while supposedly under the protection and supervision of the child welfare system. As many as 600,000 children, one percent of the population of children under the age of 18 years old, are in foster care on any given day (Tatara, 1993); and of the children in foster care, the majority are placed there because of allegations of abuse and neglect. The average age of children entering the foster care system is younger than a decade ago, and younger children remain in the system longer than do older children (Barth, Courtney, Berrick, & Albert, 1994). Critics of the child welfare system also claim that too many children are removed from their caretakers and placed into out-of-home care (Guggenheim, 1999; Wexler, 1990). Not only are many children removed inappropriately, but these children are also disproportionately African-American or minority children. Thus many critics of the child welfare system view the system as oppressive and destructive to minority families (Roberts, 1999).

A sign of the crisis of child welfare in the United States is that at least 25 state child welfare agencies are presently operating under a court order as a result of lawsuits arising out the various failings of the agencies (Schwartz & Fishman, 1999).

Perhaps the most stinging criticism of the child welfare system was contained in the initial report prepared by the U.S. Advisory Board on Child Abuse and Neglect. The Board declared that child abuse and neglect represented a national emergency. In the Board's words:

> The system the nation has developed to respond to child abuse and neglect is failing. It is not a question of acute failure of a

single element of the system; there is a chronic and critical multiple organ failure. (U.S. Advisory Board on Child Abuse and Neglect, 1990, p. x)

If this medical metaphor was insufficient to make the case, the Board concluded that the child protective system in the United States is so inadequate that the safety of the nation's children cannot be assured (U.S. Advisory Board on Child Abuse and Neglect, 1990, p. x).

If newspaper reports, legal action, and official board reports are not enough evidence, there is one important statistical fact. In the last five years, virtually all forms of violence, homicide, and abuse have declined in the United States. The Uniform Crime Reports indicate that the national rates of homicide and violent crime have decreased (U.S. Department of Justice, 1998). Even the rate of youth violence and youth homicide has decreased. Self-report data collected as part of the National Crime Victims Survey (U.S. Department of Justice, 1998) also show a decrease in rates of violent crime victimization. Domestic violence rates and intimate homicide rates have also decreased nationally since 1994 (Greenfield et al., 1998). Part of the explanation for these decreases may be more effective crime control and interventions. Part of the reason may be that the five years between 1993 and 1998 have been a period of economic advantage, with rising stock market values, low unemployment rates, and low inflation.

The booming economy and apparent effective strategies to control crime and domestic violence have had less of an effect on child maltreatment. Child abuse and neglect reports, approximately 3,000,000 per year, have leveled off (U.S. Department of Health and Human Services, 1996). Reports of sexual abuse have declined; however, there has been no overall decline in the rates of maltreatment comparable to decreases of rates of violent crime. Child fatality numbers have remained steady at around 1,200 per year (National Committee to Prevent Child Abuse, 1998).

By any indicator, as the century closes, the United States child welfare system continues to be unable to assure the safety of children.

WHY THE CRISIS? THE USUAL SUSPECTS

The crisis of child welfare is not new. Child welfare agencies have been under siege for the last three decades. The implementation of mandatory child abuse reporting in the mid to late 1960s resulted in an increase of reports submitted to agencies that were not staffed to handle the increased number of allegations of child maltreatment. In the years after the institution of mandatory reporting, definitions of child abuse and neglect were broadened, resulting in even more reports. Public awareness campaigns generated more reports, and technology, such as toll free telephone lines, made it easier to file reports. Agencies were expected to respond to maltreatment reports quickly. Here again technology, such as pagers and cell phones, created the possibility that reports could be responded to rapidly.

Of course, child welfare agency staffing never kept pace with either the number of reports or the expectation that reports would be investigated quickly. Not only were there too few child welfare workers, in absolute numbers, but the training of the staff was far below the level needed to respond to the complex and difficult nature of child maltreatment reports.

When a tragedy or crisis hits a local, county, or state child welfare agency, the response typically falls under one or more of the "round up the usual suspects" explanations and proposed solutions:

- *More Money.* We have too little money; we need more. Funding for child welfare never kept pace with the rising number of reports and the complexity of child abuse and neglect cases. Thus, child welfare agency administrators are constantly trying to secure sufficient budget allocations to hire and train staff and develop and implement appropriate policies and interventions. To a certain extent, broadened definitions, technology, and public awareness campaigns bolstered the case for more funds by generating more reports, but there has always been a significant gap between resources and caseloads.
- *More Staff.* As funds were always short, so, too, agency administrators argued that they had too few workers to meet the demands of child welfare. When a crisis or tragedy became public, the nearly automatic response was to request an increase in child protective staff. While agencies rarely received what they believed to be adequate staffing, staffing tended to increase following a tragedy or crisis.
- *More Training.* More staff would allow caseloads to be decreased, so that child welfare staff did not have to carry 40 to 60

cases each. In the unusual event that caseloads would meet the desired level of about 15 to 20 cases per worker (Child Welfare League of America, 1993), the child welfare problem was not resolved. New and old child welfare workers often receive only the most minimal pre-service training before they are assigned a caseload. It is not unusual for a child welfare worker to get 20 hours of training before being assigned a full caseload. In-service training is also minimal. Thus, agency workers and directors would often respond to a crisis with a call for new and more training for workers.

- *Blame the Judges and/or the Laws.* The final "usual suspect" is the legal system, or "the judges." Child welfare workers and administrators frequently identify their core constraint as the legal system and action or inaction of the judges. Workers claim the law requires them to make "every possible effort" to keep families together. They also claim that judges ignore caseworkers' recommendations. Legal reform and judicial training is the solution, many child welfare critics claim.

A case can be made for each and all of the above arguments. The child welfare system is understaffed, under-funded, under-trained, and limited by legal constraints and judicial decisions. Yet, each of the above problems has been addressed over the past three decades with little measurable impact. As important as the "usual suspects" are, they do not constitute the real "offender" that causes the child welfare crisis.

THE REAL FAILURES

Clearly, rounding up the usual suspects–funding, staffing, training, the legal system–has not eased the crisis of child welfare. The national emergency and the "multiple organ failure" described nearly a decade ago still exists.

I would propose that the child welfare system's problems arise less from money, staff, and management and more from lack of rigorously evaluated services and interventions. This section examines the "standard" interventions and programs that make up the child welfare system. The following section summarizes what evidence exists for the effectiveness of the standard interventions.

The Standard Interventions

Mandatory Reporting. When Kempe, Silverman, Steele, Droegmueller and Silver (1962) wrote about what they called the "battered child syndrome," a key problem with protecting children was the fact that severe child abuse was either unrecognized or not responded to by the key sentinels–physicians, nurses, and hospital personnel. Kempe himself championed the development of mandatory reporting laws that would require key medical, school, criminal justice, and social service personnel to report suspected cases of child maltreatment to a central authority. In order to encourage reporting, the central authority was to be child welfare agencies. While the police could have been the agency to receive reports, Kempe and others felt that making child abuse a crime would deter mandatory reporters from filing reports, especially reports where there was no clear evidence of an intentional inflicted injury.

The United States Children's Bureau played a pivotal role in developing model child abuse reporting laws (Nelson, 1984). The federal Child Abuse Prevention and Treatment Act of 1974 required states to conform to federal standards, including standards for reporting, in order to receive funds from the newly created National Center for Child Abuse and Neglect. In the space of ten years, mandatory reporting became the cornerstone of the nation's child welfare system.

Investigation. Once a report was received by a state, county, or local child welfare agency, the report would be screened and if the allegation met the screening standards (i.e., the suspected abuse met the state's legal criteria for maltreatment and there was sufficient evidence to initiate an investigation–names, address, etc.), the report would be assigned for investigation.

According to the National Child Abuse and Neglect Data System (U.S. Department of Health and Human Services, 1997), states received 2,025,956 reports of child maltreatment, representing just over 3 million individual child victims. Of the 970,000 child victims for whom maltreatment was indicated or substantiated and for whom there were data on type of maltreatment, 229,332 experienced physical abuse, 500,032 experienced neglect, and 119,397 experienced sexual abuse. From the reports, about 1,625,000 investigations were conducted. A main focus of the investigations was to determine whether the reports were substantiated and required an intervention.

Thirty-four percent of the more than one and one-half million investigations resulted in the report being substantiated or indicated (U.S. Department of Health and Human Services, 1998).

Responses. In theory, at least, the child welfare system has a varied toolbox with which to respond to confirmed or substantiated cases of child maltreatment. In terms of child protection, child welfare agencies have the ability to obtain *ex parte* orders allowing the child welfare department to take the custody and control of endangered children. Child welfare agencies can also petition to have a child's control and custody for a longer period of time. Title IVE of the Social Security Act of 1935 created an open-ended entitlement that provides federal matching funds to states to pay for out-of-home care for dependent children. States are required to match the federal share. In 1996 the federal share of Title IVE was $3 billion (Green Book, 1996).

For nearly the last twenty years, The Adoption Assistance and Child Welfare Act of 1980 (PL 96-272) required states, as a condition of receiving Title IVE funding, to make "reasonable efforts" to keep children with their families, or return them if they have been removed. This law enforces a long tradition of the child welfare system focusing its resources and responses at supporting and preserving families. The resources include hard and soft services. Hard services include housekeeping assistance, parenting classes, medical help, day care, and even housing. Soft services include case management, advocacy, therapy, and counseling.

Sensitive about the number of children in out-of-home care and the cost, many states implemented Intensive Family Preservation Services in the late 1970s and through the 1980s and 1990s.

Intensive Family Preservation Services were designed to be an alternative to the "business as usual" attempts at providing families resources and services. In the Intensive Family Preservation Services model, the essential service is short-term crisis intervention designed to prevent the placement of a child outside of the home. The core goal is to maintain the child safely in the home or facilitate a safe and lasting reunification. Services are meant to be provided in the client's home. The number of sessions is variable, but unlike traditional services, intensive services are available seven days a week, 24 hours a day. The length of the service is brief, typically fixed at a certain number of weeks. Caseworkers are able to deliver intensive services because they carry small caseloads, often as few as two or three cases.

The actual services delivered may be the same as the traditional child welfare services, but their delivery and intensity is different.

Of note is how few families who come to the attention of the child welfare system actually receive any services. One study of 169 investigations found that 59.7 percent of substantiated cases were offered no services other than placement (Meddin & Hansen, 1985). For those cases that were offered some kind of services, 13 percent received placement and 11 percent counseling (Meddin & Hansen, 1985). A second study found that 56 percent of all indicated cases were closed on the same day they were officially substantiated (Salovitz & Keys, 1988). While closing a case on the same day it is substantiated does not necessarily mean no services were offered or delivered, it does mean that no follow-up or monitoring took place after the case was substantiated and services were offered and/or provided.

Summary. In summary, the standard interventions or the typical "tool box" of the child welfare system consist of: (1) An investigation; (2) Some form of counseling or tangible services; and, (3) Placement of a child with monitoring and services.

This seems like a relatively limited toolbox, but the range and depth of the standard intervention is of less concern than how well the existing tools work to protect children and assist families.

THE EVALUATION DATA

It is not a surprise that efforts to respond to, prevent, and treat child maltreatment advanced at a much faster pace than efforts to evaluate the positive and negative effects of both the standard and innovative responses to the problems of child maltreatment. Once it was clear that the abuse and neglect of children were far more extensive than commonly believed, activities to treat and prevent the problem expanded rapidly. In addition, newly implemented, innovative interventions are not good candidates for scientific evaluations (National Research Council, 1998). Innovative programs often begin with a common sense or discipline-based notion of how to respond, and the response changes and is modified based on the experience and feedback of those involved in delivering and managing the intervention. Sometimes a single approach is changed, modified, and altered; other times a multi-pronged effort may add or delete components. Programs and interventions require an opportunity to evolve and mature before they can be properly evaluated. Maturity is important for three reasons. First, the often-amorphous nature of an innovative treatment may result in a "black box" evaluation, whereby the so-called "treatment" cannot be defined or categorized. Thus, even if the evaluation demonstrates that the "treatment works," it may not be clear what exactly the "treatment" was. Second, the time needed to "ramp up" the program may mean that in the early stages, the program offers a smaller "dose" of the ideal intervention and/or the program may not be delivering the actual intervention as planned to all clients. An evaluation in an early stage may fail to find effectiveness of the new program, not because the program is ineffective, but because the program is not yet being delivered as designed. Finally, innovative programs often begin with small staffs and small caseloads. The initial dose of the treatment may be quite minimal. Small sample sizes and low dosages may result in falsely accepting the null hypothesis (that the program has no significant effects).

Evaluation Studies

Notwithstanding all of the above caveats, it is surprising that almost forty years after the modern discovery of the problem of child maltreatment there are so few sound studies of the effectiveness of efforts to prevent and treat child maltreatment.

In 1994, the National Academy of Sciences established the Committee on the Assessment of Family Violence Interventions. One of the five charges to the Committee was to:

> Characterize what is known about both prevention efforts and specific interventions dealing with family violence, including an assessment of what has been learned about the strengths and limitations of each approach. . . . (National Research Council, 1998, p. 17)

After many debates, the Committee chose the following criteria to use when selecting evaluation studies for detailed analysis to meet the above charge:

1. The evaluation involved a program intervention that was designed to treat or prevent some aspect of child maltreatment, domestic violence, or elder abuse.

2. The evaluation was conducted between 1980 and 1996.
3. The evaluation used an experimental design or quasi-experimental design and included measurement tools and outcomes related to family violence; and
4. The evaluation included a comparison group as part of the study design (National Research Council, 1998, p. 21).

While appropriate standards of evidence for evaluation research, these criteria, especially criteria 2 and 4, were far below the "Gold Standard" for evaluation research, in that the criteria did not require that groups be randomly assigned.

For the period 1980 to 1996, the Committee's staff was able to identify a total of 114 evaluation studies that met the above four criteria. The search included published and unpublished studies, although the majority of the 114 studies had been published.

Of the 114 studies, 78 evaluated some aspect of the prevention and treatment of child maltreatment. Fifty studies evaluated social service interventions, four studies evaluated legal interventions, and 24 studies evaluated health care interventions.

While obvious, it is worth noting that the forty-year effort to prevent and treat the maltreatment of children yields only 78 studies that met rather minimum design standards for evaluation research.

The explanation for the paucity of evaluation research can no longer be blamed on the newness of the enterprise, as efforts to prevent and treat child abuse are at least 40, if not 200, years old. The justification is not lack of funds, given that in 1996 the federal and state governments spent nearly $10 billion on efforts to treat child maltreatment (Child Welfare League of America, 1999).

The Interventions Evaluated

In the "social service category" the programs evaluated included child-parent enrichment programs, parent training, network support services, home helpers, school-based sexual abuse prevention, intensive family preservation services, child placement services, and home health visitors. "Legal interventions" evaluated included: court-mandated treatment for child abuse offenders, court mandated treatment emphasizing child management skills, and in-patient treatment for sex offenders. Evaluations of "health care interventions" included: an identification protocol for high-risk mothers, mental health services for child victims, and home health visitor/family support programs. The largest number of evaluations was of school-based sexual abuse prevention programs and intensive family preservation programs.

Noteworthy in this summary is that almost all of the interventions or programs that were evaluated were innovative programs that were alternatives to the standard package of interventions and programs offered by child welfare systems. Interventions that were not evaluated using scientifically appropriate designs included mandatory reporting, investigations, and foster care, kinship care and other out-of-home placements. In short, not a single one of the main components of the child welfare system had been subjected to a scientific evaluation between 1980 and 1996; this, despite the fact that billions of dollars are spent each year on these interventions and despite the continued and mounting criticisms of the failings of the system.

The Findings

The one commonality of the 78 evaluations of child abuse and neglect prevention and treatment programs was, in scientific terms, a failure to reject the null hypothesis. While it may be too harsh a judgement to say these programs have not and do not work as intended, the National Research Council report did come to the following conclusion regarding social service interventions:

> Social service interventions designed to improve parenting practices and provide family support have not yet demonstrated that they have the capacity to reduce or prevent abusive or neglectful behaviors significantly over time for the majority of families who have been reported for child maltreatment. (National Research Council, 1998, p. 118)

With regard to intensive family preservation services, here, too, there was little evidence that such services resolve the underlying dysfunction that precipitated the crisis. Nor was there evidence that such services improve child well-being or family functioning.

What little research there was on out-of-home placement found that children who reside in foster care fare neither better nor worse than those who remain in homes in which maltreatment occurred.

While some programs and interventions show promise, the promise is not yet evident in empirical data that confirm that the programs actually attain their goals and objectives.

In the legal area, the main child maltreatment legal intervention, mandatory reporting, has yet to be evaluated.

Finally, there was positive and promising data from evaluations of health care interventions. Home visitation represents one of the most carefully evaluated and promising opportunities for the prevention of child maltreatment. Research reported subsequent to the National Research Council report confirmed the Committee's assessment–home visitation has demonstrated long-term effectiveness (Kitzman et al., 1997; Olds et al., 1997). Subsequent to the National Research Council's review, a review of more recent evaluations of home visitation programs concluded with a more modest and less sanguine finding. The evaluations conducted by Olds and his colleagues of their original intervention in Elmira, New York, found clear and consistent evidence of fewer substantiated child maltreatment reports among those receiving the full complement of home health visits. However, evaluations of the Hawaii Healthy Start Program and Healthy Families America found no differences in the rates of reported child abuse and neglect (Gomby, Culross, & Behrman, 1999).

WHY SO LITTLE EVIDENCE OF PROGRAM EFFECTIVENESS?

There are a number of reasons why research on child maltreatment prevention and treatment programs is generally unable to find evidence for program effectiveness. First and most pessimistically, it is possible that the programs and services, while well-intended, are, in and of themselves, not effective. It is possible that the theories (mostly informal and untested) behind the programs and services may be inaccurate or inadequate and the programs themselves, therefore, may not be addressing the key causal mechanisms that cause child maltreatment. Second, the programs or services may be effective, but they may not be implemented properly by the agencies and workers that are using the programs. For example, when the evaluation data for the Illinois Family First program were made public (Schuerman, Rzepnicki, & Littell, 1994), the data failed to support the hypotheses that the program reduced out-of-home placement, costs, and/or improved family functioning. An initial reaction was that there was considerable variation in how intensive family preservation was being implemented at the different sites in Illinois. The overall implementation was also not true to the "Homebuilders" model of intensive family preservation. Thus, the lack of support for the effectiveness of the services was blamed on the programs not being properly implemented. A third plausible explanation may be that the theory behind the program may be accurate and the program itself may be appropriate, but the "dose" may be too small. This applies to many interventions designed to prevent and treat all forms of family and intimate violence and is not unique to child maltreatment services. The National Academy of Sciences (National Research Council, 1998) concluded that the duration and intensity of the mental health and social support services needed to influence behaviors that result from or contribute to family violence, may be greater than initially estimated. With regard to social service interventions, the Committee opined that:

> The intensity of the parenting, mental health, and social support services required may be greater than initially estimated in order to address the fundamental sources of instability, conflict, stress, and violence that occur repeatedly over time in the family environment, especially in disadvantaged communities. (National Research Council, 1998, p. 118)

Thus, it is likely that more services are necessary or the length of the interventions should be increased.

With regard to theory, there are other plausible explanations for the apparent ineffectiveness of child maltreatment interventions. Many current child welfare programs assume that abuse and maltreatment are at one end of a continuum of parenting behavior. However, it is possible that this model of abusive behavior is inaccurate. It may be that there are distinct types of abusers (Gelles, 1991; 1996). Abuse may not arise out of a surplus of risk factors and a deficit of resources, but rather, there may be distinct psychological and social attributes of those caretakers who inflict serious and/or fatal injuries compared to caretakers who commit less severe acts of maltreatment. If there are different types of offenders and different underlying causes for different types of abuse, it is reasonable to assume that a "one size fits all" intervention or policy will not be effective across the board. Irrespective of the model of abuse, to date evaluations of interventions demonstrate little impact. Thus, the problem is not trying to make "one size fit all" but finding any size that fits.

Another problem with the child welfare system is the crude way behavior change is conceptualized and measured. Behavior change is thought to be a one-step process; one simply changes from one form of behavior to another. For example, if one is an alcohol or substance abuser, then change involves stopping the use of alcohol or drugs. If one stops, but then begins again, then the change has not successfully occurred. A second assumption is that maltreating parents or caretakers all want to change–either to avoid legal and social sanctions or because they have an intrinsic motivation to be caring parents. As a result, those who design and implement child abuse and neglect interventions assume that all, or at least most, parents, caretakers and families are ready and able to change their maltreating behavior. Of course, the reverse may also be true–that abusive and neglectful parents do not want to change and/or cannot change, and this explains the negative results of evaluation research.

However, research on behavior change clearly demonstrates that change is not a one-step process (Prochaska & DiClemente, 1982; 1983; 1984; Prochaska, Norcross, & DiClemente, 1994). Rather, changing behavior is a dynamic process and one progresses through a number of stages, including relapse, in trying to modify behavior. There are also cognitive aspects to behavior change that can be measured.

One of the reasons why child welfare interventions may have such modest success rates is that most interventions are "action" programs. These programs are often provided to individuals and families in what Prochaska and his colleagues call the precontemplator or contemplation stage of change (Prochaska & DiClemente, 1982; 1983; 1984). This is what others may refer to as denial or ambivalence about the need for change. For interventions to be more successful, there is the need to balance readiness for change with the immediate risk in a particular family (Gelles, 1996).

WHY SO FEW INTERVENTIONS?

Before turning to the issue of how to move ahead and use evaluation research to help improve the child welfare system, it is important to consider why there has been so little evaluation research on child welfare interventions and, equally important, why there has been so little emphasis on carrying out evaluation research. Obviously, the first answer to this question is, money. Although public and private expenditures for child welfare in the United States is in the $10 billion to

$15 billion dollar range, comparatively speaking, this is not much money. Michael Petit, Deputy Director of the Child Welfare League of America, points out that $15 billion dollars per year for child welfare is half of what the nation spends on pizza (Petit, 1999). Given the chronic gap between the demands on the child welfare system and the system's resources, it is not surprising that funds for research are minimal. Federal and foundation funds for child maltreatment are also relatively small, and those funds that are available are allocated for programs rather than research. With 3 million reports, 1 1/2 million investigations, 600,000 children in out-of-home care, and 1,200 child abuse and neglect fatalities annually, it seems obvious that scarce resources would be allocated toward "doing something," rather than "studying something."

But, when nearly forty years of "doing something" has not yielded much in the way of evidence that the "something" does any good, the answer to the question of "why so little research?" must be more than just limited funds.

An alternative answer to "lack of funds," is that those who work and administer the child welfare system are reluctant to evaluate what they do and equally reluctant to take heed of what evaluations have been carried out. In the latter case, Senator Daniel Moynihan proves the point of reluctance to take heed of results. Moynihan (1996) describes his experience chairing the Senate Finance Committee when the committee was, in 1993, considering an administration proposal to spend $930 million on family preservation. This program was proposed during a time when the Finance Committee was charged with reducing federal spending by $500 billion. Moynihan recounts that he wrote to Dr. Laura D'Andrea Tyson, then chair of the President's Council of Economic Advisors, saying that after hearings on family preservation, he had followed up on administration claims that data existed that showed that family preservation was effective. Moynihan checked out two citations offered by the administration that supposedly demonstrated the effectiveness of family preservation. The citations Moynihan obtained stated that "solid proof that family preservation services can effect a state's overall placement rate is still lacking" (Moynihan, 1996, p. 48). Despite finding no data to support the claim for the effectiveness of family preservation services, the bill passed, with Moynihan's support. Nearly $1 billion was spent on family preservation services in the next four years, and the program was re-authorized with more funding in 1997. Interestingly, between 1993 and 1997 when the legislation was re-authorized, the published results of evaluations of intensive family preservations programs also failed to find evidence of the effectiveness of this service (Heneghan, Horwitz, & Leventhal, 1996).

Part of the reason for the rejection or ignoring of data or findings that fail to support the hypothesis that a program or service is effective, is that caseworkers and administrators work in an ideographic world. By this I mean that the worldview of the child welfare system is through the lens of individual cases. Based on 30 years of personal experience, both in the field and classroom, it is my impression that caseworkers and administrators do not use a nomothetic paradigm (paradigm that looks for patterns across cases) and seek patterns. Their world is made up of individual cases and the failures and successes of those cases. Thus, effectiveness of a program is not to be found in aggregate evaluation data, but in individual case records and experiences. Thus, in many ways, the child welfare system operates on the basis of "intervention by anecdote," both good and bad anecdotes. In response to research that fails to support a claim for program or service effectiveness, workers and administrators can and do summon up a case or many cases where the service was effective. In response to media accounts of failures, caseworkers and administrators know that there are many unreported cases of program or service effectiveness.

Intervention by anecdote is bound to fail. To put much too fine a point on this issue, a blind squirrel will eventually find an acorn. That a single case or a number of cases are helped by a service proves nothing and is not justification for continued support for and funding of a service.

The larger problem is that evaluation research on child welfare interventions fails to find effects for most programs and interventions that have been evaluated. As Moynihan pointed out in his discussion of data on family preservation, the consistent pattern since the mid-1960s is that evaluation studies find no effects, few effects, or negative effects (Moynihan, 1996, p. 49). This he called "Rossi's Iron Law." The law is: "If there is any empirical law that is emerging from the past decade of widespread evaluation research activities, it is that the expected value for any measured effect of a social program is zero" (Moynihan, 1996, p. 49).

Whether they know about Rossi's Iron Law or not, agency directors and administrators must be concerned that an evaluation will conform to Rossi's law and their program will be found wanting in terms of scientific data. Rather than take a chance that a program that helps some people (policy by anecdote) will lose its funding, administrators resist having programs evaluated. If a program is evaluated, the evaluation is typically poorly funded and inadequately designed and implemented. Poor funding and an inadequate design actually enhance the likelihood of proving Rossi's Iron Law, thus creating a vicious circle that leads to no evaluations or even more poorly funded and poorly designed evaluations.

Another reason why some interventions are not evaluated is that many components of the "standard intervention," such as mandatory reporting and appointing a guardian ad litem, are mandated by law. It would be somewhat pointless to evaluate a program or intervention component that could not be changed or even modified.

Another explanation for the lack of evaluation research is that what is considered the "gold standard" for evaluation research, a randomized experiment, is often considered impractical, impossible, or unethical by agency and program directors. The notion that one group will be randomly deprived of a service, even a service with no proven value, is considered completely unethical and inappropriate. Even when an agency agrees to random assignment, they may fail to understand exactly what random assignment means. In such cases, workers may violate the random assignment protocol in order to assure that certain clients get what the workers think are effective services (see Schuerman et al., 1994, for an example of this in the Illinois Family First evaluation).

Sometimes the "gold standard" simply cannot be used. For example, in an attempt to evaluate a Children's Advocacy Center in Rhode Island we found that the program had achieved statewide status and a comparison or control group simply did not exist (Youngblood & Gelles, 1997). Moreover, the essential aspect of the intervention, keeping interviews with children to a minimum, constrained our ability to collect pre- and post-test measures from the children. Any interviews that we would conduct with the children would have contaminated the actual intervention. To resolve this problem, we relied on administrative data from the agencies involved in the cases as well as reports from parents and guardians of the children.

Finally, the innovations in the prevention and treatment of child maltreatment move much faster than evaluation research. Thus, for example, by the time a sufficient body of evaluation research on intensive family preservation services had been accumulated, intensive family preservation services were no longer the new innovative intervention. Researchers presenting their data on intensive family preservation services were told this was no longer important, as child welfare had discovered and was implementing "family conferencing."

To a certain extent, foundations are partially culpable for the pattern of limited evaluations because their priorities are typically to fund promising new programs. While foundations do often require evaluation research of their funded programs, they often promote promising results prior to the completion of the evaluation research. Some foundations rapidly move from one "cure du jour" to the next, without properly evaluating any new program.

CONCLUSION: THE SOLUTION

To a certain extent, the solution is rather simple–do more evaluation research and do it better. The crisis of the child welfare system will not and cannot be resolved until such time as we have some idea of what interventions work for what children and families, and under what conditions. Forty years of intervention by anecdote and the resistance to research and evaluation research, have yielded an expensive and complex system that fails to provide basic protection to America's vulnerable and dependent children.

There are three basic steps that need to be accomplished in order to allow for better evaluation research: (1) The first step was articulated by the National Research Council's Committee on Assessing Family Violence Interventions. The Committee pleaded for *more collaborations between researchers and programs* (National Research Council, 1998). Collaboration does not mean that program administrators throw open their doors and allow researchers to implement "gold standard" randomized field experiments. It means a genuine collaboration where both researchers and program operators understand the benefits and risks of evaluation research and both endeavor to design appropriate scientific evaluations. Such collaborations are not forged by having both groups work as partners for only 14 days in responding to requests for proposals. Sound collaborations require both groups learning about one another's language, assumptions, and paradigms. Such interactions are needed to establish the basic trust that must exist before a sound evaluation project can be put into place. (2) A second recommendation is that *funding–government, corporate and foundation–should eventually be based on accountability of a program.* In order to accomplish this, government agencies and foundations must set aside funds for evaluation research. Funding should be available at the outset of a program so that appropriate baseline data can be obtained. Funding needs to be adequate to allow for a proper design and sample. It is a relatively easy task for government agencies to include set-asides equal to 10 percent of program costs for evaluation research and it is also relatively easy to include prescriptions for acceptable designs to be used to evaluate programs and interventions. (3) Finally, *evaluation researchers must be flexible in their designs to accommodate and accept the realities of implementing and operating prevention and treatment programs for child maltreatment.* There will be many instances where practical and ethical issues constrain the ability to field a "gold standard" evaluation. These situations call for creative and innovative evaluation designs. For example, we could not use a "gold standard" design to evaluate Child Advocacy Centers. Yet, such centers need to be evaluated, as they have become a well-established and well-funded component of the child welfare system. It is not yet known whether Child Advocacy Centers actually produce the desired results of reducing trauma for children and increasing successful prosecutions. Our approach in this one case was to use a "dose response" design, whereby we assessed outcome in terms of the "dose" of the intervention and the goodness of fit of the actual intervention to the theoretical model (Youngblood & Gelles, 1997).

The crisis of the child welfare system will have to be addressed. We cannot continue to have 1 percent of America's children in foster care, 3 million reports of maltreatment each year, 1,000 homicides, and countless law suits, tragedies, and controversies plaguing the system. Rounding up the "usual suspects" as an attempt to fix the system has not worked. No amount of funding can rescue a system that cannot answer the basic question of whether anything it does is effective. It is time to find out what works, for whom, and under what conditions.

REFERENCES

Barth, R.P., Courtney, M., Berrick, J.D., & Albert, V. (1994). *From child abuse to permanency planning: Child welfare services pathways and placements.* New York: Aldine de Gruyter.

Child Welfare League of America. (1993). *Recommended caseload/workload standards: Exerpted from CWLA standards for child welfare practice.* Washington, DC: Child Welfare League of America.

Child Welfare League of America. (1999). *Child abuse and neglect: A look at the states, 1998 CWLA state book.* Washington, DC: CWLA Press.

Gelles, R.J. (1991). Physical violence, child abuse, and child homicide: A continuum of violence, or distinct behaviors? *Human Nature, 2,* 59-72.

Gelles, R.J. (1996). *The book of David: How preserving families can cost children's lives.* New York: Basic Books.

Gomby, D.S., Culross, P.L., & Behrman, R.E. (1999). Home visiting: Recent program evaluations–analysis and recommendations. *The Future of Children, 9,* 4-26.

Green Book (1996). *Background material and data on major programs within the jurisdiction of the Committee on Ways and Means.* Washington, DC: U.S. Government Printing Office.

Greenfield, L.A., Rand, M.R., Craven, D., Klaus, P.A., Perkins, C.A., Ringel, C., Warchol, G., Maston, C., & Fox, J.A. (1998). *Violence by intimates: Analysis of data on crimes by current or former spouses, boyfriends, and girlfriends.* Washington, DC: U.S. Department of Justice, Office of Justice Programs.

Guggenheim, M. (1999). *Established and emerging rights: Exploring juvenile rights under the Constitution.* Discussion presented at the University of Pennsylvania Journal of Constitutional Law, Second Annual Symposium, Philadelphia, PA.

Heneghan, A.M., Horwitz, S.M., & Leventhal, J.M. (1996). Evaluating intensive family preservation programs: A methodological review. *Pediatrics, 97,* 535-542.

Kempe, C.H., Silverman, F.N., Steele, B.F., Droegmueller, W., & Silver, H.K. (1962). The battered child syndrome. *Journal of the American Medical Association, 282,* 107-112.

Kitzman, H., Olds, D.L., Henderson, C.R., Hanks, C., Cole, R., Tatelbaum, R., McConnochie, K.M, Sidora, K., Luckey, D.W., Shaver, D., Engelhardt, K., James, D., & Barnard, K. (1997). Effect of prenatal and infancy home visitation by nurses on pregnancy outcomes, childhood injuries, and repeated childbearing. *Journal of the American Medical Association, 276,* 644-652.

Meddin, D., & Hansen, I. (1985). The services provided during a child abuse and/or neglect case investigation and the barriers that exist to service provision. *Child Abuse and Neglect, 9,* 175-182.

Moynihan, D.P. (1996). *Miles to go: A personal history of social policy.* Cambridge, MA: Harvard University Press.

National Committee to Prevent Child Abuse. (1998). *Current trends in child abuse reporting and fatalities: The results of the 1997 annual survey.* Chicago, IL: National Committee to Prevent Child Abuse.

National Research Council. (1998). *Violence in families: Assessing prevention and treatment programs.* Washington, DC: National Academy Press.

Nelson, B.J. (1984). *Making an issue of child abuse: Political agenda setting for social problems.* Chicago: University of Chicago Press.

Olds, D., Eckenrode, J., Henderson, C.R., Kitzman, H., Powers, J., Cole, R., Sidora, K., Morris, P., Pettit, L., & Luckey, D. (1997). Long-term effects of home visitation on maternal life course and child abuse and neglect: Fifteen-year follow-up of a randomized trial. *Journal of the American Medical Association, 278,* 637-648.

Petit, M. (1999). Comments made at the National Institute of Justice Law Enforcement Response to Child Maltreatment Strategic Planning Meeting, Washington, DC, March 15, 1999.

Prochaska, J.O., & DiClemente, C.C. (1982). Toward a more integrative model of change. *Psychotherapy: Theory, Research and Practice, 19,* 276-288.

Prochaska, J.O., & DiClemente, C.C. (1983). Stages and processes of self-change in smoking: Toward an integrative model of change. *Journal of Consulting and Clinical Psychology, 5,* 390-395.

Prochaska, J.O., & DiClemente, C.C. (1984). *The transtheoretical approach: Crossing traditional boundaries of change.* Homewood: Dow Jones/Irwin.

Prochaska, J.O., Norcross, J.C., & DiClemente, C.C. (1994). *Changing for good.* New York: Morrow.

Roberts, D. (1999). *Is there justice in children's rights? The critique of federal family preservation policy.* Paper presented at the University of Pennsylvania Journal of Constitutional Law, Second Annual Symposium, Established and Emerging Rights: Exploring Juvenile Rights Under the Constitution, Philadelphia, PA.

Salovitz, B., & Keys, D. (1988). Is child protective service still a service? *Protecting Children, 5,* 17-23.

Schuerman, J., Rzepnicki, T.L., & Littell, J.H. (1994). *Putting families first: An experiment in family preservation.* New York: Aldine de Gruyter.

Schwartz, I.M., & Fishman, G. (1999). *Kids raised by the government.* Westport, CT: Praeger.

Tatara, T. (1993). *U.S. child substitute care flow data for FY 1992 and current trends in the state child substitute care populations (VCIS Research Notes, No. 9, pp. 1-11).* Washington DC: American Public Welfare Association.

U.S. Advisory Board on Child Abuse and Neglect. (1990). *Child abuse and neglect: Critical first steps in response to a national emergency.* Washington, DC: U.S. Government Printing Office.

U.S. Department of Health and Human Services. (1996). *Study findings: Study of the national incidence and prevalence of child abuse and neglect: 1993.* Washington, DC: U.S. Government Printing Office.

U.S. Department of Health and Human Services. (1997). *Child maltreatment 1996: Reports from the states to the National Center on Child Abuse.* Washington, DC: U.S. Government Printing Office.

U.S. Department of Health and Human Services. (1998). *Child maltreatment 1997: Reports from the states to the National Center on Child Abuse.* Washington, DC: U.S. Government Printing Office.

U.S. Department of Justice. (1998). *Uniform crime reports for the United States,*

1997. Washington, DC: U.S. Department of Justice, Federal Bureau of Investigation.

Wexler, R. (1990). *Wounded innocents: The real victims of the war against children*. Buffalo, NY: Prometheus Press.

Youngblood, J., & Gelles, R.J. (1997). *Measuring the impact of an intervention on the well-being of victims of sexual abuse*. Paper presented at the 5th International Family Violence Research Conference, Durham, NH.

Assessing Family Violence Interventions: Linking Programs to Research-Based Strategies

Rosemary Chalk

SUMMARY. The introduction of family violence treatment and prevention programs during the past few decades has occurred in the absence of scientific evidence that could indicate the types of benefits to be gained by the use of these programs as well as the types of clients who would benefit from them. Although a broad patchwork of interventions has emerged in social service, law enforcement, and health care settings, few of these programs have been evaluated in a systematic manner. The use of comparison groups in family violence program evaluation studies is also rare. As a result, evaluation studies currently provide limited guidance in the design of family violence prevention and treatment programs.

Violence in Families: Assessing Prevention and Treatment Programs is a recent report on family violence prepared by the National Research Council and the Institute of Medicine that identifies a set of methodological issues designed to improve the quality of family violence evaluation research. The report provides an in-depth analysis of 114 evaluation studies of interventions in the area of child maltreatment, domestic violence, and elder abuse and includes policy and research recommendations designed to improve the quality of evaluation studies in this field.

Two key areas–research infrastructure and the development of ap-

---

Address correspondence to: Rosemary Chalk, BA, Senior Program Officer, Institute of Medicine, 2101 Constitution Avenue, NW FO 3121, Washington, DC 20418.

[Haworth co-indexing entry note]: "Assessing Family Violence Interventions: Linking Programs to Research-Based Strategies." Chalk, Rosemary. Co-published simultaneously in *Journal of Aggression, Maltreatment & Trauma* (The Haworth Maltreatment & Trauma Press, an imprint of The Haworth Press, Inc.) Vol. 4, No. 1 (#7), 2000, pp. 29-53; and: *Program Evaluation and Family Violence Research* (ed: Sally K. Ward, and David Finkelhor) The Haworth Maltreatment & Trauma Press, an imprint of The Haworth Press, Inc., 2000, pp. 29-53. Single or multiple copies of this article are available for a fee from The Haworth Document Delivery Service [1-800-342-9678, 9:00 a.m. - 5:00 p.m. (EST). E-mail address: getinfo@haworthpressinc.com].

29

propriate theories, measures, and datasets that can support more rigorous evaluations–require attention to improve the capacity of the evaluation research field to inform family violence policy and practice. The lack of opportunities for long-term collaboration between researchers and service providers presents an important challenge in developing research on the multiple pathways to services and the implementation and effects of service interventions. *[Article copies available for a fee from The Haworth Document Delivery Service: 1-800-342-9678. E-mail address: <getinfo@haworthpressinc.com> Website: <http://www.HaworthPress.com>]*

KEYWORDS. Evaluation studies, policy, research, child maltreatment, domestic violence, elder abuse

INTRODUCTION

Over the past three decades a patchwork of specialized interventions has emerged in social services, health care, and law enforcement agencies to address the problem of family violence (including child maltreatment, domestic violence, and elder abuse). Examples of such efforts include child and adult protective services, battered women's shelters, specialized police and prosecution policies and practices, and training programs designed to enhance the diagnostic, treatment, and referral skills of health care professionals.

Many of these family violence interventions have resulted from the influence of advocacy movements for the protection of women and children. As greater awareness of the complex dimensions of the problem of family violence grows within social service, law enforcement, and healthcare agencies, service personnel are experimenting with different ways of responding to the needs of children, adolescents, and adults who have experienced violence within their homes.[1] Generally characterized as family violence treatment and prevention programs, these efforts have emerged largely in the absence of research demonstrating their effectiveness in reducing the incidence, severity, or harmful consequences of violence among family members. In many cases, federal agencies and private foundations play important roles in supporting the development of family violence programs, although the service system is commonly administered through state and local organizations.

The result of this combination of efforts is a highly fragmented set of treatment and prevention programs in a variety of institutional settings. Wide variation exists among programs that bear similar labels (such as family preservation services, domestic violence arrest programs, or battered women's shelters), and the intensity, mix, and skills of services associated with individual programs can also vary over time within a single site. Demonstration efforts that suggest positive effects in one locale are often copied or adapted in other settings prior to an in-depth understanding of critical components that may have contributed to their success. Broad reforms in areas such as out-of-home placement of children, arrest policies, evidentiary standards, and medical referrals have occurred largely in the absence of compelling evidence that a specific approach will achieve desirable change in either individual or group behavior.

Family violence treatment and prevention programs now represent a major source of economic investment in our society, but the absence of cohesive and integrated efforts obscures the scale and costs of that investment. Although research efforts are underway to estimate the cost of the problem of family violence itself, such studies do not yet have the capacity to identify program investments or distinguish among costs for different types of service components. For example, Dorothy Rice and her colleagues at the University of California at San Francisco estimate that reliable cost indicators are difficult to obtain because of significant variation in prevalence estimates, definitions, and measurement issues (Rice, Max, Golding, & Pinderhughes, 1996). They observed that a commonly cited annual figure of $1.7 billion published by Straus (1986) is frequently quoted as seriously underestimating the true cost of family violence. Other reported figures range from $5-10 billion (also generally regarded as underestimates) to $67 billion, but the latter figure includes a significant amount of nonmonetary costs (for pain and suffering) that involve debatable assumptions.

Although reliable cost data are imprecise, we can say, with confidence, that the problem of family violence has a significant impact on the health and well-being of children, adults, and families in our society and that extensive activity is underway within the service sector systems to address it. For example, one observer has suggested that Massachusetts state courts alone issued almost 100,000 restraining orders for domestic violence during the period 1992-1994 (Adams, 1994).

EXAMINING THE EVIDENCE
OF FAMILY VIOLENCE PROGRAM EFFECTS

The tremendous scale of effort and investment in family violence programs have stimulated attention to the dynamics and structure of public and private agency efforts. Recognizing that many family violence prevention and treatment programs are relatively immature (compared with the areas of substance abuse, teen pregnancy, community violence, or child health, for example), several expert panels have called for evaluations of ongoing efforts to inform program development and oversight as well as strategic efforts designed to improve agency coordination and program investments.[2] Recent emphasis on the importance of service accountability and outcomes-based performance measures in a variety of service settings has also stimulated interest in the evaluation of family violence interventions. A growing evaluation literature has emerged, focused on individual family violence prevention and treatment programs, which reveals some insights about promise and pitfalls.[3] Yet several formidable challenges inhibit efforts to move from the evaluation of single programs to the assessment of broad strategies in the areas of social service, healthcare, and law enforcement. The explicit recognition of these challenges is perhaps a first step in their resolution.

First, many family violence programs are driven by perceptions of individual need (as reported in victim accounts of abuse and violence) rather than a theory of change based on population-based epidemiology studies. The *victim-response approach* has been highly effective in attracting public attention and resource commitments, but it provides a shallow foundation for measurement and evaluation of long-term outcomes or program effects. Furthermore, evaluation studies of individual programs are often unable to control for non-programmatic factors that may influence results (such as characteristics of the client base, leadership styles within the program, levels of community support, or incentives and sanctions that exist outside the scope of the program that contribute to its effects). Most evaluation studies focus on program effects for clients who actually used or, more often, completed, a service intervention rather than comparing the characteristics of clients who received one set of services with those who received something different or perhaps nothing at all. The absence of appropriate comparison groups in the family violence evaluation literature is perhaps its most fundamental flaw.

Second, *a variety of different, and sometimes competing, theories of change* drive family violence interventions but such theories often remain obscure and ill-defined in statements of program mission or objectives. Battered women's shelters, for example, are described as havens of safety, refuge, support, and empowerment. The same shelter may provide some or all of these roles according to the needs of individual clients. Ideally, the mix of services would be tailored to each client's own profile. Each dimension of the program conveys important assumptions about the nature of the problem that is to be addressed for the client; sometimes it is simply the persistent presence of social support, rather than the intensity or content of any single component, that influences outcomes. Assessing the impact of shelters is complicated by the multiple dimensions of their mission: does this type of intervention focus on direct services tailored to the victim's immediate needs or is its role designed to develop resources within the community (such as employment, housing, and childcare) that can assist clients in transforming or moving away from abusive relationships? The child maltreatment field reveals similar tensions, as service providers often work in ambiguous situations where the best interest of the child needs to be weighed against the rights and obligations of other family members.

Uncertainty, ambiguity, role conflict, and lack of adequate measures are not unique to the field of family violence studies. Assessing the critical components of positive parenting, social support, or deterrence, for example, are formidable challenges in many other areas of study. Solutions to these challenges are not easy, especially in the absence of solid infrastructures to support knowledge exchange efforts as well as interdisciplinary studies focused on theoretical and measurement aspects of family violence. Even when another area of study (the field of parenting literature, for example) makes significant progress in areas such as classifying critical components within parenting styles or identifying conflict resolutions practices within parent-child interactions, family violence researchers and program providers are unlikely to benefit until "accidental collisions" facilitate the exchange of new assessment measures or instruments across research areas.

Third, the *tremendous diversity and array of interventions* that have emerged over the past few decades remain largely undocumented in the research literature. The basic components and strategies imbedded in these interventions are often highly individualized and context dependent, shifting from case to case and community to community. Relying upon victim-driven frameworks (rather than standardized protocols), service providers adjust and adapt their activities to situational needs, resulting in varying strengths, duration, and intensity of services. As a result, although a broad array of treatment and prevention interventions focused on family violence has emerged in various institutional settings (including health services, social services, and law enforcement), the experiences and lessons learned from these interventions remain obscure in the research literature. Even when well-documented programs that have a clear mission and consistent program components emerge, weak research measures and the transience of the client base can impede systematic studies.

A fourth factor that challenges evaluation studies of family violence programs is *the range of heterogeneity and difficulty* in the lives of the clients themselves, both victims and offenders. Recognizing that no clear and consistent profile of an "abusive parent" or "batterer" exists, researchers are increasingly turning to the study of the convergence of risk factors in studies of family violence. The ecological theory of child maltreatment, for example, suggests that individual risk factors need to be considered within a framework that considers these factors within the context of family dynamics, neighborhood or community practices, and social norms. The occurrence of family violence is often seen as behavior that is influenced both by individual factors as well as the absence or presence of situational factors that influence the choice of stressor or conflict resolution strategies. Yet the multiple interactions of health and social problems (such as depression, social isolation, and economic insecurity) in troubled families who experience parent/child or partner violence create major challenges for researchers as well as service providers who seek to isolate individual behavior patterns, events, or risk and protective factors that are linked directly to the experience of violence.

The ecological approach, in turn, suggests that no single program or service intervention can achieve significant impact for large numbers of at-risk children. A comparable approach has emerged in the field of teen pregnancy prevention, for example, where limited success with single factor prevention strategies has evolved into broader efforts that seek to build on the positive assets of youth by broadening their educational and community service opportunities. The ecological approach encourages the identification and linkage of key components, at adequate strength, focused on the right population group (generally individuals who are seen to be at high risk for involvement in family violence incidents either as victims or offenders). This strategy has also been described as determining what works best for whom, under what circumstances. Learning how to substitute "time outs" as a form of child discipline may help reduce the use of physical punishment, for example, but it is unlikely to be effective in working with parents whose problems involve emotional maltreatment, sexual abuse, or child neglect.

Given these challenges, it is not surprising to discover that limited progress has been made in evaluation studies of family violence interventions. What is more impressive, perhaps, is that researchers and service providers remain optimistic that a science-based approach can yield stronger and more sustainable program interventions. Incentives to work with stronger theory-based approaches in building programmatic interventions have also been shaped by larger forces in social service, healthcare, and law enforcement organizations, the result of a growing emphasis on measuring performance, outcomes, and programmatic effectiveness. The shift towards greater reliance on empirical evidence in the development of family violence interventions thus represents an important landmark in the evolution of strategies to address child maltreatment, domestic violence, and elder abuse.

MOVING FROM PROGRAMS TO STRATEGIES: THE NRC-IOM STUDY

In order to improve the synthesis of and access to research in this field, and to improve the quality of both future programs and the evaluation of family violence interventions, the National Research Council and the Institute of Medicine in 1994 organized a committee representing law enforcement, social service, health care, and evaluation research and practice to assess family violence prevention and treatment services.[4] The study was supported by a consortium of federal agencies within the U.S. Department of Health and Human Services and the Department of Justice and the Carnegie Corporation of New York.[5] The result is a book-length report titled *Violence in Families: Assessing Prevention and Treatment Programs* (Chalk & King, 1998).[6]

One of the first tasks of the NRC-IOM study was to survey the research literature on family violence interventions and to classify studies on the basis of their methodology and study design. Examining numerous on-line research databases in consultation with numerous practitioners and state agency officials, the study team identified 114 evaluation studies conducted from 1980 to 1996 that were of sufficient quality to provide inferences about the effects of specific interventions in the area of child maltreatment, domestic violence, and elder abuse. The primary selection criteria for this set of studies was the existence of a comparison or control group within the evaluation design (such studies are known as quasi-experimental studies) which allowed the researcher to compare the relative effects of the intervention under study to what might be expected in its absence. If the research subjects are randomly assigned to treatment and control groups, the study design can reduce sources of bias that might affect its results. Randomized studies are common in clinical research, but they are rare in law enforcement or social service settings.

The 114 studies are distributed unequally over the three fields (child maltreatment, domestic violence, and elder abuse) that formed the framework for the NRC-IOM study (Table 1). The distribution of these studies does not reflect the distribution of the interventions themselves but instead conveys the state of the empirical research literature about intervention outcomes and effects. Within the group of 114 evaluation studies, 78 studies fall within the area of child maltreatment, 34 studies involve domestic violence interventions, and two studies focus on elder abuse. In considering the institutional settings, it is important to note that slightly more than half of the selected evaluations (59) involve social service interventions, most of which (50)

TABLE 1. Total Number of Quasi-Experimental Evaluations of Family Violence Interventions, 1980-1996

Service Sector	Type of Family Violence		
	Child Maltreatment	Domestic Violence	Elder Abuse
Social service	50	7	2
Legal	4	9	0
Health care	24	8	0
Total	78	34	2

Source: Committee on the Assessment of Family Violence Interventions, National Research Council and the Institute of Medicine (Chalk & King, 1998:28).

focus directly on child maltreatment. In contrast, 19 of the 23 studies that examined domestic violence interventions involved law enforcement initiatives (compared to only seven in the child maltreatment area). The two elder abuse intervention studies both involve social service programs.

In conducting this analysis, the NRC-IOM committee was not able to look in detail at the many challenging issues that surround the development and implementation of family violence interventions, such as project design, development, finding, implementation, or coordination. Committee members met with service providers through a workshop and five site visits to selected programs in Seattle, Miami, Dallas, New York, and Boston. The extent of regional variation in treatment and prevention programs was notable; in some communities health or social service sectors take the lead in developing family violence interventions, in others law enforcement agencies provide leadership and resources. Community-based programs are obviously a key part of the service delivery system, but these vary in form, intensity, and range of services. Most programs emphasize a particular type of family violence (child or adult), most focus on responding to victims or perpetrators (rather than on prevention), and most are attempting to deal with large caseloads with modest resources. Beyond these general observations, the report does not provide extensive material about the nature of the programs themselves.

One of the committee's goals was to strengthen the research base by providing a conceptual framework for evaluation studies of family violence interventions. The absence of such a framework discourages efforts to examine the relative effects of different types of therapeutic interventions, and also inhibits the ability of researchers and policymakers to compare the merits of comprehensive versus single program approaches in family violence treatment and prevention efforts. Each type of family violence has its own service arrangements: some are designed as therapeutic, rescue, or emergency protection efforts; others serve social support, punitive, or deterrent roles. The NRC-IOM report maps these interventions by type of strategy within a systems framework; the result is a patchwork of services that shows minimal overlap and few connections among the separate parts (Table 2). This type of service arrangement system can be described as a "loosely coupled" rather than tightly connected set of services.

Two options lie ahead in the development of family violence inter-

TABLE 2. Array of Services for Family Violence by Service Sector and Purpose

Sector	Prevention	Case Identification/ Risk Factor Detection	Short-Term Victim Protection/Risk Assessment/Treatment	Long-Term Intervention
Social services	Education programs	Surveys	Shelters	Peer support groups
	Service provider training programs	Case reports	Batterers' treatment programs	Education and job training
	Community coordinating councils	Child protective services	Family preservation services	Housing (transitional and permanent)
	Comprehensive community service		Parenting practices and family support	Child and elder placement
	Community support groups			
Health	Service provider training programs	Health reports	Home visitation and family support	Mental health services for victims
		Emergency room procedures		Mental health services for offenders
		Diagnostic protocols		
Law enforcement	Service provider training programs	Uniform crime reports	Temporary restraining orders	Offender incarceration
		National crime victimization surveys	Arrest procedures	Sentencing guidelines
			Batterers' treatment programs	Conditions of probation and parole
			Victim advocates	

Source: Committee on the Assessment of Family Violence Interventions, National Research Council and Institute of Medicine (Chalk & King, 1998).

ventions: (1) the field can continue to grow in this locally-driven and loosely coupled fashion, or (2) a more coordinated, centralized, and focused infrastructure can emerge to guide and integrate the development of services, allowing flexibility at the local level. Each approach has positive as well as negative features. For example, the contextual and situational character of the existing array of services may be desirable because victim response interventions can address individuals and groups at different stages and provide multiple entry points for services and support. Yet one could make an equally compelling argument that this approach lacks the skeletal structure to attract and support large amounts of resources and to provide basic measures of outcomes and accountability for the investments that are made in the treatment and prevention of family violence. Perhaps it is best to view the broad array of family violence services within an evolutionary perspective, recognizing that a diverse range of program experimentation and innovative practice is necessary in dealing with a complex and relatively new phenomenon in order to identify critical components that deserve investments and replication for a broader population in designing long-term service strategies. Identification of these critical components is thus an essential step in moving from "promising" approaches to best practice standards and performance criteria in designing strategies to address family violence.

From this perspective, the field of family violence interventions is entering a new stage of maturation that requires strong evidence of outcomes and effects to sustain large increases in the current level of public and private resources. In the early stages of discovering and addressing a new social problem, local, state, and national governments are often eager to put money aside for community-based rescue efforts. It is important for such programs to build a track record of experience that illuminates the nature and scope of the needs of the clients they serve and the strengths and deficiencies in existing service systems to meet these needs. Such rescue efforts, however, now need to fit into larger networks of health and social service systems that can provide long-term care and follow-up referrals for clients within settings that are responsive to the full health and social well-being of family members. For offenders, the specialized response units in law enforcement agencies need to integrate their efforts into the activities of those agencies responsible for sanctions and oversight so that an effective web of social control can be implemented to reduce and prevent incidents of family violence.

All too often, however, expectations emerge that the specialized and emergency response efforts by themselves can "cure" the problem of family violence. In this regard, sponsors and the public at large want to know "what works?" In an era of performance based standards and outcomes-based accountability, public agencies are increasingly asked to set goals and benchmarks that can serve as the criteria by which their efforts are to be judged. It is no longer sufficient to request resources because it's the right thing to do; public and private investments are now being judged by questions about program effectiveness, cost, and evidentiary standards, rather than simply humanitarian needs.

Recognizing that the literature on family violence evaluation studies is not easily compiled or analyzed, the NRC-IOM committee used their framework of research-based evidence to highlight key findings within the knowledge base that could provide the foundation for critical components of broad based prevention and treatment strategies. This study was not designed to find the two or three programs that "work" or "cure" family violence, but represented instead an important step in building the necessary research infrastructure that will stimulate a new generation of family violence interventions and research studies.

The methodological challenges of family violence evaluation studies are daunting, and they reflect the reasons why this field is often viewed as a stepchild within the child and family services arena. In conducting rigorous evaluations of family violence services, a researcher must take a program that was often assembled by advocates and community service personnel with small amounts of foundation or government agency funding, and put it under the lens of research methods that are traditionally designed for theory-driven interventions and strong quantitative measures. Furthermore, the study population who are the clients and users of family violence interventions are often not compliant or eager research subjects. They are difficult to locate and difficult to retain in long-term studies. Their circumstances are often characterized by crisis situations and multiple problems that represent pragmatic barriers to their participation in scientific research projects. A range of safety, privacy, and other ethical and legal concerns pervade the development of family violence interventions that often discourage research on their impact and effectiveness.[7]

Finally, the service providers who administer family violence interventions are generally more interested in helping people, especially victims, in the short run than advancing the state of empirical knowledge about service interventions. They often are too busy to fill out additional forms for program evaluators who may appear briefly and depart without providing good answers or even useful questions. The information systems within social service, public health, and law enforcement agencies often are inadequate to provide reliable case record data and include extensive duplication as well as a lack of extensive detail regarding the type or frequency of agency contacts, services provided, or consequences of the agency interaction.

As a result, the question of "goodness of fit" in matching appropriate evaluation techniques to the state of development of family violence interventions raises a number of intriguing concerns. In a chapter on evaluation research, the committee's report raises a number of specific methodological concerns about effect size, sample size, selection of effects and methods, and other topics that deserve particular attention in the conduct of research evaluations. The report also calls for the creation of ongoing collaborative partnerships between researchers and practitioners that can provide a foundation for the exchange of theory-driven knowledge and practice-based insights (also called craft knowledge).

These concerns have attracted attention within the federal research agencies. The Department of Justice has already issued two research solicitations in the area of domestic violence that draw on the report's findings.[8] DOJ expects to issue five grant awards of approximately $100,000 each to support practitioner-researcher collaborations as envisioned in the NRC-IOM study. An additional four to six research awards will be granted by DOJ to support research evaluations of law enforcement policies and programs that include experimental research designs to improve the overall quality of ongoing research efforts. In addition, an RFA on child neglect has been issued with support from NIH, NIJ, and the Children's Bureau that cites the study, calls attention to the set of methodological concerns related to definitions and measurement raised in the report, and provides funding to support research to address them.

The role of the federal government in designing and improving service system reforms remains ambiguous, however. Neither Congress nor the Clinton Administration seems eager to launch broad-based family violence programs during periods of tight fiscal controls on federal discretionary spending. The primary responsibility for these efforts remains with the states as part of their basic mission in the areas of social services, law enforcement, and public health. Research on service reforms is commonly not a priority area in any single service setting. Service system interventions, traditionally a stepchild in biomedical research agencies, has remained elusive.

The pitfalls of using evidence-based reports to achieve reforms in family violence practices and policies thus remain significant. Each state and local agency operates within its own culture, and the programs and services that it offers are often shaped by the surrounding social, political, and economic context. Federal agencies and small groups of professionals may be able to change organizational behaviors in areas where little resistance occurs from interest groups or other actors within the agency's environment. While rapid reforms occurred in the past few decades that allowed public agencies to be more responsive to the problem of family violence, these often occurred in the form of "add-ons" or contractual arrangements rather than requiring significant investments in permanent personnel or resources for training existing employees. It will be more difficult to achieve changes or establish programs that require greater investments of effort, resources, and professional training. Implementing recommendations such as those presented within the NRC-IOM report, therefore, will require stronger leadership and support within state-level agencies to overcome the bureaucratic inertia that challenges professionals seeking to introduce evidence-based initiatives and changes in service strategies.

INTEGRATING RESEARCH INTO PRACTICE AND POLICY

The NRC-IOM report included six conclusions that provide a base for considering the current state of interactions among family violence research, practice, and policy:

1. *Findings from small-scale studies are often adopted into policy and professional practice without sufficient independent replication or reflection on their possible shortcomings.* All too often, family violence services and evaluation studies focus on single programs rather than broad interventions or strategies. The rate of diffusion of innovative policies and programs focused on family violence seems remarkably high when compared with other social policy areas. Consider, for example, the short time in which states throughout the country adopted mandatory reporting laws for child abuse and neglect. Or the rate at which police departments adopted the practice of incorporating victim advocates into their interactions with victims of domestic violence. Child advocacy centers are another example of novel approaches to prevention and treatment that have developed very quickly.

In other areas, however, routine practices and service delivery systems are extremely slow and resistant to change in addressing family violence. The child protective services system is perhaps an important example of a service intervention that consistently focuses predominantly on casework, child protection, and foster care rather than family support. A recent article by Patricia Schene (1998) discusses this point in greater detail, pointing out that although federal legislation made repeated efforts in the 1970s to give the states resources that could be used to address the social service needs of children and families, three-fourths of these funds were devoted to foster care rather than to services to support and preserve families. The author suggests, however, that the level of resources necessary to support families in distress has never been sufficient to meet the demand and also respond to the needs of children who do require placement. But the policy shifts from child protection to family preservation to expedited adoption proceedings are ones that need to be viewed with concern–in each case the knowledge base that guides the basic assumptions of the policy process is weak and composed largely of anecdotal stories or studies without rigorous designs.

2. *Interventions exist in an uncoordinated system of services whose effects interact on the problem of family violence in a way that presents a major challenge to their evaluation.* The rush to "do something" has resulted in a broad array of services in a variety of institutional settings–a wealth of program experimentation that is extensive but uncoordinated. The committee observed that the existing array of programs, interventions, and strategies within health, social services, and law enforcement settings is highly fragmented and documentation of the existing set of treatment and prevention services for family violence is poor. The preoccupation with the development and analysis of particular programs, as opposed to the assessment of interventions and strategies, has created research and service environments that are tightly clustered around individual components within the service system rather than examining the quality of interactions, strengths, and shortcomings within the system of family violence services as a whole.

3. *Prevention efforts have emerged in some areas (such as home visitation services and child witness to violence interventions) that show some promise of impact on the problem of family violence by concentrating services on populations and communities at risk.* The problem of family violence has many roots, and the challenge for prevention is to find those that are significant and can be changed. Different paradigms govern the design of preventive interventions in child maltreatment, domestic violence, and elder abuse, and these variations inhibit our ability to discern approaches that can be trans-

ferred across fields and institutional settings. For example, in addressing child maltreatment, the focus of prevention is often designed to give the parent, especially the mother, the resources she needs to cope with the developmental needs of the child without resorting to violence or neglect. In domestic violence, the focus is generally on empowering the victim, usually the woman, to see other options for herself in moving away from an abusive relationship and providing the necessary protections and resources that can allow her to act on her choices. We still know so little about elder abuse, but the issue of prevention is more complicated in this area because the competency of the senior adult to make well-informed and autonomous decisions is often in question.

The goal of many preventive interventions is to reach individuals, families, and communities *before* family violence is a problem. Although this is admirable, the heterogeneity of the profiles of victims and batterers suggests that multiple approaches will be necessary to reach a significant sample of the community. If there is a tipping point, in which behavioral changes within a small group will affect the actions of the larger at-risk population, its dimensions remain unknown. In the interim, the NRC-IOM committee believed that significant potential exists to design preventive interventions focused on at-risk populations, and that some programs, such as home visitation, have demonstrated important benefits that deserve attention.

4. *An increasing emphasis on the need for integrated services is stimulating interest in comprehensive and cross-problem approaches that can address family violence in the context of other problem behaviors.* The recognition that different family members may experience different forms of family violence, and that family violence is linked in yet poorly understood ways to other social behaviors such as alcoholism, substance abuse, crime, homelessness, and runaway youth, has stimulated efforts to foster greater coordination among separate programs and services. It is thought that comprehensive efforts have an increased chance of achieving favorable outcomes because they have the capacity (in theory) to address a wide array of dysfunctional behavior and, in some cases, involve multiple family members or community members. The child witness to violence intervention programs, for example, represent an important effort to link the impact of domestic violence on children with the need for preventive interven-

tions before the child herself is injured or begins to mimic the abusive behavior.

But the evaluation studies of comprehensive community-based interventions are inconsistent. First, moving from theory to an on-the-ground intervention requires an enormous investment of resources, personnel, and leadership that can divert attention away from victim services towards internal programmatic needs. Secondly, since service providers in different institutional settings may use different theories of change, comprehensive approaches require efforts to establish a single consistent programmatic philosophy. For example, one study of a program that attempted to integrate domestic violence and substance abuse treatment reported that the substance abuse counselors worked from a paradigm in which their clients were viewed as having a clinical disorder that required them to move towards a medical model of treatment. The domestic violence counselors, on the other hand, worked from a philosophy of behavioral accountability, in which a client who reported that he was out of control in dealing with an intimate partner was viewed as lacking accountability and motivation to change. The substance abuse clients were viewed as sick folks who needed help to overcome their addictions; the domestic violence clients (the same individuals) were taught that they had to take charge of their lives and be held accountable for their actions. The service providers in each unit were reluctant to refer clients to each other because they simply did not trust the paradigms that governed the separate elements of this cross-problem program.

6. *The duration and intensity of the mental health and social support services needed to influence behaviors that result from or contribute to family violence may be greater than initially estimated.* All too commonly, family violence treatment and prevention programs focus on single incidents and short periods of support in areas such as parenting skills, mental health, and batterer treatment. Many treatment programs are less than six weeks, which may simply be inadequate to resolve problems that are pervasive, multiple, and chronic. Efforts to address fundamental sources of conflict, stress, and violence that occur repeatedly over time within family environments may require extensive periods of support or follow-up services to sustain the positive effects achieved in short-term interventions. If clinical signs of mental illness are involved, such as depression, post-traumatic stress

disorder, or schizophrenia, more intensive therapeutic interventions may be required to complement social support services.

NEXT STEPS:
RESEARCH AND POLICY RECOMMENDATIONS

The NRC-IOM study offers two sets of recommendations in the areas of policy and research. The six policy recommendations are derived from the analysis of existing research studies of family violence interventions. They include:

- *State reporting laws addressing family violence should be examined to determine whether and how early case detection leads to improved outcomes for victims or families.* Since no evaluation studies exist that can demonstrate the value of mandatory reporting systems compared with voluntary reporting procedures, the committee recommends that states refrain from enacting mandatory reporting laws for domestic violence until such systems have been tested and evaluated by research.
- *Health care and social service providers should develop safeguards to strengthen their documentation of abuse and histories of family violence in individual and group records.* The voluntary disclosure of abuse histories in victim interactions with health care providers requires serious attention to determine the best means by which documentation of family violence experiences can be conveyed to different service providers over the lifetime of the patient. Such documentation can be important in determining relationships between early, acute, or chronic experiences with violence and stress-related health disorders or developmental outcomes that may not appear until many years after the initial experiences, when health care providers have often changed. The importance of confidentiality and privacy in safeguarding abuse histories should not be underestimated, however. Efforts to record abuse histories need to be accompanied by safeguards to ensure that such documentation does not lead to victim stigmatization, encourage discriminatory practices, or lead to practices that distract service providers from treating problems that might be mistakenly attributed to an abuse history.
- *Collaborative strategies should be encouraged in law enforcement settings to improve the batterer's compliance with treatment*

and the certainty of the use of sanctions in addressing domestic violence. The series of arrest studies conducted in the 1980s provide empirical support for the use of deterrence in dealing with some, but not all, batterers. The uneven effects of arrest, however, call into question the reliance of law enforcement officers on arrest as the sole or central component of their response, especially in communities where domestic violence cases are not routinely prosecuted and sanctions are not imposed. What remains to be determined is whether collaborative approaches have the ability to establish deterrence for larger numbers or different types of batterers, at what cost, and how that strategy compares with the effects of arrest-only interventions.

• *Courts should adopt early warning systems to detect failure by offenders to comply with or complete treatment as well as to detect signs of new abuse or retaliation against victims.* This recommendation, along with the one before it, is designed to determine if efforts to create a web of social control for offenders can deter domestic violence. Since the research base does not yet suggest a specific treatment model that is appropriate for most batterers, courts need to be more vigilant in their oversight of treatment referrals. Such oversight could include stronger enforcement for referral orders, penalties for failure to comply with program requirements, and the development of different treatment components that can address the needs of different types of batterers.

• *Home visitation programs should be particularly encouraged for first-time parents living in social settings with high rates of child maltreatment reports.* Home visitation and family support programs constitute one of the most promising areas of child maltreatment prevention. Studies in this area have experimented with different levels of treatment intensity, duration, and staff expertise. Evaluation studies of home visitation services suggest that such interventions can achieve positive effects for first-time mothers who delay additional pregnancies and reduce the financial and social stresses that burden households with large numbers of young children, improve child care for infants and toddlers, and increase knowledge about the availability of community services for mothers and children.

- *Although intensive family preservation services are an important part of family support services, they should not be required in every situation in which a child is recommended for out-of-home placement.* Evaluations of intensive family preservation services have focused primarily on their effects on placement rates and the duration of placement. These studies have often not examined the impact of such services on child health, safety, and well-being, or the level of family functioning.

The committee's research recommendations offer several principles to guide research sponsors in their selection of evaluation studies:

- An intervention should be mature enough to warrant evaluation.
- An intervention should be different enough from existing services that its critical components can be evaluated.
- Service providers should be willing to collaborate with the researchers and appropriate data should be accessible in the service records.
- Satisfactory measurement processes should exist to assess client outcomes.
- Adequate time and resources should be available to conduct a quality assessment.

With these principles in mind, the NRC-IOM committee identified a set of interventions that are the focus of policy attention and service innovation efforts but have not received significant attention from research. This set of interventions is recommended as strong candidates for future evaluation studies in the report's research agenda. It includes: (1) family violence training for health and social service providers and law enforcement officials; (2) universal screening for family violence victims in health care and child welfare settings; (3) comprehensive community initiatives; (4) shelter programs and other domestic violence services; (5) protective orders; (6) child fatality review panels; (7) mental health and counseling services for child and adult victims of family violence; (8) child witness to violence prevention and treatment programs; and (9) elder abuse services.

In addition, four research topics were highlighted in the NRC-IOM report as ones that merit further development to inform family violence policy and practice. These include: cross-problem research (such as the relationship between substance abuse and family violence);

studies of family dynamics and processes that interact with family violence; cost analysis and service system studies; and social setting issues that can influence the design of treatment, support, prevention, and deterrence strategies.

In addressing the role of public health in family violence interventions, the report observes that improved strategies are needed to achieve a balance between risk and protective factors to develop both case detection and social support approaches and also to establish safeguards to protect the rights of privacy and confidentiality of individuals and families. Although managed care models may encourage prevention efforts, especially if patients are followed over extensive periods of time, cost containment models may impose new limits on the abilities of health care providers to ask about their clients' experience with violence, to provide counseling services to become a point of consistent interaction with their patients, and to engage in nonreimbursable collaborative ventures with other agency personnel designed to improve the quality care for the community as a whole.

Furthermore, the emergence of comprehensive and collaborative interventions focused on family violence prevention and treatment raises a host of questions about the value of addressing multiple risk and protective factors in community settings. The NRC-IOM committee acknowledges that although comprehensive community interventions are one of the most popular and fastest growing areas of activity in family violence interventions, no single model of service integration, comprehensive services, or community change can be endorsed at this time. These interventions have the potential to reduce the scope and severity of family violence, and represent an exciting prevention model. But several key factors deserve further consideration as part of their development:

- What are the resource requirements of comprehensive community interventions?
- Do adequate measures exist to examine the critical domains in which changes are expected to occur as a result of a community intervention?
- Are the strategies that are developed in one area (such as domestic violence) useful in addressing other forms of family violence or the relationships between family and community violence?

- What lessons can be drawn from program design and evaluation experiences in other areas of prevention research, especially with regard to study design, sample recruitment and retention, and measurement, that can help inform the field of family violence interventions?

THINK STRATEGICALLY, ACT LOCALLY

In the decades ahead, research will provide new insights that can lead to improved services, policy and practice in addressing family violence. But the integration of research knowledge and the development of interventions will require consistent and explicit attention to interactions among science, health care, law enforcement, and social services within their regional context. Collaborative partnerships are needed to address these interactions that can be tested in a variety of community settings and governance structures. Such efforts will need to address the resource and organizational constraints that inhibit moving promising initiatives from the stage of demonstration projects to sustained practices within large systems of ongoing services. This task is made more difficult because the large bureaucratic structures associated with law enforcement, social service, and, to a more limited extent, public health and health care have not been receptive to using innovative research knowledge in the design of human services.

The NRC-IOM committee identified a series of opportunities to build these partnerships and improve collaboration between service providers and researchers, focusing on ways to develop knowledge about what works, for whom, and under what conditions: (1) improving descriptions of existing community services; (2) documenting the theory of change that guides service interventions; (3) describing the stages of implementation of the service program; and (4) describing the client referral, screening, and baseline assessment process. Team building efforts are needed to address the dynamics of collaboration and to foster greater opportunity for functional partnerships that build a common respect for research requirements and service information needs. To achieve this goal, the committee urges the establishment of a series of consensus conferences on relevant outcomes, and appropriate measurement tools, to strengthen and enhance the design and evaluation of family violence interventions.

An integrated research foundation, the development of reliable measures and large datasets, careful descriptions of the goals of an intervention and the characteristics of clients, and documentation of the services that were actually provided, all provide important opportunities for such partnerships. But institutional and policy leadership is needed to ensure that such efforts have the resources that will be needed to establish enduring relationships and resist advocacy efforts to endorse programmatic innovations that have not been tested in reliable research studies.

NOTES

1. See for example, *Understanding Child Abuse and Neglect* (National Research Council, 1993) and *Understanding Violence Against Women* (Crowell & Burgess, 1993).

2. The NRC reports cited in footnote 1 included recommendations in these areas.

3. For examples of studies that include randomized designs, see research on the Elmira, NY home visitation programs (Olds et al., 1986, 1988, 1994, 1995, and 1997); the Spousal Arrest Replication Program (Berk et al., 1992a; Dunford et al., 1990; Ford and Regoli, 1993; Hirschel and Hutchison, 1992; Pate and Hamilton, 1992; Sherman and Berk, 1984a,b; and Steinman, 1988, 1990), and evaluations of intensive family preservation services (Schuerman et al., 1994; Pecora et al., 1992).

4. Committee members included Patricia King (chair), Jacquelyn Campbell, David Cordray, Diana English, Jeffrey Fagan, Richard Gelles, Joel Greenhouse, Scott Harshbarger, Darnell Hawkins, Cindy Lederman, Elizabeth McLoughlin, Eli Newberger, Joy Osofsky, Helen Rodriguez-Trias, Susan Schechter, Michael Smith, Bill Walsh, Carole Warshaw, and Rosalie Wolf. Rosemary Chalk was the project study director.

5. Federal sponsors included the Centers for Disease Control and Prevention, the National Institute of Justice, the Administration of Families and Children, the National Institute of Mental Health, the Maternal and Child Health Bureau, and the Substance Abuse and Mental Health Services Administration. The study was housed within the Board on Children, Youth, and Families, a joint activity of the National Research Council and the Institute of Medicine in Washington, DC.

6. The full text of the report is available in electronic form from the National Academy Press and is posted on the web at www.nap.edu. An abbreviated summary of the report has been published in the *American Journal of Preventive Medicine* (May 1998, 14(4): 289-292). This report is the latest in a series of family violence research studies prepared through the National Research Council and the Institute of Medicine, including *Understanding Child Abuse and Neglect* (National Research Council, 1993), *Understanding Violence Against Women* (Crowell and Burgess, 1996), and an earlier 4-volume series on *Understanding Violence* (Reiss and Roth, 1993 and 1994) that includes a lengthy background paper by Jeff Fagan and Angela Browne on domestic violence research.

7. A discussion of these concerns can be found in Chapter 9 of *Understanding Child Abuse and Neglect* (National Research Council, 1993).

8. See U.S. Department of Justice, National Institute of Justice, "Research and Evaluations on Violence Against Women" research solicitation, April 1998; "Research on Violence Against Women: Syntheses for Practitioners" research solicitation, June 1, 1998. Additional research solicitations are expected to be published in 1999 by the U.S. Department of Health and Human Services.

REFERENCES

Adams, S.L. (1994). Restraining order trend analysis and defendant profile. *Executive Exchange*, 2-3.

Berk, R.A., Campbell, A., Klap, R., & Western, B. (1992a). A Bayesian analysis of the Colorado Springs spouse abuse experiment. *Journal of Criminal Law and Criminology, 83*(1), 170-200.

Berk, R.A., Campbell, A., Klap, R., & Western, B. (1992b). The deterrent effect of arrest in incidents of domestic violence: A Bayesian analysis of four field experiments. *American Sociological Review, 57*, 698-708.

Chalk, R., & King, P. (Eds.). (1998). *Violence in families: Assessing prevention and treatment programs*. Washington, DC: National Academy Press.

Crowell, N., & Burgess, A. (Eds.). (1996). *Understanding violence against women*. Washington, DC: National Academy Press.

Dunford, F.W., Huizinga, D., & Elliott, D.S. (1990). The role of arrest in domestic assault: The Omaha experiment. *Criminology, 28*, 183-206.

Ford, D.A., & Regoli, M.J. (1993). *The Indianapolis domestic violence prosecution experiment. Final Report*. Indianapolis, IN: Indiana University.

Hirschel, J.D., & Hutchison, I.W. (1992). Female spouse abuse and the police response: The Charlotte, North Carolina experiment. *Journal of Criminal Law and Criminology, 83*(1), 73-119.

National Research Council. (1993). *Understanding child abuse and neglect*. Washington, DC: National Academy Press.

Olds, D.L., & Kitzman, H. (1990). Can home visitation improve the health of women and children at environmental risk? *Pediatrics, 86*(1), 108-116.

Olds, D.L., & Kitzman, H. (1993). Review of research on home visiting for pregnant women and parents of young children. *The Future of Children, 3* (3), 53-92.

Olds, D.L., Henderson, C.R., Chamberlin, R., & Tatelbaum, R. (1986). Preventing child abuse and neglect: A randomized trial of nurse home visitation. *Pediatrics, 78*(1), 65-78.

Olds, D.L., Henderson, C.R., Tatelbaum, R., & Chamberlin, R. (1988). Improving the life-course development of socially disadvantaged mothers: A randomized trial of nurse home visitation. *American Journal of Public Health, 78*(11), 1436-1445.

Olds, D.L., Henderson, C.R., & Kitzman, H. (1994). Does prenatal and infancy nurse home visitation have enduring effects on qualities of parental caregiving and child health at 25 to 50 months of life? *Pediatrics, 93*(1), 89-98.

Olds, D.L., Henderson, C.R., Kitzman, H., & Cole, R. (1995). Effects of prenatal and infancy nurse home visitation on surveillance of child maltreatment. *Pediatrics, 95*(3), 365-372.

Olds, D.L., Eckenrode, J., Henderson, Jr., C.R., Kitzman, H., Powers, J., Cole, R., Sidora, K., Morris, P., Pettitt, L.M., & Luckey, D. (1997). Long-term effects of home visitation on maternal life course and child abuse and neglect. *Journal of the American Medical Association, 278*(8), 637-643.

Pate, A.M., & Hamilton, E.E. (1992). Formal and informal deterrents to domestic violence: The Dade County Spouse Assault Experiment. *American Sociological Review, 57,* 691-697.

Pecora, P.J., Fraser, M.W., & Haapala, D.A. (1992). Client outcomes and issues for program design. In K. Wells & D.E. Biegel (Eds.), *Family preservation services: Research and evaluation.* Newbury Park, CA: Sage.

Reiss., A.J., & Roth, J.A. (Eds.). (1993). *Understanding and preventing violence, Volume 1.* Washington, DC: National Academy Press.

Reiss, A.J., & Roth, J.A. (Eds.). (1994). *Understanding and preventing violence, Volume 3.* Washington, DC: National Academy Press.

Rice, D.P., Max, W., Golding, J., & Pinderhughes, H. (1996). *The cost of domestic violence to the health care system. Final Report.* Washington, DC: U.S. Department of Health and Human Services.

Schene, P.A. (1998). Past, present, and future roles of child protective services. *The Future of Children, 8*(1), 23-38.

Schuerman, J.R., Rzepnicki, T.L., & Littell, J.H. (1994). *Putting families first: An experiment in family preservation.* New York, NY: Aldine de Gruyter.

Sherman, L.W., & Berk, R.A. (1984a). The specific deterrent effects of arrest for domestic assault. *American Sociological Review, 49*(2), 261-272.

Sherman, L.W., & Berk, R.A. (1984b). *The Minneapolis domestic violence experiment.* Washington, DC: Police Foundation.

Steinman, M. (1988). Evaluating a system-wide response to domestic violence: Some initial findings. *Journal of Contemporary Criminal Justice, 4,* 72-186.

Steinman, M. (1990). Lowering recidivism among men who batter women. *Journal of Police Science and Administration, 17*(2), 124-132.

Straus, M. (1986). The cost of intrafamily assault and homicide to society. *Academic Medicine, 62,* 556-561.

Research Synthesis in Family Violence: The Art of Reviewing Research

David B. Sugarman
Sue Boney-McCoy

SUMMARY. The present article discusses the application of quantitative research synthesis techniques to family violence research. While examples are taken from a number of general areas in family violence, we focus on the application of these review methods to evaluation research in particular. Although this is not a "how-to" manual for conducting quantitative or meta-analytic reviews, we present a general description of the meta-analytic process and then address both meritorious and problematic aspects of quantitative research synthesis. The paper examines the manner in which quantitative research synthesis reconceptualizes the review process, the problems often confronted when conducting a meta-analysis, and the way in which these techniques complement the traditional narrative literature review. To demonstrate the applicability of these techniques to evaluation research in family violence, a small meta-analysis of the Spousal Assault Replication Program (SARP) is presented. *[Article copies available for a fee from The Haworth Document Delivery Service: 1-800-342-9678. E-mail address: <getinfo@haworthpressinc.com> Website: <http://www.HaworthPress.com>]*

KEYWORDS. Meta-analysis, evaluation research, violence, family

In a recent Presidential Column for the American Psychological Society, Loftus (1998) recalls admonishing new graduates at the Uni-

---

Address correspondence to: David B. Sugarman, PhD, Professor of Psychology, Rhode Island College, 600 Mt. Pleasant Avenue, Providence, RI 02908.

[Haworth co-indexing entry note]: "Research Synthesis in Family Violence: The Art of Reviewing Research." Sugarman, David B., and Sue Boney-McCoy. Co-published simultaneously in *Journal of Aggression, Maltreatment & Trauma* (The Haworth Maltreatment & Trauma Press, an imprint of The Haworth Press, Inc.) Vol. 4, No. 1 (#7), 2000, pp. 55-82; and: *Program Evaluation and Family Violence Research* (ed: Sally K. Ward, and David Finkelhor) The Haworth Maltreatment & Trauma Press, an imprint of The Haworth Press, Inc., 2000, pp. 55-82. Single or multiple copies of this article are available for a fee from The Haworth Document Delivery Service [1-800-342-9678, 9:00 a.m. - 5:00 p.m. (EST). E-mail address: getinfo@haworthpressinc.com].

55

versity of Portsmouth, England, to ask two questions when evaluating claims about human behavior. The first question that she advised students to ask was "What is the evidence?" With this recommendation, she cautioned against accepting claims as fact merely because they appeal to sentiment or common sense (p. 3). This dictum applies equally well to family violence researchers, particularly when we are called to guide the design of interventions or social policy. We must base our recommendations on empirical evidence, not on lay-theories, folk wisdom, or the political "flavor-of-the-day." Does a specific treatment program reduce domestic violence recidivism? Does children's witnessing of parental violence have a negative impact later in life? Will school-based programs to reduce dating violence really work? Such questions must be informed by scientifically sound, empirical research.

The second question that Loftus (1998) counseled students to ask was, "What EXACTLY is the evidence?" (p. 27) because the *type* as well as the *presence* of empirical evidence used to support claims about human behavior requires evaluation. Those engaged in family violence research must confront this second issue because not all empirical research is of equal quality. The range of criticisms that might be leveled at a particular study is very broad. Were adequate control groups used? Were participants randomized to level of treatment? Is the study's design prospective or retrospective? How representative is the sample of the target population? We need to scrutinize the quality as well as the quantity of the evidence from which we draw our conclusions and generate public policy.

Traditionally, members of the family violence research community have evaluated the results of empirical research with narrative or qualitative reviews of the literature. These reviews span a wide range of areas: partner violence risk factors and correlates (e.g., Gleason, 1997; Hotaling & Sugarman, 1986; Holtzworth-Munroe, Bates, Smutzler, & Sandin, 1997; Holtzworth-Munroe, Smutzler, & Bates, 1997; Jackson, 1999; Kaufman Kantor & Jasinski, 1996; Sugarman & Hotaling, 1989), sequelae of partner violence (Giles-Sims, 1996; Holtzworth-Munroe, Smutzler, & Sandin, 1997; Wolak & Finkelhor, 1996), prevention and intervention issues regarding domestic violence (Chalk & King, 1997; Hamby, 1996; Rhodes & McKenzie, 1998) as well as a great many other family violence issues. Although the narrative review approach has contributed much to our understanding of family violence, behavioral and social scientists have encouraged the application of *meta-analytic* or *quantitative research synthesis* strategies (Cooper & Hedges, 1994; Hedges & Olkin, 1985; Rosenthal, 1984, 1991). Within the field of psychology, in general, quantitative research reviews have become more common. For example, the percentage of citations in the psychological computerized database, PsycInfo, containing the keywords "meta-analysis" or "meta-analytic," has increased from .1% in 1977 to more than 5% in 1997. However, family violence researchers have only recently begun to address the questions of "What is the evidence?" and "What EXACTLY is the evidence?" with quantitative techniques.

The present paper offers family violence researchers a brief discussion of quantitative research synthesis techniques. It is not a "how-to" manual for conducting quantitative reviews; these guides are readily available (e.g., Cooper, 1982; Cooper & Hedges, 1994; Rosenthal, 1995; Rothstein & McDaniel, 1989). Instead, we present a general description of the meta-analytic process and then address both meritorious and problematic aspects of quantitative research synthesis. Specifically, we highlight the ways in which quantitative research synthesis reconceptualizes the review process, we discuss several problems that are often met when conducting a meta-analysis, and we emphasize the ways in which meta-analytic techniques complement rather than replace narrative literature reviews.

THE META-ANALYTIC RESEARCH PROCESS

A quantitative research review (meta-analysis) involves five steps. First, reviewers must clearly identify a research hypothesis or research question for which they desire to evaluate the empirical evidence. Clear identification of the hypothesis or question to be examined is critical, because it determines the data points (e.g., the research studies) that will be included in the analysis. Examples of such a specific question might be "How strong is the relationship between social desirability and self-reports of partner violence?" or "How strong is the impact of an intervention program to decrease the amount of dating violence in high schools?"

Once a specific hypothesis or question has been identified, reviewers systematically search the research literature for empirical studies that focus on the issue addressed by the review. This step typically commences with a thorough search of computerized literature databases (e.g., PsycInfo and Sociofile), continues with perusal of the reference sections of the articles thus identified, and concludes with directly contacting authors who have published research on the topic to inquire about the existence of additional, applicable, research that has not been published. The search for unpublished studies includes an attempt to discover data that failed to be published because they did not succeed to support a particular hypothesis. Once the studies have been obtained, the third step involves developing a database of statistical information from all of the studies. This database includes *effect sizes* from each study that result from empirical testing of the research hypothesis under scrutiny. The two most common effect sizes used in meta-analytic reviewing are Cohen's *d* and the Pearson *r*. Variables that might moderate the size of the effect across samples (e.g., participant gender) are also included in the meta-analytic database. If sufficient information to calculate effect sizes is not given in a particular study, reviewers attempt to gather this information directly from the study's author. With the fourth step, reviewers perform the necessary statistical analyses on the obtained effect sizes. This analysis typically involves the calculation of the *overall average effect size* (usually weighted by sample size) and a test of *homogeneity* (Q_W) that evaluates the variation among the effect sizes. A significant Q-statistic (based on the chi-square distribution) indicates heterogeneity among effect sizes and leads reviewers to attempt to identify the source of this variance. For example, does one find significantly larger effect sizes with male samples than with female samples? Or, do clinical sample studies exhibit significantly larger effect sizes than studies using community samples? Investigation of such moderating effects produces some of the richest and most interesting results from a meta-analytic review, and multivariate techniques have been successfully applied to effect size data sets (cf. Raudenbush, Becker, & Kalaian, 1988). The fifth and final step of a quantitative review is to write the research synthesis (Rosenthal, 1995).

RECONCEPTUALIZING
THE RESEARCH REVIEW PROCESS

Quantitative Reviews: Similarity to Primary Research

Perhaps the greatest difference between the traditional, narrative, literature review and the meta-analytic review is that in the latter, meta-analysts construe the review process more as primary research than as simply "reviewing" the research of others. Unlike the narrative review, the quantitative review requires that numeric data are collected and statistically analyzed. The chief difference between a quantitative review and primary research is that the data in the quantitative review derive from previously conducted research. However, the collection and statistical analysis of these "data points" requires reviewers to treat the review process with the same scientific rigor that they would apply to primary research.

For example, consider the "sample" on which quantitative reviewers base their analyses. Each effect size can be considered analogous to a "participant" in primary research. Quantitative reviewers must provide detailed information about how they sampled the universe of relevant studies, including the specific literature search techniques (e.g., the "keywords" or "subject headings" entered into PsycInfo) that were used to obtain their sample. Just like primary researchers, meta-analysts are concerned with the representativeness of their samples. If a study is dropped from the meta-analytic database, this deletion must be discussed and justified. Narrative reviews, by contrast, are often based on unsystematic samples of studies that are limited or indeterminate in their representation of studies on the topic.

Other aspects of the procedures involved in conducting quantitative research reviews parallel those used in primary research. For example, primary researchers who conducted an observational investigation on the aggressive classroom behavior of children from homes where there was or was not the presence of marital violence would have to indicate how "aggressive behavior" was operationally defined and offer evidence of inter-rater agreement. Similarly, in conducting a meta-analytic review on the relationship between witnessing parental violence and aggressive behavior during childhood, reviewers would have to develop a coding scheme for various study characteristics and obtain inter-rater agreement on these qualities.

The quantitative review has the advantage of making explicit the decisions and the procedures used in generating reviewers' conclusions, increasing the reliability of these reviews (Zakzanis, 1998). This information permits other reviewers to replicate the results of a quantitative research synthesis, to extend our understanding of the research by adding new or previously "lost" studies, or to examine a moderator variable not included in the initial review. For example, Sugarman and Frankel (1996) reported that the overall effect size between men's self-reports of their attitudes toward women and their perpetration of marital violence was not statistically significant. However, Hanson (1998) replicated this analysis with the inclusion of a number of newly located effect sizes and found a significant average effect size across this collection of studies.

Focus on Effect Size, Not Significance Level

Narrative literature reviews typically focus on the results of published, inferential statistical tests (significance tests) to assess support for a hypothesis. Studies that report *significant* results (in the predicted direction) are considered to support the hypothesis. Studies that do not report significant results weaken support for the hypothesis. Reliance on significant results, whether the critical alpha level is set at $p = .05$, .01, or .001, may yield erroneous conclusions about the empirical support for a hypothesis for three reasons.

First, tests of significance are influenced by two factors: (1) the size of the effect obtained and (2) the sample size (Rosenthal, 1984, 1991). With a large enough sample, even the smallest effect will be statistically significant. By the same token, small sample sizes can produce non-significant results despite the presence of large effects. When narrative reviewers qualitatively synthesize research findings, their reliance on significance levels can result in erroneous conclusions because of differences in sample size or the power of the particular statistical tests applied. In addition, the significance level does not indicate the *direction* of an observed effect and cannot be used to systematically assess the extent to which results in the "opposite" direction from that predicted influence the overall pattern of findings for the hypothesis. While other quantitative techniques have been developed for confronting some of these issues, these techniques are more advisable when the analysis of effect size estimates cannot be performed (Becker, 1994; Bushman, 1994). By focusing on the size of the effects obtained rather than on whether a test statistic has surpassed a critical value, quantitative research synthesis improves the accuracy of reviewers' conclusions.

A second limitation of our traditional focus on significance levels is the nearly mandatory requirement of statistical significance for publication (see Begg & Berlin, 1988, for review). Due to this publication bias, we do not know the number of non-significant findings that are hidden away in our colleagues' desk drawers (Rosenthal, 1979). Quantitative review of the literature addresses this issue in two ways. First, because meta-analysts may conduct more exhaustive searches of the research on a topic (both published and unpublished), they may be more likely to discover unpublished, null findings than would the typical qualitative reviewer. They might also be more likely to uncover studies yielding substantial effect sizes that failed to be accepted (or even submitted) for publication due to failure to achieve statistical significance. Second, meta-analytic techniques allow the quantitative reviewer to calculate the number of studies with "null findings" (an effect size of zero) that would be required to "wash out" the effect indicated by those studies that were available for analysis. Both aspects of meta-analysis are likely to enhance the accuracy of conclusions derived from such a review of the literature. See the following sources for a discussion of the relative merits of focusing on significance levels (Abelson, 1997; Chow, 1988; Harris, 1997) or on effect sizes (Cohen, 1994; Hunter, 1997; Schmidt, 1996).

A third problem with focusing on significance levels is their limited utility for translating research findings into real-world implications. Using police reports, Sherman and Berk (1984) reported a significantly lower 6-month recidivism rate for men who were arrested after assaulting their wives than men who were either offered mediation or separated from their partner, $r = .13$, $d = .25$, $p = .022$. Based on the significance level alone, this finding would suggest that mandatory spouse arrest might be a sound public policy to institute. However, one can use the effect size estimate to conduct a more detailed cost-benefit analysis of this intervention.

Estimating the Utility of an Intervention

To assess the impact of a policy or intervention, Rosenthal and Rubin (1982) suggested the use of a very simple and intuitive display, the binomial effect size display (BESD). The BESD addresses the impact that a particular treatment, procedure, or policy has on a measure of success rate (i.e., cure rates, recidivism rates, improvement rates). The display exhibits the increase in success rate that can be attributed to the new treatment or procedure relative to a control treatment. The treatment group success rate is calculated by adding one half of the observed correlation to .50; the control success rate is computed by subtracting one half of the observed correlation from .50.

To evaluate the intervention's impact, one subtracts the control success rate from the treatment success rate and then divides this figure by the treatment success rate. One converts the obtained value into a percentage by multiplying by 100. For example, The BESD for the Sherman and Berk's (1984) police report finding is given in Table 1. The treatment success rate is .5627 and the control success rate is .4373. Consequently, this suggests that there is a 22.3 percent decrease in recidivism ((.5627 − .4373)/.5627*100) when arrest of the violent spouse occurs, in contrast to the other two intervention conditions (separation and mediation). Consequently, if a jurisdiction reports a 6-month recidivism incidence rate of 5,000 cases, one would expect that the initiation of a mandatory arrest policy would reduce this number to 3,885 cases in that time period.

Armed with information about the potential elimination of 1,115 cases, a policy analyst could begin to evaluate the costs and benefits of this policy initiative. What would be the health, social, and economic benefits associated with this reduction in partner violence recidivism? What would be the direct costs of this policy (e.g., the additional cost to the investigatory and prosecutory branches of the criminal justice system, or the additional legal costs for the defendant)? What are the opportunity costs that are foregone if one decides to fund this new policy initiative? By focusing on effect size estimates instead of significance levels, program evaluators can obtain more precise projections of program efficacy.

Reconceptualizing Replication

A chief concern in any review of empirical literature is the extent to which a particular finding or effect has been *replicated* across studies. Social and behavioral researchers readily accept the notion that if a study produces statistically significant results that are in the same

TABLE 1. Binomial Effect Size Display of Sherman and Berk's (1984) Minneapolis Spouse Arrest Study Using 6-Month Recidivism Based on Court Records (r = .1254).

Recidivism Status After 6 Months

Treatment	Repeats Offense		Does Not Repeat Offense	
Arrest	.50 − r/2	.4373	.50 + r/2	.5627
Separation + Mediation	.50 + r/2	.5627	.50 − r/2	.4373

direction as reported in previous research, then the study has "replicated" the earlier finding. In contrast, if several studies fail to reveal statistically significant findings, narrative reviewers typically conclude that they have failed to establish the hypothetical effect. In the event that two studies offer contradictory findings (e.g., Study 1 finds a statistically significant effect and Study 2 does not), narrative reviewers would conclude that there has been a failure to replicate the effect.

As noted by Rosenthal (1990), this emphasis on significance levels may lead reviewers to erroneous conclusions. Additionally, it requires that we make a dichotomous decision (replication versus non-replication) as to whether two studies replicate each other. Rosenthal argues that a more useful conceptualization of replication focuses on effect sizes, giving less consideration to statistical significance and allowing a continuous, as well as binary, decision regarding replication.

As an example, Rosenthal (1984, 1991) presents hypothetical data about Dr. Smith, whose original study found a significant effect ($t(78) = 2.21$, $p < .05$), and Dr. Jones, whose replication of Dr. Smith's work did not yield a significant finding ($t(18) = 1.06$, $p > .30$). If we focus on the statistical significance level, we would conclude that the studies did not replicate each other. Interpretation of the two effect sizes, however, yields a different conclusion. Rosenthal shows that Dr. Jones's replication study ($d = .50$, $r = .24$) exhibited the *identical* effect size as did Dr. Smith's original study ($d = .50$, $r = .24$). Although Dr. Smith's finding did not reach statistical significance, it did replicate the effect (the *effect size*) obtained by Dr. Jones.

Rosenthal (1990) points to two continuous indicators of the degree of replication or robustness. The first statistic, Cohen's q, tests the significance of the observed difference between two effect sizes (rs). One can then evaluate the degree of heterogeneity between these effect sizes. Alternatively, a meta-analyst could calculate a coefficient of robustness of replication computed by dividing the average effect size by the variance of the effect sizes. Robustness coefficients do not have an intrinsic meaning but can serve as comparison indicators across research domains. For example, one may conclude that a research domain with a robust coefficient of 2.0 would exhibit a stronger tendency of replication than a domain with a 0.5 coefficient.

In addition to suggesting that statistical significance is not *necessary* for replication, Rosenthal's approach also demonstrates that it is not *sufficient*. For example, consider the hypothetical case of Dr. Adams and Dr. Bower. Dr. Adams finds that self-referred violent husbands are more likely to benefit from a specific battered treatment program than court-mandated violent husbands, $t(36) = 3.10, p < .01$, $r = .46$. Attempting to replicate Adams's treatment findings, Dr. Bower reports significant results in the same direction, $t(220) = 2.04, p < .05, r = .14$. These studies do replicate each other with regard to the direction of the effect and statistical significance; however, the magnitude of these effects differs tremendously. Dr. Adams's study had an effect size ($r = .46$) that was more than triple that of Dr. Bower's study ($r = .14$); a meta-analytic test for homogeneity of effect sizes shows that this difference is statistically significant ($Q_w(1) = 3.78, p = .05$). Consequently, the meta-analytic reviewer would conclude that Dr. Bower's study represents only a weak replication of Dr. Adams's study and would attempt to discern why these two studies showed such discrepant effect sizes.

Another example from the family violence literature further illustrates the usefulness of measuring replication by assessing the homogeneity of effect sizes from several studies. Sugarman and Hotaling (1997) conducted a meta-analytic review of studies testing the relationship between social desirability and partner violence. Across the 18 effect sizes obtained, an average effect size (r) of $-.179$ was found. These estimates, however, exhibited statistically significant variability ($Q_w(17) = 39.95, p < .001$); in other words, they represented only partial "replication" of the effect because they were not homogeneous. These findings suggested that some factor or factors moderated the size of the effect. One candidate for a "moderator variable" in this review was the *type* of violence in which the respondents reported engaging ("minor" or "severe," as indexed by the Conflict Tactics Scales). Interestingly, after the effect size from the only study that examined the relationship between social desirability and *"severe"* partner violence was removed from this data set, the remaining 17 effect sizes were shown to be statistically homogeneous ($Q_w(16) = 20.94, p = .18$). Among the 17 studies concerning "minor" partner violence, the average effect size (r) was $-.158$ ($N = 1,872$); by contrast, the effect size from the only study involving "severe" partner violence (Saunders, 1992) was $r (180) = -.38$. This analysis suggested that the relationship between admitting to perpetration of intimate violence and social desirability is different (stronger) for "severe" violence than for "minor" violence. "Replication" in this instance was found most strongly when studies that measured only one type of violence were examined. If the reviewers had focused simply on the direction and significance of results, rather than on the homogeneity of the effect sizes, this moderating effect might not have been detected.

Assessing the Impact of Moderator Variables

When a data set of effect sizes exhibits heterogeneity, as in the previous example, meta-analysts seek to identify moderator variables that contribute to the observed variation of these effect sizes. Although narrative reviewers also seek to understand discrepancies in research literature, their tools for doing so are less precise than those used in a quantitative review. For example, Jumper (1995) examined the relationship between child sexual abuse and adult psychological adjustment as assessed by psychological symptomatology, depression, and self-esteem. Focusing on the analysis of self-esteem, Jumper reported an average effect size (r) of .17 based on 2,362 subjects across 12 studies. In addition, he noted that the variation among these effect sizes was greater than would be expected by chance ($Q_w(11) = 85.95$, $p < .001$). To account for this effect size variability, Jumper conducted a moderator analysis and classified the studies based on four characteristics: sample source (community, clinical, student, or other); abuse definition (contact abuse, non-contact abuse, consensual); date of publication (1978-1987 versus 1988-1991); and participant gender (male, female). Each of these study characteristics accounted for significant variability in the effect sizes obtained. To illustrate, Jumper reported that the data from the nine female samples analyzed (average $r = .24$, $p < .05$, $N = 1,740$) reflected a significantly stronger relationship between child sexual abuse and adult self-esteem ($Q_b(1) = 29.61$, $p < .001$) than did the data from the three male samples (average $r = -.02$, $p = $ ns, $N = 622$).

The examination of moderator variables permits meta-analysts to directly test the impact of specific theoretically or methodologically important variables. Consequently, one may detect boundary conditions for a particular effect. In addition to revealing the absence of an association between child sexual abuse and adult self-esteem for samples of men, Jumper (1995) found non-significant average effect sizes for four studies in which students were sampled, average $r = -.02$, $p = $

ns, N = 1,011, for four studies in which the definition of abuse could include non-contact forms of abuse (e.g., exposure), average r = $-.02$, p = ns, N = 1011, and for seven studies for which the publication date was 1988-1991, average r = .07, p = ns, N = 879. Although it is possible that Jumper might have discerned all of these moderator relationships from qualitative perusal of the literature, meta-analysis provided him with a powerful tool for identifying, quantifying, and partitioning the variance in effect size for the relationship between child abuse and adult self-esteem.

Translating Research into Policy

Perhaps one of the strongest arguments for doing quantitative research syntheses is an increased ability to translate findings into practically applicable information. It is especially useful for guiding policy formation in instances where the research literature yields inconsistent results. Meta-analysis affords a quantitative resolution to conflicting research findings that is somewhat more systematic than that provided by narrative reviews.

We offer an example of the way in which meta-analysis could be used to address one of the most important policy-related questions that has been studied by researchers in our field: the efficacy of mandatory arrest policies for reducing recidivism among perpetrators of intimate violence. As noted previously, Sherman and Berk's (1984) landmark Minneapolis Police Arrest study found that domestic violence recidivism was lower when the male participant was arrested than if the police separated the man from the woman or attempted to mediate the situation (r = .1254, see Table 2). This study received considerable attention, and it is commonly believed that it served as one of the factors that motivated the widespread implementation of mandatory arrest laws during the 1980s (Buzawa & Buzawa, 1993).

When one examines published reports of efforts to replicate the Minneapolis study, however, the picture becomes somewhat more murky. As described by Schmidt and Sherman (1993), data from three cities (Omaha, Charlotte, and Milwaukee) indicated an *increase* in recidivism as a result of mandatory arrest; data from three others revealed a *decrease* in recidivism as a consequence of arrest (Sherman, 1993). Schmidt and Sherman (1993) stated that these apparently conflicting results "have clouded the issue for police and policymakers" (p. 603), and Binder and Meeker (1993) decried what they la-

TABLE 2. Summary Statistics and Effect Size Estimates for the Impact of Police Arrest on Spousal Assault Recidivism Prevalence Rate as Assessed by Police Reports at Six Months (derived from Garner, Fagan, & Maxwell, 1995, Table 1)

Study	nt	nc	%t	%c	d	95% CI	r	p
Charlotte	214	436	18.2%	15.6%	−.0701	−.23/+.09	−.0351	.3718
Colorado	421	58	19.2%	19.3%	+.0025	−.27/+.28	+.0013	.9779
Dade Co.	465	442	19.1%	20.6%	+.0376	−.09/+.17	+.0188	.5713
Milwaukee	624	297	25.8%	25.2%	−.0137	−.15/+.12	−.0069	.8349
Minneapolis	93	237	6.5%	14.8%	+.2522	+.01/+.49	+.1254	.0225
Omaha 1	111	136	14.4%	22.1%	+.2064	−.04/+.46	+.1030	.1057
Omaha 2	109	221	17.4%	16.3%	−.0295	−.26/+.20	−.0148	.7891
OVERALL	2037	1827	20.1%	18.9%	+.0279	−.04/+.10	+.0140	.3854

Note: $Q_w(6)$ = 7.299; p = 0.2941; mean d (studies weighted by 1): +0.0551; nt, Arrest condition sample size; nc, Comparison condition sample size; %t, Percent of recidivism in the Arrest condition; %c, Percent of recidivism in the Comparison condition; d, Cohen's d statistic; 95%CI, 95% confidence interval for the d statistics; r, Pearson correlation; p, probability level of r.

beled "the uniform failure to reproduce the original results" of the Minneapolis arrest study (p. 886).

The failure to replicate the Minneapolis findings, however, may have been overstated. Garner, Fagan, and Maxwell (1995) reported findings from the six studies of the Spousal Assault Replication Program (SARP) studies as well as from the original Minneapolis sample, and we analyze these data here. We first examined the overall intervention effect using *police arrest data* as the measure of recidivism. When we apply meta-analytic techniques to these reported effect sizes (see Table 2), we find that the average effect size (weighted by sample size) approaches a zero value, d = .028; r = .014, and is statistically non-significant, p = .39, even given the large cumulative sample size, N = 3,864. More importantly, these results showed that the variation among the observed effect sizes could be readily attributed to chance, $Q_w(6)$ = 7.30, p = .29. That is, the effect sizes from the seven studies (including the original, Minneapolis sample) are statistically homogeneous, indicating *successful replication*. Because the overall effect size is not significantly different from zero, and the contributing effect sizes are homogenous, these studies provide evidence that mandatory arrest has essentially *no* overall main effect on recidivism when one uses *police arrest reports* to assess recidivism–not inconsistent effects (at least as demonstrated by *these data*).[1]

Six of these seven studies also assessed recidivism using *victim surveys*, and the meta-analysis of these data, offered in Table 3, reveals two very interesting points. First, based on victim reports, police arrests reduced violence recidivism significantly more than interventions involving mediation and separation, $d = .11$, $r = .06$, $p = .009$, $N = 2245$. Second, the variation among these six effect sizes may be accounted for by chance, $Q_w(5) = 9.88$, $p = .08$, and we can therefore conclude that these effect sizes replicate each other. Applying the binomial effect size display, this suggests that there is a 5.2% decrease in recidivism associated with an arrest intervention in contrast to mediation and separation.

In this example, a meta-analytic review of data that focuses on effect size produces very different conclusions than narrative reviews of these findings that consider only p values and the direction of effects. First, for both police arrest and victim survey data, the published evaluation research *do* report findings that "replicate" each other. We grant that a detailed analysis of methodological differences among these replication studies is highly important (see Garner & Maxwell, this issue); however, in examining these differences, one can lose sight of the fact that the simplest explanation of the variability

TABLE 3. Summary Statistics and Effect Size Estimates for the Impact of Police Arrest on Spousal Assault Recidivism Prevalence Rate as Assessed by Victim Surveys at Six Months (derived from Garner, Fagan, & Maxwell, 1995, Table 1)

Study	nt	nc	%t	%c	d	95% CI	r	p
Charlotte	112	236	58.9%	62.8%	+.0801	−.15/+.31	+.0401	.4617
Dade Co.	199	182	25.1%	39.0%	+.3010	+.10/+.50	+.1491	.0035
Milwaukee	624	297	32.4%	31.0%	−.0299	−.17/+.11	−.0150	.6499
Minneapolis	52	115	17.3%	30.4%	+.2994	−.03/+.63	+.1487	.0544
Omaha 1	84	112	34.5%	47.3%	+.2606	−.02/+.54	+.1297	.0693
Omaha 2	77	165	37.7%	41.8%	+.0845	−.19/+.36	+.0423	.5114
OVERALL	1148	1107	33.5%	41.7%	+.1102	+.02/+.20	+.0550	.0091

Note: $Q_w(5) = 9.822$; p = 0.0805; mean d (studies weighted by 1): +0.1659; nt, Arrest condition sample size; nc, Comparison condition sample size; %t, Percent of recidivism in the Arrest condition; %c, Percent of recidivism in the Comparison condition; d, Cohen's d statistic; 95%CI, 95% confidence interval for the d statistics; r, Pearson correlation; p, probability level of r.

among these findings is randomness or chance, an explanation supported by the homogeneity of the effect sizes involved. Second, these analyses reveal that, at least for victim survey data, we find a small, statistically significant, effect of arrest on spouse assault recidivism. This finding can be used by public policymakers to aid in judging the cost-effectiveness of this policy. As a final point, these conclusions do not negate the examination of interaction effects hypotheses such as the "stake-in-conformity" hypothesis (Toby, 1957) that have emerged from researchers' attempts to explain the differential findings from the SARP studies.

COMMON PROBLEMS WITH META-ANALYSIS

Despite their advantages, several problems may arise with quantitative research reviews. We will discuss some of the more frequently encountered difficulties, both as a caution to prospective meta-analysts and as a guide for primary researchers who wish to make their research "friendly" to quantitative reviewers.

Calculating Effect Sizes

In pandemic proportions, primary researchers report insufficient information to permit the meta-analyst to compute effect size estimates. Although particularly prevalent when reporting non-significant findings, this problem commonly occurs with significant results as well. In older research, authors' failure to report standard deviations along with means has spelled frustration for many a meta-analyst. In more recent research, sophisticated, multivariate analysis is often reported at the expense of basic, bivariate effect size information. For example, primary researchers may report the standardized discriminant function coefficients of risk factors between violent and non-violent dating relationships; however, they do not give the zero-order correlations between the individual risk factors and group membership.

A quantitative reviewer can apply three strategies to the problem of missing effect size information. The first approach is to request the needed statistical information from the original authors. Unfortunately, this strategy becomes less effective as the study's age increases due to the decreased availability of the original data. Second, a reviewer can eliminate from the research synthesis those studies that have insufficient statistical information to compute effect sizes. This approach has drawbacks because it may eliminate a sizable proportion of studies. This problem is magnified if the number of studies in the population is relatively small. The third approach is statistical in nature. The meta-analyst could calculate the average effect size by combining significance level (often denoted as "vote-count" data) and effect size information from different studies (Bushman & Wang, 1996). However, this approach is computationally intensive and may deter some researchers.

Primary researchers are strongly urged to include basic, bivariate effect size information in all of their published research, or to make such data readily available for several years after publication. By making it easy to obtain this information, they will encourage others to include their findings in quantitative reviews and perhaps increase the frequency with which such reviews are performed.

Effect Size Non-Independence: When Multiple Effects Come from the Same Study or Sample

A major assumption that underlies the statistical techniques of quantitative research synthesis is that the effect sizes that are included in the meta-analytic "database" are independent from each other (see Cooper, 1989, pp. 76-79). This assumption is often ignored by quantitative reviewers, and its violation serves as a major threat to the proper interpretation of meta-analytic results. Non-independence of effect sizes can result from a number of factors, but the most common is using multiple measures to assess the focal construct. For example, Saunders, Lynch, Grayson, and Linz (1987) compared violent and non-violent men regarding their attitudes about marital violence. They used an inventory of beliefs about wife beating that has five subscales assessing different aspects of this construct (e.g., the offender's degree of responsibility and whether the beating was justified). Consequently, five effect sizes could be computed for this study, one for each of the marital violence beliefs. The subscales, however, were not independent of each other, meaning that the effect sizes produced by them were correlated. How would one use these effect sizes in a quantitative review?

Although several strategies are available, each approach has limitations. One strategy is to simply ignore the fact that some of the effect sizes in the meta-analytic database are correlated with each other. If the sample of effect sizes is relatively large and most of these effects are *not* correlated with each other, this "denial" strategy may introduce only a very small amount of error into the calculations of average effect size and homogeneity. For example, the level of non-independence may be minor if only two of 100 studies reported a pair of correlated effect sizes. On the other hand, if there are relatively few studies, then this strategy becomes highly inappropriate (see Walsh, 1947).

An alternative approach is to compute a "study-level" or composite effect size by averaging these multiple effect sizes. This procedure requires that the meta-analyst take into account the average correlation among these correlated effect sizes. For example, Table 4 represents hypothetical correlations among three measures of psychopathology (depression, anxiety, and irritability) and the frequency of sexual victimization during childhood and adolescence. The average correlation among the three psychopathology measures is .365. This results in a composite r of .64 ($d = 1.67$), which could be entered into the meta-analytic database to represent the results of this study. Since the measures are correlated, one should not conduct a moderator analysis using all three psychopathology measures; however, this does not prohibit separate meta-analyses for the different constructs. The correlation of these effect sizes would simply prohibit the statistical comparison of the average effect sizes across psychopathology measures. A final strategy was offered by Gleser and Olkin (1994), who suggested retaining the individual effect sizes but taking into account their intercorrelations via a regression model approach.

TABLE 4. Hypothetical Data Examining the Relationship Between Psychopathology and the Frequency of Childhood and Adolescent Sexual Victimization (N = 150).

| | Victimization Frequency | | | | | |
Measure	1	2	3	r	d	p
1. Depression	---			.60	1.46	<.001
2. Anxiety	.50	---		.55	1.31	<.001
3. Irritability	.34	.24	---	.45	1.00	<.001

Software Limitations

Given the availability and simplicity of the formulas for the computation of effect sizes and their associated variance estimates (see Rosenthal, 1994, pp. 237-238), meta-analysts might appear to require only a calculator to conduct a quantitative review. However, growth in the use of meta-analytic techniques has resulted in statisticians' attempts to confront some of the problems that have emerged (e.g., effect non-independence, combining effect size and vote-count information). As a result, some of the more basic analyses, such as examining the impact of a categorical moderator variable (Hedges, 1982), required reviewers to use spreadsheet programs for computation and data management.

Several specific meta-analytic computer programs have been developed to aid reviewers (Johnson, 1989; Mullen, 1989; Rosenberg, Adams, & Gurevitch, 1997; Schwarzer, 1989). Although these programs are helpful, they are characterized by some limitations. First, they differ with respect to their general meta-analytic approach. Johnson's (1989) D-Stat program relies on Hedges and Olkin's (1985) approach, which translates study outcomes into standard deviation units (Hedge's g), and corrects these estimates for small sample size (using Cohen's d). The d statistics are aggregated and their homogeneity is examined. Finally, the impact of categorical and continuous moderator variables is assessed. Rosenthal's (1984, 1991) strategy underlies Mullen's (1989) BASIC computer program. This approach involves converting study outcomes into a standard normal metric (Z scores associated with one-tail probabilities for observed statistical significance levels; Fisher's r-to-Z transformation of effect sizes). Weighted mean Zs are then computed and examined through the application of diffused or focused comparisons. Finally, Schwarzer's (1989) META program applies Hunter and Schmidt's (1990) approach. This strategy does not correct the effect estimate for sample size prior to computing mean effects; however, it does correct for a number of statistical artifacts (i.e., the reliability of the independent and dependent variables, sampling error). Johnson, Mullen, and Salas (1995) compared these three approaches and found that the techniques of Rosenthal (1984, 1991) and Hedges and Olkin (1985) produce convergent meta-analytic findings. In contrast, Hunter and Schmidt's (1990) techniques result in more conservative statistical significance evaluations of the effect sizes and larger estimates of the impact of moderator variables. In a more recent comparison of these techniques, Schmidt and Hunter (1999) reported that the three analytic strategies produced comparable results.

In addition to the differences between these approaches, the programs themselves offer different statistical options. Both Mullen's (1989) and Schwarzer's (1989) programs permit cluster analysis and generate stem-leaf plots of the data. Johnson's (1989) D-Stat program does not have these capabilities but it does evaluate the impact of effect size outliers and allows for the regression analysis of multiple moderator variables on the effect sizes. To further complicate this issue, the data management strategies for these programs do not permit easy translation from one meta-analytic program to another meta-analytic program, or even to more conventional statistical packages (e.g., SAS, SPSS). Finally, these programs are limited in terms of types of effect size estimates that are calculated. While Johnson's (1989) program focuses on the *d* statistic, the other two programs use the *r* statistic. In addition, none of these programs have a strategy for integrating odds-ratio or logit data into their analyses, and all of these programs assume the independence of effect sizes (often an unwise assumption). However, future software development will address these shortcomings.

The Issue of Research Quality

A criticism that is often directed at meta-analytic reviews is that they often include methodologically weak studies (e.g., Mansfield & Busse, 1977). The presumption is that these "poorer" studies bias the average effect size, underestimating or overestimating it depending on the circumstances. This point needs to be well heeded, as researchers cannot afford to draw conclusions or inform social and public policy based on seriously flawed data. Therefore, quantitative researchers must decide on the criteria for judging study quality and decide whether poor quality studies are to be included in the review. Obviously, one strategy is to only consider "high quality" studies, with study quality operationalized in terms of research design. For example, one might decide to include only studies that use comparison groups (e.g., comparing the self-esteem of battered women versus non-battered women). Such a strategy would exclude single-group correlational designs (e.g., correlating battering frequency and self-esteem for a group of battered women in a shelter). Alternatively, one might consider publication in a peer-reviewed journal as an operationalization of high quality; however, this strategy results in a clear publication bias (see Begg, 1994; Begg & Berlin, 1988).

A second strategy that a quantitative review can use is to code the various studies for methodological factors that may influence effect size (Wortman, 1994) and to use these factors as moderator variables. For example, Wagner (1997) conducted a very thorough narrative review of the risk factors associated with adolescent suicidal behavior that identified child abuse as a consistent risk factor for this behavior. In his qualitative analysis of the child abuse-attempted suicide relationship, he noted that better designed studies appeared to exhibit stronger effects. To test this conclusion, we collected the 23 articles that he cited with respect to the abuse-suicide relationship. We eliminated only a single article (Hernandez, Lodico, & DiClemente, 1993) because it did not offer sufficient statistical information for the computation of an effect size. Several steps were taken in this analysis. First, we coded effect size estimates separately for males and females in the three studies that disaggregated participants by gender. Second, for each of the nine studies that used multiple measures of abuse (usually physical and sexual abuse), we combined these effect size estimates together to insure that the impact of these studies would not be overestimated. Because none of these nine studies reported the correlation between these two dependent variables, we assumed the correlation between physical abuse and sexual abuse to be .30 (David Finkelhor, personal communication, May 29, 1997) in order to compute the combined effect size. This procedure resulted in a total of 25 effect sizes; three effects ($N = 254$) focused on the relationship between child abuse and suicide completion, and the remaining 22 effect sizes ($N = 12,321$) assessed the child abuse-suicide attempt association. Third, we coded for several study characteristics based on Wagner's coding scheme (1997, pp. 264-267, Table 3).

For this context, we were interested in the moderator effect that research design would have on the abuse-suicide attempt relationship. Wagner (1997) coded the following four types of designs (increasing in quality of temporal sequencing): (1) correlational studies without controls for variable sequencing; (2) retrospective studies that possibly controlled for variable sequencing; (3) retrospective studies that did control for variable sequencing; and (4) prospective studies. The results of our moderator analysis are offered in Table 5; study quality has a significant impact on effect size ($Q_b(3) = 43.71, p = .001$).

If one does not consider the single, prospective study, Wagner's (1997) conclusions about design are supported. One finds that the better controlled studies (at least, with respect to the temporal priority of variables) had larger effect sizes. However, the single prospective study (Brent et al., 1993) generated a statistically non-significant effect size in the direction counter to expectation, $d = -.23; r = -.11; N = 134, p = .19$. This anomaly may be due to the fact that there is only a single effect size within this category; however, it does indicate that more prospective studies are required to thoroughly address the relationship between child abuse and suicide.

A second insight from this analysis focuses on the fact that the three other categories of design quality are not homogeneous in their effect size estimates. Other factors besides study quality can contribute to heterogeneity of effect sizes, and these factors may differ from one category to another. If one examines only the nine retrospective studies that controlled for variable sequencing, one finds that a second methodological factor (the operationalization of abuse) accounts for a significant proportion of effect size variance, $Q_b(2) = 17.11, p < .001$ (see Table 6). These findings suggest that operationalizing abuse as physical violence produced a significantly larger effect size than if a social service contact measure or a combining of physical and sexual abuse measures were used.

TABLE 5. Moderator Analysis of the Child Abuse-Attempted Suicide Relationship Using Design Type as the Grouping Variable (based on Wagner, 1997)

Type of Design	k	d+	95% CI	r	Q_w	p
Correlational without controls for variable sequencing	9	+.0999	+.07/+.13	+.0499	103.56	<.001
Retrospective with possible controls for variable sequencing	3	+.2971	+.19/+.40	+.1469	24.83	<.001
Retrospective with controls for variable sequencing	9	+.4607	+.34/+.58	+.2244	37.80	<.001
Prospective	1	−.2312	−.80/+.34	−.1147	0.00	1.000
OVERALL	22	+.1365	+.11/+.17	+.0681	209.90	<.001

Note: k = number of studies, d+ = mean Cohen's d statistic, 95% CI, 95% confidence interval associated with the Cohen's d statistic, r = Pearson correlation associated with the Cohen's d statistic, Q_w = Test of homogeneity, p = probability level of the homogeneity test.

TABLE 6. Moderator Analysis of the Child Abuse-Attempted Suicide Relationship for Only Retrospective Design Studies with Established Variable Sequence Using Predictor Variable as the Grouping Variable (based on Wagner, 1997)

Predictor Variable	k	d+	95% CI	r	Q_w	p
Physical abuse	2	+1.2858	+.87/+1.70	+.5408	5.39	.067
Contact with social services	2	+.4222	+.23/+.61	+.2065	0.45	.790
Physical and sexual abuse	5	+.3547	+.19/+.52	+.1746	14.85	.011
OVERALL	9	+.4607	+.34/+.58	+.2244	37.80	<.001

Note: k = number of studies, d+ = mean Cohen's d statistic, 95% CI, 95% confidence interval associated with the Cohen's d statistic, r = Pearson correlation associated with the Cohen's d statistic, Q_w = Test of homogeneity, p = probability level of the homogeneity test.

In sum, coding for variables that assess research quality (e.g., type of design, type of sample, construct measurement) can aid reviewers in determining how robust the reported effects are and the boundary conditions that may limit generalizability. Clearly, evaluation researchers are interested in a variety of design and methodological variables. These could include moderator variables such as the type of design (pre-test/post-test only versus post-test treatment/control comparison), the treatment dosage (12 weeks, 24 weeks, etc.), the source of treatment participants (self-referred versus court-mandated), the post-test time frame (six months, one year), or the specific assessment measure (court records versus victim surveys). For example, in the previously presented SARP meta-analysis, one can ponder why arrests had a small, significant statistical impact on victim survey reports of recidivism but not on court record reports. More importantly, this strategy permits reviewers to quantitatively test their assumptions regarding the association between research quality and outcome.

A ROLE FOR THE NARRATIVE REVIEW

Although quantitative reviewing has steadily increased, narrative literature reviews retain an important role in the field of family violence. First, we need to recognize the importance of narrative reviews during the fledgling stage of any research area. Although meta-analytic techniques can be applied to as few as two effect sizes, reviewers may be better served to rely on their insight or clinical experience when only a small number of studies exist. In these situations, the large number of potential moderators and their likely correlations across the small number of studies render it almost impossible to study effect size heterogeneity. Second, even with the advent of better "vote-counting" methods (e.g., Bushman & Wang, 1996), reviewers may need to return to a narrative style to include the results of those studies that provide insufficient statistical information to compute an effect size. For example, Sugarman and Hotaling (1997) noted in their analysis of the relationship between intimate violence and social desirability that their average effect size estimate may be an overestimate due to the number of studies that reported insufficient statistical information. They also point out that these eliminated studies usually involved the use of clinical scales, in contrast to scales solely used to assess the social desirability construct. Third, meta-analyses may overlook information from a number of sources. Quantitative reviews do not offer evidence derived from single case designs, qualitative research, expert judgement, and non-quantitative data from quantitative studies; however, these sources of information may serve to generate new hypotheses.

CONCLUSION

In the recent National Research Council report on assessing prevention and treatment programs for family violence (Chalk & King, 1997), considerable attention was given to the methodological problems that confront researchers in this area. This report concluded that because of poor research quality, our research base is "insufficient to provide confident inferences to guide policy and practice, except in a few areas" (p. 68). Although this report suggested a number of improvements to family violence evaluation research (e.g., common definitions and measures, appropriate use of treatment and control groups, culturally sensitive research designs and measures), it was surprisingly devoid of any recommendations about the communication of research findings and their integration. Effect size was only mentioned in a section on sample size and statistical power (pp. 76-77), and a discussion of meta-analysis was conspicuously absent.

If we as researchers are committed to the evaluation of family violence-related policies and programs, then we need to ask Loftus' (1998) questions about the nature of research evidence with more rigor and systematic treatment. We must not be satisfied with knowing only whether a program worked or not (i.e., revealed a significant effect or not); rather, we must require an assessment of how *well* it worked (i.e., obtain an effect size). This latter information permits more accurate evaluation of the cost effectiveness of a program. Furthermore, we need to know the boundary conditions that limit the effectiveness of a program (e.g., do studies of dating violence prevention programs show a larger effect with high school students than with middle school students?) and the robustness of the evaluation process itself (e.g., do studies that randomize to treatment condition have larger effect sizes than those studies that do not?).

To answer Loftus's questions, both primary researchers and literature reviewers must think meta-analytically. Primary researchers should be aware of the statistical information that they need to report in their studies to aid quantitative reviewers. In contrast, literature reviewers must think like primary researchers, treating each finding as a study participant. It is this partnership that will reduce the occurrence of unsupported or poorly supported claims and allow us to understand what "exactly" the evidence is for the effectiveness of programs designed to reduce or eliminate family violence.

NOTE

1. These data reported recidivism six months after the index incident. Several other measures of effect size might be derived from these studies, and analyses of these alternative data could yield different results from those presented here. The results discussed in the present paper are offered simply as an illustration of the way in which replication might be differently approached by narrative and quantitative reviewers; it does not represent a thorough meta-analysis of the arrest literature.

REFERENCES

Abelson, R. P. (1997). On the surprising longevity of flogged horses: Why there is a case for the significance test. *Psychological Science, 8*(1), 12-15.

Becker, B. J. (1994). Combining significance levels. In H. Cooper & L. V. Hedges (Eds.), *The handbook of research synthesis* (pp. 215-230). New York, NY: Russell Sage Foundation.

Begg, C. B. (1994). Publication bias. In H. Cooper & L. V. Hedges (Eds.), *The handbook of research synthesis* (pp. 399-409). New York, NY: Russell Sage Foundation.

Begg, C. B., & Berlin, J. A. (1988). Publication bias: A problem in interpreting medical data. *Journal of the Royal National Cancer Institute, 81*, 107-115.

Binder, A., & Meeker, J. W. (1993). Implications of the failure to replicate the Minneapolis experimental findings. *American Sociological Review, 58*, 886-888.

Brent, D. A., Kolko, D. J., Wartella, M. E., Boylan, M. B., Moritz, G., Baugher, M., & Zelenak, J. P. (1993). Adolescent psychiatry inpatients' risk of suicide attempt at 6 month follow-up. *Journal of the American Academy of Child and Adolescent Psychiatry, 32*, 95-105.

Bushman, B. J. (1994). Vote-counting procedures in meta-analysis. In H. Cooper & L. V. Hedges (Eds.), *The handbook of research synthesis* (pp. 193-213). New York, NY: Russell Sage Foundation.

Bushman, B. J., & Wang, M. C. (1996). A procedure for combining sample correlation coefficients and vote counts to obtain an estimate and a confidence interval for the population coefficient. *Psychological Bulletin, 111*(3), 530-546.

Buzawa, E. S., & Buzawa, C. G. (1993). The impact of arrest on domestic violence. *American Behavioral Scientist, 36*(5), 558-574.

Chalk, R., & King, P. A. (Eds.) (1997). *Violence in families: Assessing prevention and treatment programs.* Washington, DC: National Academy Press.

Chow, S. I. (1988). Significance test or effect size? *Psychological Bulletin, 103*, 105-110.

Cohen, J. (1994). The earth is round ($p < .05$). *American Psychologist, 49*, 997-1003.

Cooper, H. M. (1982). Scientific guidelines for conducting integrative research reviews. *Review of Educational Research, 52*, 291-302.

Cooper, H. M. (1989). *Integrating research: A guide for literature reviews* (2nd Ed.). Newbury Park, CA: Sage.

Cooper, H., & Hedges, L. V. (Eds.) (1994). *The handbook of research synthesis.* New York, NY: Russell Sage Foundation.

Garner, J., Fagan, J., & Maxwell, C. (1995). Published findings from the Spouse Assault Replication Program: A critical review. *Journal of Quantitative Criminology, 11*(1), 3-28.

Garner, J., & Maxwell, C. (this issue). What are the lessons of the police arrest studies? *Journal of Aggression, Maltreatment & Trauma.*

Giles-Sims, J. (1996). The aftermath of marital violence. In J. L. Jasinski & L. M. Williams (Eds.), *Partner violence: A comprehensive review of 20 years of research* (pp. 44-72). Thousand Oaks, CA: Sage Publications.

Gleason, W. J. (1997). Psychological and social dysfunctions in battering men: A review. *Aggression and Violent Behavior, 2*(1), 43-52.

Gleser, L. J., & Olkin, I. (1994). Stochastically dependent effect sizes. In H. Cooper & L. V. Hedges (Eds.), *The handbook of research synthesis* (339-356). New York, NY: Russell Sage Foundation.

Hamby, S. L. (1996). Partner violence: Prevention and intervention. In J. L. Jasinski & L. M. Williams (Eds.), *Partner violence: A comprehensive review of 20 years of research* (pp. 210-258). Thousand Oaks, CA: Sage Publications.

Hanson, R. K. (1998, July). *Attitudes as a risk factor for wife abuse: Only for the socially well-adjusted?* Paper presented at Program Evaluation and Family Violence Research: An International Conference, Durham, NH.

Harris, R. J. (1997). Significance tests have their place. *Psychological Science, 8*(1), 8-11.

Hedges, L. V. (1982). Fitting categorical models to effect sizes from a series of experiments. *Journal of Educational Statistics, 7*(2), 388-395.

Hedges, L. V., & Olkin, I. (1985). *Statistical methods for meta-analysis.* Orlando, FL: Academic Press.

Hernandez, J. T., Lodico, M., & DiClemente, R. J. (1993). The effects of child abuse and race on risk-taking in male adolescents. *Journal of the National Medical Association, 85*, 593-597.

Holtzworth-Munroe, A., Bates, L., Smutzler, N., & Sandin, E. (1997). A brief review of the research on husband violence: Part I. Maritally violent versus nonviolent men. *Aggression and Violent Behavior, 2*(1), 65-99.

Holtzworth-Munroe, A., Smutzler, N., & Bates, L. (1997). A brief review of the research on husband violence: Part III. Sociodemographic factors, relationship factors, and differing consequences of husband and wife violence. *Aggression and Violent Behavior, 2*(3), 285-307.

Holtzworth-Munroe, A., Smutzler, N., & Sandin, E. (1997). A brief review of the research on husband violence. Part II: The psychological effects of husbands' violence on battered women and their children. *Aggression and Violent Behavior, 2*(2), 179-213.

Hotaling, G. T., & Sugarman, D. B. (1986). An analysis of risk markers in husband-to-wife violence: The current state of knowledge. *Violence and Victims, 1*(2), 101-124.

Hunter, J. E. (1997). Needed: A ban on the significance test. *Psychological Science, 8*(1), 3-7.

Hunter, J. E., & Schmidt, F. L. (1990). *Methods of meta-analysis: Correcting error and bias in research findings.* Newbury Park, CA: Sage.

Jackson, S.M. (1999). Issues in the dating violence research: A review of the literature. *Aggression and Violent Behavior, 4*(2), 233-247.

Johnson, B. T. (1989). *DSTAT: Software for the meta-analytic review of research literatures.* Hillsdale, NJ: Erlbaum.

Johnson, B. T., Mullen, B., & Salas, E. (1995). Comparison of three meta-analytic approaches. *Journal of Applied Psychology, 80*(1), 94-106.

Jumper, S. A. (1995). A meta-analysis of the relationship of child sexual abuse to adult psychological adjustment. *Child Abuse and Neglect, 19*(6), 715-728.

Kaufman Kantor, G., & Jasinski, J. L. (1996). Dynamics and risk factors in partner violence. In J. L. Jasinski & L. M. Williams (Eds.), *Partner violence: A comprehensive review of 20 years of research* (pp. 1-43). Thousand Oaks, CA: Sage Publications.

Loftus, E. (1998). Who is the cat that curiosity killed? *APS Observer, 11*(5), 2, 27.

Mansfield, R. S., & Busse, T. V. (1977). Meta-analysis of research: A rejoinder to Glass. *Educational Research, 6*, 5.

Mullen, B. (1989). *Advanced BASIC meta-analysis: Procedures and programs.* Hillsdale, NJ: Erlbaum.

Raudenbush, S. W., Becker, B. J., & Kalaian, H. (1988). Modeling multivariate effect sizes. *Psychological Bulletin, 103*(1), 111-120.

Rhodes, N. R., & McKenzie, E. B. (1998). Why do battered women stay? Three decades of research. *Aggression and Violent Behavior, 3*(4), 391-406.

Rosenberg, M. S., Adams, D. C., & Gurevitch, J. (1997). *MetaWin, Ver 1.0: Statistical software for meta-analysis with resampling tests.* Sunderland, MA: Sinaurer Associates.

Rosenthal, R. (1979). The "file drawer problem" and tolerance for null results. *Psychological Bulletin, 86,* 638-641.

Rosenthal, R. (1984). *Meta-analytic procedures for social research.* Beverly Hills, CA: Sage.

Rosenthal, R. (1990). Replication in behavioral research. *Journal of Social Behavior and Personality, 5*(4), 1-30.

Rosenthal, R. (1991). *Meta-analytic procedures for social research* (Rev. Ed.). Beverly Hills, CA: Sage.

Rosenthal, R. (1994). Parametric measures of effect size. In H. Cooper & L. V. Hedges (Eds.), *The handbook of research synthesis* (pp. 231-244). New York, NY: Russell Sage Foundation.

Rosenthal, R. (1995). Writing meta-analytic reviews. *Psychological Bulletin, 118,* 183-192.

Rosenthal, R., & Rubin, D. B. (1982). A simple, general purpose display of magnitude of experimental effect. *Journal of Educational Psychology, 74,* 166-169.

Rothstein, H. R., & McDaniel, M. A. (1989). Guidelines for conducting and reporting meta-analyses. *Psychological Reports, 69,* 759-770.

Saunders, D. G. (1992). A typology of men who batter: Three types derived from cluster analysis. *American Journal of Orthopsychiatry, 62*(2), 264-275.

Saunders, D. G., Lynch, A. B., Grayson, M., & Linz, D. (1987). The inventory of beliefs about wife beating: The construction and initial validation of a measure of beliefs and attitudes. *Violence and Victims, 2*(1), 39-57.

Schmidt, F. L. (1996). Statistical significance testing and cumulative knowledge in psychology: Implications for training of researchers. *Psychological Methods, 1,* 115-129.

Schmidt, F. L., & Hunter, J. E. (1999). Comparison of three meta-analysis methods revisited: An analysis of Johnson, Mullen, and Salas (1995). *Journal of Applied Psychology, 84*(1), 144-148.

Schmidt, J. D., & Sherman, L. W. (1993). Does arrest deter domestic violence? *American Behavioral Scientist, 36*(5), 601-609.

Schwarzer, R. (1989). *META-programs, Vers. 5.3.* Berlin, Germany: Author.

Sherman, L. W. (1993). Implications of a failure to read the literature. *American Sociological Review, 58,* 888-889.

Sherman, L. W., & Berk, R. (1984). The specific deterrent effect of arrest for domestic assault. *American Sociological Review, 49,* 261-272.

Sugarman, D. B., & Frankel, S. L. (1996). Patriarchal ideology and wife-assault: A meta-analytic review. *Journal of Family Violence, 11*(1), 13-40.

Sugarman, D. B., & Hotaling, G. T. (1989). Dating violence: Prevalence, context, and risk markers. In M. A. Pirog-Good & J. E. Stets (Eds.), *Violence in dating relationships: Emerging social issues* (pp. 3-32). New York, NY: Praeger.

Sugarman, D. B., & Hotaling, G. T. (1997). Intimate violence and social desirability: A meta-analytic review. *Journal of Interpersonal Violence, 12*(2), 275-290.

Toby, J. (1957). Social disorganization and stakes in conformity. *Journal of Criminal Law and Criminological Police Science, 48*, 12-17.

Wagner, B. M. (1997). Family risk factors for child and adolescent suicidal behavior. *Psychological Bulletin, 121*(2), 246-298.

Walsh, J. E. (1947). Concerning the effect of intraclass correlation on certain significance tests. *Annals of Mathematical Statistics, 18*, 88-96.

Wolak, J., & Finkelhor, D. (1996). Children exposed to partner violence. In J. L. Jasinski & L. M. Williams (Eds.), *Partner violence: A comprehensive review of 20 years of research* (pp. 73-112). Thousand Oaks, CA: Sage Publications.

Wortman, P. M. (1994). Judging research quality. In H. Cooper & L. V. Hedges (Eds.), *The handbook of research synthesis* (pp. 97-109). New York, NY: Russell Sage Foundation.

Zakzanis, K. K. (1998). The reliability of meta-analytic review. *Psychological Reports, 83*(1), 215-222.

EXPERIMENTAL DESIGN
AND ALTERNATIVES

What Are the Lessons
of the Police Arrest Studies?

Joel H. Garner
Christopher D. Maxwell

SUMMARY. The six domestic violence police arrest experiments and several precursor studies stand unique in their research contribution to criminology and public policy. Together, these studies have significantly informed the debate about the deterrent effects of criminal justice sanctions and about the importance of how police can respond effectively to domestic violence. The strong methodological rigor of the six arrest experiments was a notable accomplishment, and set new standards for

This research was supported in part by awards from the National Institute of Justice, Centers for Disease Control and Prevention and the Harry Frank Guggenheim Foundation. Points of view are those of the authors and do not necessarily represent the views of the organizations providing financial support.

Address correspondence to: Joel Garner, PhD, Joint Centers for Justice Studies, Inc., 13 Willowdale Drive, Shepherdstown, WV 25443.

[Haworth co-indexing entry note]: "What Are the Lessons of the Police Arrest Studies?" Garner, Joel H., and Christopher D. Maxwell. Co-published simultaneously in *Journal of Aggression, Maltreatment & Trauma* (The Haworth Maltreatment & Trauma Press, an imprint of The Haworth Press, Inc.) Vol. 4, No. 1 (#7), 2000, pp. 83-114; and: *Program Evaluation and Family Violence Research* (ed: Sally K. Ward, and David Finkelhor) The Haworth Maltreatment & Trauma Press, an imprint of The Haworth Press, Inc., 2000, pp. 83-114. Single or multiple copies of this article are available for a fee from The Haworth Document Delivery Service [1-800-342-9678, 9:00 a.m. - 5:00 p.m. (EST). E-mail address: getinfo@haworthpressinc.com].

83

future criminological research. Early reviews synthesizing many results from the six arrest experiments typically concluded that the deterrent effect of arrest was not significant, however, these reviews generally did not meet the methodological rigor of the five replication experiments. Two recent attempts using different approaches for systematically combining results across multiple studies have concluded that there is a significant deterrent effect from arrest. This finding is variant from early reviews. Based upon data gathered from victim interviews, these two studies suggest that contemporary policies requiring preferred or mandatory arrest may be providing protection for victims though there is little change in the prevalence of police response over time. These studies have also taught us that methodological rigor is required throughout the scientific process, and not just during the data collection and analysis stages. The authors conclude that for several reasons there will likely be no further research testing for the effect of arrest on domestic violence and that current debate concerning how other aspects of the criminal justice system should respond to domestic violence seems less willing to be informed by the rigorous research and experimentation. *[Article copies available for a fee from The Haworth Document Delivery Service: 1-800-342-9678. E-mail address: <getinfo@haworthpressinc. com> Website: <http://www.HaworthPress.com>]*

KEYWORDS. Deterrence, spouse assault, victim interviews, National Academy of Sciences, National Institute of Justice

INTRODUCTION

In reviewing what is known about the effectiveness of treatment or prevention programs in the area of domestic violence, the National Academy of Sciences (Chalk & King, 1998) surveyed over 2,000 studies published between 1980 and 1996. Of these studies, the Academy identified only 114 that (1) involved an intervention designed to treat some aspect of child maltreatment, domestic violence or elder abuse, (2) used an experimental or quasi-experimental design, and (3) measured and used violence as an outcome measure. Among the roughly six percent of the published studies of sufficient methodological value to warrant consideration by the Academy were seven studies that tested the deterrent effectiveness of the police making an arrest (or issuing an arrest warrant) for misdemeanor assaults against a spouse or intimate partner. These are the "police arrest studies" reviewed in this paper.

The first of these seven studies, the Minneapolis domestic violence experiment (Sherman & Berk, 1984a), is among the most visible (Sherman & Cohn, 1989) and highly cited research articles in criminology (Cohn & Farrington, 1996). That experiment found that when suspects in misdemeanor spouse assault incidents were not arrested, the prevalence of official recorded re-offending within six months was 21%; this rate was 50% higher than the 14% re-offending rate of similarly situated suspects who were arrested. Similar results were obtained when re-offending was measured by interviewing victims.

The published results of the six other experiments into the effectiveness of arrest (Black, Berk, Lilly, & Rikoski, 1991; Dunford, Huizinga, & Elliot, 1989; Hirschel, Hutchison, Dean, Kelley, & Pesackis, 1991; Pate, Hamilton, & Annan, 1991; Sherman et al., 1991) generated a variety of measures, analyses and inconsistent findings, leading the National Academy to conclude that "arrest in all misdemeanor cases will not on average produce a discernable effect on recidivism" (Chalk & King, 1998, p. 176). Our substantive assessment of the evidence available to the Academy is similar to their conclusion but we have also argued (Garner, Fagan, & Maxwell, 1995) that there is insufficient evidence in the published findings of these experiments to assess the effectiveness of arrest as a deterrent to spouse assault.

The nature of our disagreement with the Academy's report is derived from three considerations. First, not all the possible findings from these six experiments (known collectively as the Spouse Assault Replication Program, or SARP) have been published. Thus, the published evidence is only a small proportion of the complete set of possible findings. Second, while each of the SARP experiments uses multiple measures of violence as outcomes, there is no single measure of violence used consistently in the published reports. For instance, the Minneapolis experiment counted threats of violence as violence; none of the subsequent publications define violence as including threats of violence. In addition, the published research uses a wide variety of analytical approaches and it is difficult, if not impossible, to separate the diverse findings from the diverse measurement and analytical techniques reported (Garner et al., 1995).

Our third consideration cuts to a basic but often an ignored tenet of science–the reproduction of findings by independent scholars. Despite the fact that the raw data from these experiments have been publicly archived for more than five years, there are no published reports by independent scholars confirming the original results of any of these experiments through secondary analysis of the original data. This is a potentially serious threat to establishing the reliability of any findings about the deterrent effectiveness of arrest and, we suspect, an often unrecognized threat to many other criminological research findings (e.g., Blumstein, Cohen, & Gooding, 1983; Laub & Sampson, 1989; Visher, 1986).

This paper is a review of the design, implementation and results of these same experiments; in addition, we report here the results of a recently completed reanalysis of the raw data from five of these experiments that directly addresses the problems associated within the inconsistent use of different measures and analysis. Our multi-site reanalysis uses more consistent methods and measures and brings higher methodological standards to assessing the police arrest studies. Our analysis provides a more favorable assessment of the deterrent effects of arrest than the Academy's or any other qualitative or quantitative review of the published literature on the police arrest studies.

WHAT ARE THE POLICE ARREST STUDIES?

For purposes of this review, we have identified a number of publications that we believe constitute the heart and soul of research on the deterrent effectiveness of arrest for misdemeanor spouse assault. These studies include the original reports on the findings of the Minneapolis experiment, the original reports on the six replication studies, and publications that reanalyze the data from one or more of these studies. Our selection captures those documents that derived findings about the effectiveness of arrest by analyzing the data about victims, suspects and police behavior directly from individual cases. Purposely excluded from our review are publications that involve commentaries on published findings from the police arrest studies but do not involve any original data analysis.

Precursor Studies

Our goal in this essay is to establish what we have learned (or should have learned) from this series of experiments. To determine what we know now that we did not know then, it is useful to review a number of publications that can, in different ways, be considered precursors to the Minneapolis domestic violence experiment. Some of these precursors relate directly to research on alternative police responses to domestic violence; others relate to the changing standards for criminological research in the 1970s.

In 1968, the *New York Times Magazine* (Sullivan, 1968) reported on an innovative program in which 18 New York City police officers volunteered to be trained to use psychology to handle family crisis problems. A subsequent report was published by the then newly created National Institute of Law Enforcement and Criminal Justice (Bard, 1970). This research asserted the value of an alternative to traditional law enforcement approaches to addressing domestic violence. Bard and Zacker (1971) recommended that the police be trained in new ways to respond to domestic violence. In this program, the police would calm down the situation, separate the parties, listen to the concerns of each of the disputants and attempt to address the immediate problem that was underlying the current dispute. The police were also trained to give the victim a phone number to call to obtain information about a variety of social services. Arresting one or both of the parties was not part of this approach. This approach was touted as integrating the psychologist's knowledge of human behavior with the coercive authority of the law in a manner that promoted collaboration among the police and other social service agencies.

The Bard study had several important methodological characteristics. First, it involved the comparison of police behavior in two New York City precincts. In one precinct some of the officers were trained by Bard and in the control precinct no officers were trained in these new procedures. The experimental precinct was the predominantly African-American 30th precinct; the comparison precinct was the predominately Puerto Rican 24th precinct.[1] Thus, the Bard design was a non-equivalent control group (Campbell & Stanley, 1966), a design with many known weaknesses. A second pertinent characteristic of the Bard study was that the primary outcome measure used was the number of assaults on police officers. Bard reported that during the experimental program there were no assaults on the 18 trained police officers. However, he also reported that there were two assaults against other police officers in the experimental precinct and only one assault in the entire comparison precinct. Thus, there were more, not fewer, assaults to officers in the precinct where the program had been implemented (Bard & Zacker, 1972, p. 74). Bard also compared the number of family related homicides in the two years before the implementation of the program with the first two years of the program. In the 30th precinct where Bard had trained 18 officers, the number *increased* from one to five (Bard & Zacker, 1972, p. 72). In the comparison precinct, the number of family related homicides remained constant at two over both periods.

Despite the weak design and results that indicated that the program had negative results on officers and victims, Bard's research was, in its day, quite influential. In addition to the visibility in the *New York Times*, between 1971 and 1976, the demonstration and testing divisions of the National Institute of Justice[2] spent millions of dollars paying officers overtime to attend training that encouraged the use of Bard's intervention program in more than a dozen police departments across the United States. Elements of the program were promoted by the International Association of Chiefs of Police and discussed positively in the widely distributed Law Enforcement Bulletin (Mohr & Steblein, 1976). Police Family Crisis Intervention had become a major, if not the dominant, law enforcement approach to addressing domestic violence. In 1976 a National Institute of Justice (NIJ) funded evaluation of six demonstration sites (Wylie, Basinger, Heinecke, & Rueckert, 1976) reported that the demonstration program had been implemented in widely diverse manners in each of the six sites. In addition, a pre-program/post-program time series comparison in these six sites revealed that family related assaults and arrests were up in two sites and level in the other four. Despite the evaluation's negative program findings, the evaluators advocated their own untested version of police family violence intervention training (Wylie et al., 1976). The lesson here is that, unlike drugs and medicines, Federal financial support for a social intervention does not necessarily mean that there is a body of knowledge supporting the efficacy of that intervention.

There is another study which, we believe, should be seen as a precursor to the police arrest studies. In a sample of domestic violence assaults and homicides over a two-year period, Katherine Milton and her colleagues (Police Foundation, 1977) reported that in 85% of the incidents the police had been called to the scene at least once before; in 50% of the incidents, the police had been called five times or more. These findings contradicted a common presumption that there was little that the police could do about domestic violence (American Bar

Association, 1981; International Association of Chiefs of Police, 1967). The 1977 Police Foundation study documented that domestic violence was repetitive and highly visible to the police. What was not clear from this research was what the police should do. In the *Foreword* to that 1977 report, James Q. Wilson, Vice Chairman of the Police Foundation, reviewed the alternative policies available and asserted

> At present we lack any reliable information as to the consequences of following the different approaches. Gathering such information in a systematic and objective manner ought to be a high-priority concern of local police and prosecutors. (Wilson, 1977, p. v)

It would be four more years before Chief Anthony Bouza and the Minneapolis Police Department accepted Wilson's challenge and implemented the first police arrest study.

A Methodological Sea Change

Between the publication and dissemination of Bard's research and the 1980 funding and 1984 dissemination of the Minneapolis domestic violence experiment, there was a sea change in the nature of criminological research. In 1974, Lipton, Martinson, and Wilks (1975) reviewed the published research on effectiveness of rehabilitative treatments and concluded that "nothing worked." Their review was limited to treatments implemented in a correctional setting and did not include law enforcement programs like police family crisis interventions but, as a result of their very negative assessment, the ideological underpinnings for all treatment programs were shattered. In 1979, a panel of the National Academy of Sciences (Sechrest, White, & Brown, 1979) concurred with Martinson's substantive assessment and added detailed critiques of the methodological weakness of much of the published research on rehabilitation. The Academy's methodological critiques asserted that much of the prior criminological research had used unstandardized measures of recidivism, rarely had even roughly equivalent treatment and control groups, did not control for different times at risk, and failed to measure the delivery of treatment and control conditions. Although not explicitly addressed by the Academy, Bard's research did not meet any of these methodological standards.

In another highly controversial arena, Issac Erhlich's econometric assessment supporting the deterrent effects of criminal sanctions was included in the U.S. Department of Justice's *amicus curiae* brief supporting the constitutionality of the death penalty (Bork, 1974). The resulting substantive and methodological disputes over the value of criminal justice sanctions as an effective crime control strategy were addressed in a separate report by the National Academy of Sciences (Blumstein, Cohen, & Nagin, 1978). Among other issues, this Academy's deterrence report emphasized the value of experimental designs as a means to assess the impact of changes in levels of criminal sanctions (Zimring, 1978).

These highly visible public debates over the relative effectiveness of rehabilitation and of deterrence, and the Academy's repeated critiques of the methodological weaknesses of prior research provided support for the use of stronger research designs in Federally supported research at the National Institute of Justice. In 1979, NIJ created the Crime Control Theory Program and issued the first of many solicitations for research on rehabilitation, deterrence and incapacitation. Unlike prior NIJ research solicitations, this program was open to all and the review and assessment of research proposals were conducted by independent panels composed entirely of experienced researchers and not solely by NIJ management and staff. In 1980, the new Director of Research at the Police Foundation, Lawrence W. Sherman, submitted a proposal to the Crime Control Theory Program that called for a rigorous test of deterrence theory; the idea was to use an experimental design to assess the deterrent effect of arrest on the crime of spouse assault. The rest is history.

The Minneapolis Domestic Violence Experiment

The basic history of the Minneapolis Domestic Violence Experiment is an often told story. The Minneapolis police department agreed to implement an experimental design, where one of three alternative responses to incidents of misdemeanor domestic violence–arrest, separation, or counseling, would be determined on an equal probability basis. Sherman and his colleagues collected and analyzed data from the experimental incidents, from official police records of the subsequent criminal behavior of the suspects, and from interviews with victims. The findings of this study were reported in a Police Foundation Report (Sherman & Berk, 1984a), in the *New York Times* Science

Section (Boffey, 1983), in many electronic and print media (Sherman & Cohn, 1989) and in several peer-reviewed scientific journals (Berk & Sherman, 1988; Sherman & Berk, 1984b).

Much has been made of the methodological rigor of the Minneapolis design but two other comparisons with the prior research on police family crisis intervention programs are, we think, instructive. First, Sherman and Berk's study made victim safety, not police officer safety, the sole measure of success for alternative police responses to domestic violence. Following the Minneapolis experiment, victim safety is certainly the paramount and perhaps the only criteria for assessing the effectiveness of alternative police responses to domestic violence. Second, both reforms were based on research, were supported by NIJ, generated widely distributed reports, and received favorable media coverage. However, in the case of police family crisis intervention training, the favorable press reports came first (1968), followed by extensive NIJ promotion (1972 to 1975) leading up to a more thoroughly researched assessment (1976). In the Minneapolis study, rigorous research was conducted first (1981-1983), followed by media attention (1983), and peer reviewed publications (1984).

There are other, less well known, aspects of the Minneapolis experiment. First, the project was implemented in full collaboration with a Minneapolis based domestic violence coalition; in fact, the release of the initial findings of the experiment was set to follow the broadcast of the coalition sponsored documentary on domestic violence on Minneapolis public television. Second, the experiment was not implemented throughout Minneapolis but only in two precincts and among a small number of volunteer officers who had a major role in determining how the experimental design would be implemented. Third, unlike the Police Family Crisis Intervention program, the National Institute of Justice did not publish a single document on the study or its results. Neither did it hold a large conference to discuss the study's findings or fund a single demonstration program to promote the use of arrest. The visibility of this research was due almost entirely to actions of individuals outside of NIJ.

Sherman and Berk (1984a) employed two common scientific criteria in assessing the results of the Minneapolis experiment. First, they reported that differences between treatments were "statistically significant." Second, they emphasized that the analyses of official records were consistent with the results of the victim interviews. As Sampson and Laub (1993) have noted, tests of statistical significance are, technically, irrelevant since the underlying statistical justification for these tests assumes that the experimental incidents were drawn as a random sample of some population, which they obviously were not. These tests, however, are commonly used in non-random samples as a standard criterion for distinguishing real effects from spurious effects. The finding that the results were consistent across two measures was a less formal but perhaps more persuasive way of arguing that the results were real and not due to the selection of a particular source of information about subsequent violence.

A complete understanding of the Minneapolis experiment also requires a close reading of the original reports by the original authors and a reanalysis of the publicly archived data. For instance, the original reports (Sherman & Berk, 1984a, 1984b) analyze 314 eligible experimental cases; however, 16 cases for which randomized treatments had been assigned were excluded because "no treatment was applied or the case did not belong in the study" (i.e., a fight between a father and son) (Sherman & Berk, 1984a, footnote on p. 264). Second, the 314 experimental incidents were not analyzed as the treatments were randomly assigned; neither were they analyzed as the treatments were delivered. Rather the original investigators used an innovative technique to "correct" for the misapplication of treatments (Sherman & Berk, 1984a, p. 267), a calculation that has not been fully documented in any technical reports or reproduced by independent scholars. From the published reports by Sherman and Berk, it is impossible to determine the extent to which the direction, size and statistical significance of the original Minneapolis experiment depends upon the exclusion of 16 experimental cases or the use of statistical corrections for the misapplication of treatments.

These issues were addressed in Gartin's (1991) detailed attempt at the reconstruction of the archived data from the Minneapolis experiment (Berk & Sherman, 1993). Gartin generally confirms the original findings but found that the existence of statistically significant effects for arrest were dependent on data source or on the analytical models used. Gartin (1991, p. 253) reports that, despite considerable missing data problems, the "analyses reported by Sherman and Berk (1984a) are reproducible" but that the weight of the evidence "seems to indicate that there was not as much of a specific deterrent effect for arrest" as the results from the original reports seemed to suggest. Gartin's

general confirmation of the Minneapolis results is a significant contribution to the scientific evidence and adds some reliability to the
original findings. There are many experiments in criminal justice;
there are few confirmations that the findings of those studies can be
reproduced from the original data by independent scholars.[3]

We recount these details because we have learned that many commentators on the Minneapolis experiment appear to either (1) not
understand basic research methods, (2) not have read the reports of
this experiment very closely or (3) have chosen to describe the experiment in ways which do not conform with the actual events. For
instance, the often repeated assertion that Sherman and Berk did not
consult and collaborate with local domestic violence reform activists
(e.g., Pence, 1998) is simply without a factual basis. There are numerous other errors and irrelevancies in much of the commentaries on the
Minneapolis experiment, and the traditional recommendation that
scholars rely on original source documents and not second-hand assumptions or corruptions about what was or could have been done
seems particularly relevant to the literature on this experiment. The
Minneapolis experiment is not above criticism. However, the rarely
noted but *actual* exclusion of more than 5% of the experimental cases
could as easily have compromised the rigor of this experiment as the
often-noted *speculation* that officers who volunteered to conduct the
research and helped design its protocols might have imperfectly implemented the random assignment. There is another lesson from the
Minneapolis experiment. An earlier reanalysis of the Minneapolis data
may have provided more reasonable expectations about how effective
arrest alone would be as a treatment for reducing domestic violence.
Such a reanalysis, however, requires the kind of hard work and scholarship that few commentators seem prepared to contribute, prior to
publishing critical assessments of other people's scientific products.

The Decision to Replicate

The importance of the Minneapolis experiment stems from its test
of theory, its rigorous experimental design, its visibility in the popular
press, its apparent impact on policy and the fact that it was replicated.
Support for replication was widespread. The original authors urged
replication (Sherman & Berk, 1984b). Early praise for the study's
design among criminological scholars was tempered by a preference
for replication (Boffey, 1983; Lempert, 1984). It is less well known

that a highly influential Department of Justice Task Force recommending the adoption of a pro-arrest policy nationwide also recommended replication of the Minneapolis experiment (U.S. Attorney General, 1984). There were, however, serious objections to replication, primarily from within NIJ. One concern was that, since the results of the Minneapolis experiment were in conformity with the political preferences of the current administration, the results from a replication were unlikely to be more supportive of these political preferences and could directly undermine the administration's position. Another concern was that any replication would be expensive and multiple replications would consume a substantial portion of the modest research budget at NIJ. In this instance, the political director of NIJ chose to follow the scientific advice instead of the political or budgetary advice. Of equal note, the reformers on the Attorney General's Task Force promoting the use of arrest simultaneously favored additional research on the effectiveness of arrest as a deterrent to spouse assault.

The decision to replicate the Minneapolis experiment turned out to be easier than the decisions on how to replicate. What aspects of the Minneapolis study should be copied and what aspects should be changed? How many new sites should be implemented and how would NIJ select the departments and the researchers to implement the replications in those sites? Perhaps the most important question was, would any police department other than Minneapolis agree to randomly assigning treatments to suspects? At the time, there were few scientific or administrative examples to guide this process.

The ultimate resolution of these issues was the initiation of six new experiments, one that began in 1985 (Omaha) and five additional sites initiated in 1986. NIJ required that each replication must involve experimental comparisons of alternative police responses to misdemeanor spouse assault incidents and measure victim safety using both official police records and victim interviews (NIJ, 1985). Other aspects of the design were left to the preferences of the local teams of researchers and implementing police agencies. Seventeen law enforcement agencies competed to be part of the replication program even though this program, unlike the NIJ Police Family Crisis Intervention programs of a decade earlier, did not provide additional financial resources to the department or to participating officers. The replication effort was research, not a demonstration, program and there were no Federal subsidies to the participating departments.

The main lesson of the events from 1983, when the Minneapolis results were initially released, to 1986 is that it was actually possible to replicate the design of the Minneapolis experiment but that this effort was neither instantaneous nor easy. In fact, the program's design imposed a number of administrative burdens on the participating departments and none of the police arrest studies would have been possible without the willingness of law enforcement agencies throughout the country to participate in rigorous research examining their own behavior on an issue of considerable public controversy. Like Minneapolis, these departments had risen to Wilson's challenge to gather systematic and empirical evidence of the consequences of their actions on the victims of domestic violence.

The Omaha Experiments

There were two police arrest experiments implemented in Omaha, Nebraska between 1986 and 1989. One of these experiments (Dunford, Huizinga, & Elliot, 1990) closely copied the design of the Minneapolis Experiment: it involved the random assignment of arrest, separation and counseling in misdemeanor domestic violence incidents. The second experiment (Dunford, 1990), implemented simultaneously with the first, involved the random assignment of an arrest warrant in misdemeanor domestic violence incidents when the offender was not present when the police arrived. The Omaha studies found (and later studies confirmed) that when probable cause existed to make an arrest, the offender was absent more than 40% of the time. The first, and perhaps most important, lesson of the Omaha experiments is that police practices can be no better than 60% effective if they are limited to treating offenders who wait for the police to arrive. Using a variety of measures, Dunford (1990) found that warrants were consistently associated with less re-offending and that in several but not all of their measures, these comparisons exceeded the traditional tests of statistical significance. Based on the partial support from the statistical tests and the consistent direction of the effects of using warrants, Dunford (1990) suggested that the use of warrants deserved further investigation.

The substantive conclusions of the Omaha offender-present experiment did not confirm the original Minneapolis findings published by Sherman and Berk (1984a). In the Omaha offender-present experiment, Dunford and his colleagues reported that arrested offenders were more likely to re-offend based on official police records and less likely to re-offend based on victim interviews. Neither of the Omaha results, however, were sufficiently large to be statistically significant and Dunford et al. (1990), concluded that arrest "neither helped nor hurt victims in terms of subsequent conflict" (p. 204).

The selection of Omaha as a site came about in ways not dissimilar to the selection of Minneapolis as a site. For instance, the principal investigators, Sherman and Dunford, had prior personal and professional relationships with the police chiefs in Minneapolis and Omaha, respectively, and this facilitated but did not ensure the departments' willingness to participate. In Minneapolis, the new reform chief was not particularly popular with the department and Sherman needed to negotiate with mid-level management and recruit the volunteer officers. During the operation of the experiment in Omaha, the chief was fired, re-hired and then fired again. The experiments were successfully implemented because of the social and professional skills of the principal investigators and their ability to collaborate with the police departments that implemented the research.

What lessons are to be drawn from the Minneapolis and Omaha results? The results are different but the experiments, while similar, were not conducted using the same measures or methods. For instance, in the victim interviews in Minneapolis, both violent acts and threats of violence were counted as failures and half of the re-offending instances involved threats only. In Omaha, only actual violence with injury to the victim was included in the measure of re-offending. Despite the more restrictive definition of new violence in the Omaha study, the proportion of victims that reported new violence in Omaha was over 40%; in the Minneapolis study the level of new violence reported in victim interviews was about 26%. In Omaha, Dunford and his colleagues compared treatments as randomly assigned and did not use statistical corrections for the misapplication of treatments. There are numerous other methodological differences between the two studies and it is difficult, if not impossible, from these two published works to determine whether the nature of police responses to domestic violence was different in Minneapolis and Omaha or whether some or all of the methodological differences generated the diverse results.

The publication of diverse findings is a common practice in social research but it can be disconcerting to policy makers who are trying to inform, if not base, policy on research findings. While there are methodological improvements in the Omaha offender-present study–notably researcher not police officer control of randomization and a much higher proportion of victims interviewed–both studies approach the standards for research advocated by the National Academy of Sciences. A major lesson of the Minneapolis and Omaha studies is that rarely will one social experiment, no matter how well designed and implemented, tell us very much and a second experiment, even one designed as a replication, does not add that much more knowledge. This would be true if the Omaha results were exactly the same as the Minneapolis results, but the disparate results emphasize the weakness of a scientific literature or a public policy based on one or two studies. In its wisdom, the management of NIJ had foreseen the limitations of just two police arrest studies and had found the funds and the will to initiate six replications.

The Omaha experiments reported on the prevalence of re-offending, the frequency of re-offending and the time to first new offense. The original publications on the Minneapolis experiment (Sherman & Berk, 1984a, 1984b) had reported only on the prevalence of re-offending. A 1986 National Academy of Sciences report (Blumstein, Cohen, Roth, & Visher, 1986) had encouraged the use of these alternative dimensions of criminal careers and victimization and the Omaha and other police arrest studies adopted the use of these alternative measures. In addition, Berk and Sherman (1988) reanalyzed the Minneapolis data using a survival model and continued to find statistically significant deterrent effects. Dunford and his colleagues reported that in both official records and in victim interviews some victims reported multiple new offenses and that the total number of new offenses was higher for arrested suspects than for suspects not arrested. Neither of these effects was statistically significant. In their analysis of the time to first failure, they found effects in the direction of deterrence in the victim interviews but in the other direction in the official records; neither findings were statistically significant. The lesson here is that arrest could decrease the proportion of suspects with new offenses but increase the total number of new offenses against a smaller number of victims.

The use of alternative measures and data sources means that there are not just one or two but many effects from each of the police arrest studies and a serious evaluation of the effectiveness of arrest requires a clear specification of which effects are important and which are not.

Unfortunately, our theories of deterrence and our understanding of how arrest and other treatments might improve the safety of women are not sufficiently well developed to specify exactly which measure or methods are the best tests of effectiveness. This is not simply a methodological issue but a central concern for individuals concerned with policy and for individuals concerned with testing theory. For the purposes of this paper, we have generally limited our discussion to the prevalence of re-offending but our choice is based on the need for parsimony and does not reflect theoretical or policy preference.

The Charlotte Experiment

The Charlotte experiment (Hirschel & Hutchison, 1992; Hirschel, Hutchison, & Dean, 1992) followed the Minneapolis and Omaha models of testing three police actions–arrest, separation and counseling, and used official records and victim interviews to assess re-offending among randomly assigned treatments. Omaha and Minneapolis, however, were mid-sized Midwestern cities with relatively low crime and low unemployment. The racial composition of the Minneapolis sample was almost predominately White (57%) or Native American (18%). In Omaha, the sample was about 50% White and 50% African-American. Charlotte is a southern city with relatively high crime, high unemployment and the experiment there had a relatively large (70%) minority population. The evidence from Minneapolis and Omaha may be inadequate to address the effectiveness of alternative police responses in this very different context.

The published results of the Charlotte experiment were similar to those obtained in Omaha: in the official records, arrest was associated with increased re-offending and in the victim interviews, arrest was associated with reduced re-offending. In Charlotte, as in Omaha, neither of these effects were statistically significant and Hirschel and his colleagues argued that their experiment provides "no evidence that arrest is a more effective deterrent to subsequent assault" (Hirschel et al., 1992, p. 29). There are, however, two possible interpretations of the results obtained in Charlotte and in Omaha. One interpretation is that there is, in fact, no difference between arrest and other treatments. The second interpretation is that the research designs used in these studies are not capable of detecting differences that do exist. Despite the experimental design, the Omaha study had only 330 experimental cases (and 242 interviews), so the Omaha design is unlikely to be able to detect effects as big as those found in the Minneapolis study. The 686 experimental cases (and 338 interviews) in the Charlotte study meant that the analysis of official records was powerful enough to detect the kinds of effects reported in the official records in Minneapolis but not the effects reported in the 338 victim interviews.[4]

The results of the Minneapolis, Omaha and Charlotte studies agree on one point: there is no large or even medium sized deterrent effect for arrest. The Minneapolis results suggest that there is a small to medium sized effect; the Omaha and Charlotte studies did not find even small effects but their designs are generally not strong enough to detect modest or small effects (Cohen, 1988; Garner et al., 1995). The main lesson is this: three relatively small studies are not sufficient to answer the two central issues of this research: does arrest deter spouse assault, and, if it does, by how much?

The Milwaukee Experiment

In Milwaukee, teams of researchers and police managers, in cooperation with local domestic violence service providers, designed and implemented an experiment that obtained 1,200 experimental cases and interviews with 921 victims (Sherman, 1992; Sherman et al., 1991; Sherman et al., 1992). The results of this experiment were consistent with the results found in Omaha and Charlotte: there was no statistically significant difference in the re-offending rates in official records and in victim interviews based on whether the suspect was arrested or not. In Milwaukee, on both measures, the arrested suspects had higher rates of re-offending in both the victims interviews and official records. Because of the random assignment of treatments and the larger sample size, there is no confusion in the Milwaukee study between non-existence effects and weak designs. In fact, the statistical power of the Milwaukee study was sufficient to detect even small effects but no such effects were found.

The design of the Milwaukee experiment involved some innovative approaches to better understand the effectiveness of alternative police responses to domestic violence. First, in order to assess the underlying mechanism of how arrest might deter future violence, this experiment examined differences between on-scene arrest with a short period of incarceration and on-scene arrest with a longer period of incarceration. Using official police records and victim interviews, the study found no statistically significant differences between these two arrest treatments. Second, the Milwaukee study used a third measure of re-offending–records of police calls to the local shelter. Using this measure, the Milwaukee study found statistically significant results showing arrest associated with higher rates of re-offending (Sherman et al., 1991). While the uniqueness of this measure makes direct comparison of these results with the results from the other police arrest studies difficult, the evidence obtained from the shelter data clearly does not support the notion that arrest deters subsequent violence. Third, the Milwaukee design called for interviewing some of the arrested suspects immediately after they were arrested. While the nature of these interviews limits their utility, the idea of suspect interviews is important. In fact, deterrence theory (Maxwell, 1998; Zimring & Hawkins, 1971) posits changes in suspect behavior but the design of the police arrest studies was to interview victims.

The Experiments in Metro-Dade

The experiment in alternative police responses to domestic violence in Dade County (Pate et al., 1991) found statistically significant deterrent effects for arrest when re-offending is measured by victim interviews; the official records also showed arrest to be associated with decreased re-offending but the effect was not statistically significant.[5] This was the first confirmation of the statistically significant effects observed in Minneapolis and increased the likelihood that there is a deterrent effect for arrest. With the addition of the Dade findings, we can observe that, using victim interviews, four of the five experiments had found effects in the direction of deterrence; in two of these experiments, the effects were statistically significant. Using official records, two of the five experiments had found effects in the direction of escalation and in only one experiment (Minneapolis) were these effects statistically significant. Minneapolis had established the importance of measuring the safety of victims; the emerging pattern suggests the importance of how victimization is measured, by victim interview or by police records.

There were two experiments implemented in Dade. The first was the replication of the Minneapolis experiment with just two treatments, arrest and no arrest. The second experiment used the same incidents as the first but randomly assigned half the cases to a program of follow-up services that was already in place in Dade County. This second experiment was larger and more rigorous than the Minneapolis, Omaha and Charlotte experiments and just as rigorous as the replication experiment in Dade County. Pate et al. (1991) report that there were no differences in the official records and in the victim interviews between those victims who had been given the follow-up police services treatment and those who had not. The statistical power of this experiment was sufficient to warrant the conclusion that these services did not protect the victims of domestic violence. The results of this second experiment were never published and have received no attention in the voluminous literature of alternative police responses to domestic violence. The study was not even mentioned in either of the recent National Academy of Sciences reports (Chalk & King, 1998; Crowell & Burgess, 1996), despite the fact that it meets all of the Academy's criteria for research quality. Given the extensive interest in post arrest follow-up services for victims of domestic violence, continued inattention to the nature and results of the one true experiment on the limited ability of these services to actually help victims ignores the best available evidence and may put the safety and lives of women at unnecessary risk.

The Colorado Springs Experiment

In the largest police arrest study ever conducted, the Colorado Springs Police Department (Berk, Campbell, Klap, & Western, 1992a; Black et al., 1991) randomly assigned 1,660 domestic violence incidents to four treatment groups–arrest, separation, on-scene counseling and post incident counseling. The results of this experiment in many ways mirror the results reported in Dade County–a statistically significant deterrent effect existed when re-offending is defined using victim interviews but the deterrent effect found in the official records was not statistically significant. The results of the Dade and Colorado Springs experiments breathed new life into the diverse findings from the police arrest studies but they did not resolve whether the weight of the available evidence favored or opposed the deterrence argument.

The size of the Colorado Springs experiment strengthened its design but it also created numerous implementation problems for the Colorado Springs Police Department. The study's design called for interviewing all of the victims shortly after the experimental incident and at about six months after the experimental incident. Had they accomplished those goals they would have completed 3,320 interviews. In addition, the Colorado Springs study attempted to interview three fourths of the victims by phone on a bi-weekly schedule for up to three months. Had they accomplished that goal they would have completed another 6,225 interviews for a total of 9,545 interviews. They actually interviewed 1,350 or 84% of the victims at least once and completed a total of 6,032 interviews. The extensive interviewing, however, raises another question: did the attention and surveillance involved in the interviewing process contribute to or detract from the safety of the victims. This issue is relevant to all of the police arrest studies where the assigned treatment was not just arrest but arrest with follow-up interviews; however, the interview intensive study in Colorado Springs highlights the importance of this design feature. Ironically, prior to Maxwell (Maxwell, 1998), there were no published results based on the victim interviews from Colorado Springs.

The Atlanta Experiment

There was a seventh police arrest study initiated in the Atlanta Police Department but, as of 1999, this project has not produced a final report to NIJ or published any findings from this research and it is unlikely that it ever will. Given the conflicting findings from the other six experiments, the evidence from Atlanta could have contributed much to the issue of the effectiveness of arrest as a response to spouse assault. Implementation failures happen, but the fact that this project did not produce an accounting of why the study was not completed means that we learned next to nothing from this $750,000 investment. The failure of the Atlanta project, however, highlights the accomplishments of the other studies: despite innumerable obstacles, eight police arrest studies were competently and, in some aspects, expertly implemented in six jurisdictions.

Summarizing the Site Specific Results

The existence of diverse findings from the police arrest studies raises the central issue of this paper: how can the information in these studies best be understood. Since the publication of reports and articles on the design, implementation and findings of the six police arrest studies, several assessments of the meaning and lessons of these experiments have been produced. Four of these prior assessments warrant note.

The National Academy of Sciences review (Chalk & King, 1998, p. 176) conclusion that arrest will not "produce a discernable effect on misdemeanor spouse assault" was arrived at through a qualitative judgment by a small group of scientific and policy experts. However, the Academy's review did not indicate a specific methodology for weighing and integrating the large body of evidence from the police arrest studies. Furthermore, the Academy's report did not provide any criteria for how large an effect would need to be to be "discernable." Most importantly, however, the Academy's assessment was based on a qualitative review of the available literature and, like all of the qualitative assessments, it is limited to the information in the printed reports from the police arrest studies.

The second notable assessment of the results of the police arrest studies is Sherman's (1992) *Policing Domestic Violence*. This book length review stands as a detailed accounting and an intellectual *tour de force* on the origins, implementation, findings and interpretation of the police arrest studies by the individual who conceived and implemented the Minneapolis study and who first called for its replication. Sherman's personal contributions and experience brought great authority to an assessment of this literature but, in his assessment, he, too, had to rely heavily on the published findings from other people's research. Unlike the Academy, however, Sherman has an explicit method for synthesizing the results of the six police arrest studies. His essential approach is to count the number of jurisdictions whose findings generally support deterrence–Minneapolis, Dade, and Colorado Springs, and the number of sites whose findings lean in the other direction–Omaha, Charlotte and Milwaukee and then compare the characteristics of those studies. Counting the number of individual studies supporting and not supporting a hypothesis has been a common way to assess a large number of common studies but this method of synthesizing research has several known weaknesses (Bushman, 1993; Hedges & Olkin, 1980, 1982). For instance, this method assumes that studies with 330 incidents are equivalent to those with 1,600 incidents, that one study with a large deterrent effect is equivalent to one study with a small escalation effect (and vice versa), and that each jurisdiction has a single and easily identified "finding" for or against deterrence. While Sherman's use of an explicit method is to be preferred over the Academy's unarticulated judgment call, the assessment methods in *Policing*

Domestic Violence can produce inaccurate estimates of the specific deterrent effects of arrest on domestic violence.

Qualitative reviews, however, are only one method for assessing a large set of scientific evidence (Glass, 1976; Rosenthal, 1978) and a growing body of research has argued that qualitative assessments of the findings from individual studies are, in most instances, inadequate for assessing the true effect of social interventions (Cook & Leviton, 1980; Cooper & Hedges, 1993; Hedges & Olkin, 1985). This research tradition recommends the use of more systematic and quantitative methods to summarize the overall effect of a large body of research. This approach takes each study as a research subject and uses the published findings from each study to compute a standardized effect across all studies. Sugarman and Boney-McCoy (1999) describe the use of these analytical techniques in family violence research generally and apply those techniques to the police arrest studies. They summarize information on the prevalence of new offending and find, on average across all five SARP experiments and the Minneapolis experiment, that there is no effect for arrest when victim safety is measured using the official police data, but that there is a modest deterrent effect for arrest when victim safety is measured using data from victim interviews. Sugarman and Boney-McCoy's meta-analysis was able to determine, contrary to the qualitative accounts in the literature reviews or the individual site reports, that there are no statistically significant differences in the effect of arrest between sites. Sugarman and Boney-McCoy's review, however, is limited to measures of the prevalence of new offending because the original publications do not provide sufficient information to compute standardized effect sizes for measures of frequency of new offenses or the time to first new offense. In addition, their meta-analysis does not control for differences in interview completion rates, differences in the kinds of cases that were included in each site, or other variable design characteristics in the police arrest studies.

A very different review and assessment of the police arrests studies was published in three companion articles (see: Berk, Campbell, Klap, & Western, 1992b; Pate & Hamilton, 1992; Sherman, Smith, Schmidt, & Rogan, 1992). These assessments analyzed the raw data from four (Omaha, Milwaukee, Colorado Springs and Dade County) of the six police arrest studies and found that arrest deterred employed suspects but did not deter unemployed suspects. The employment findings fit nicely with the hypotheses about the role of an individual's stakes in conformity[6] in the effectiveness of criminal justice sanctions but do not fit as nicely with the application of a consistent policy of either using or not using arrest in all cases of domestic violence. While the secondary analysis of raw data can be a rigorous and robust method of synthesizing the results of diverse research publications (Boruch, Wortman, & Cordray, 1981; Bryant & Wortman, 1978; Hyman, 1972), there are numerous methodological limitations of the specifics of these four analyses (Garner et al., 1995, pp. 21-24). For instance, only one of these articles uses data from as many as four of the five new police arrest studies, none of these articles uses the same prevalence or frequency measures and none of these studies uses outcome measures derived from the victim interviews.

NEW FINDINGS FROM A MULTI-SITE ANALYSIS

Our earlier detailed literature review and critique of the published reports from the police arrest studies (Garner et al., 1995) concluded that the site specific reports do not provide sufficient information to understand the exact effect of arrest on subsequent misdemeanor spouse assault. Among other things, that review established that none of the site specific publications employed the same outcome measures or methodological approach used in the Minneapolis study and that the publications from the new police arrest studies had no common approach to measurement issues or analytical methods. Our review, however, could not determine the extent to which the diversity of measures and methods influenced the diversity of findings from the police arrest studies. At that time, we urged caution in accepting the published results until a multi-site analysis using common data and a consistent analytical approach was available. That time is at hand.

We have recently completed a multi-site analysis of the individual records from the five new police arrest studies (Maxwell, 1998; Maxwell, Garner, & Fagan, forthcoming, 2000).[7] Using incident level data from all five new police arrest studies, consistent definitions for eligible cases, common measures for defining the prevalence, frequency and time to first new act of aggression, and a common analytical approach that controlled for site characteristics, the highly variable rate at which victims were exposed to interviews, and the age, race, criminal history and employment and marital status of suspects, we found that arrest had a modest but consistent deterrent effect on subsequent aggression by male offenders against their female partners. In analyzing the prevalence, frequency and time to failure in official records and the prevalence and frequency of re-offending in the victim interviews, the only analyses possible across all five sites, we found that arrest was always associated with reduced re-offending. However, only when we measured re-offending based on victim interviews did those reductions meet the traditional criteria for statistical significance. Like Sugarman and Boney-McCoy (1999), we tested whether there were different effects in any of the sites and in none of our analyses were the differences between sites statistically significant. Our findings support the view that the deterrent effect in this multi-site analysis is not dependent upon the jurisdiction in which the study was conducted but is dependent upon the nature of the outcome measures used.

Most of the prior research evaluating the SARP experiments relied on less rigorous methodological approaches to the synthesis of information across studies, were limited to official records only, and used *ad hoc* qualitative criteria for assessing the site differences. Interestingly, the meta-analysis by Sugarman and Boney-McCoy (1999), which did not suffer from these limitations, obtained findings on the prevalence of new offending similar to our own–no statistically significant differences in the official records and a statistically significant deterrent effect in the victim interview data. However, the similar findings from their meta-analysis and our secondary analysis of individual level data may be coincidental. For instance, they used all the cases from six experiments; we used individual level data from five experiments and then removed about 15 percent of the cases because they were not assaults by adult males on adult females or were repeat experimental cases. We included threats of violence and property damage in our analysis;[8] the published studies synthesized by Sugarman and Boney-McCoy typically do not. We are encouraged by the similarity in our findings and their findings, but a detailed comparison of how our methods, measures and analyses are different from those employed by Sugarman and Boney-McCoy (and which are to be preferred for which purposes) is beyond the scope of this paper.

We were able to go beyond what was possible in their meta-analysis and compute tests of the frequency of re-offending and of the time to first failure. We found that the direction of all of our tests favored the deterrence hypothesis and that out of five tests, the two tests using victim interview data were statistically significant. We argue that the effect of arrest was real but modest: reductions in subsequent aggression varied from four to 30%, depending upon the source of the data (official records or victim interviews) and the measure of re-offending (prevalence, frequency or time to failure) employed (Maxwell et al., forthcoming, 2000). We call these effects modest for several reasons. First, in three of the five tests, the effects did not reach statistical significance. Second, other effects were much larger than those for arrest. For instance, the suspect's age and prior criminal history were associated with increases in re-offending from 50 to 330%. Third, regardless of site, outcome measures, or treatment delivered, most suspects did not re-offend. Consistent with other studies (Langan & Innes, 1986), the police arrest studies have found consistent desistence from re-offending once the police have been called. Our finding is that arrested suspects desisted at higher rates than suspects who were not arrested. Lastly, we determined that the effect for arrest was modest because, even among the arrested cases, a substantial proportion of victims–on the order of 30%–reported at least one new offense and those who were re-victimized reported an annual average of more than five new incidents of aggression by their partner. However consistent the deterrent effect of arrest may be in our analysis, it is clearly not a panacea for the victims of domestic violence.

THE LESSONS OF THE POLICE ARREST STUDIES

The police arrest studies command a unique place in criminology and in our understanding of alternative police responses to domestic violence. Beginning with the Minneapolis experiment, they changed the nature of public debate from the safety of police officers to the safety of victims and demonstrated how good research could contribute to the policies and practices of the police. These studies heralded the use of higher methodological standards for criminological research and continue to inform a central theoretical debate in criminology over the deterrent effects of legal sanctions.

These qualities are rare (to non-existent) in criminological research in general and in most investigations into the nature of domestic violence in particular. Few studies can match the methodological rigor, implementation fidelity, theoretical contribution or impact on policy of any of these studies; as a group they may be unsurpassed by any other multi-site collaborative effort in social research on crime and justice. Despite these qualities, it is unlikely that another police arrest study will ever be conducted. The policy debate on alternative police responses to domestic violence is no longer about alternatives to arrest but alternatives to what the police and other agencies should do after an arrest. Random assignment between arrest and other treatments was ethically appropriate only when policymakers agreed that they had insufficient evidence to choose among them. The police arrest studies took advantage of that unusual historical moment and experimented with the lives of over 10,000 victims and suspects (and their families). As a result, we now know far more about the nature of domestic violence and the ability of arrest to improve the safety of victims. Although the size of the deterrent effect of arrest is modest, the empirical and political support for arrest is unlikely to evaporate sufficiently to warrant new tests like the Minneapolis and replication experiments. There may be additional reviews of this research and even more reanalyses of its data, but this research program is finished collecting data and implementing experiments.

The police arrest studies were, to say the least, imperfect. Sites were selected based on the willingness of police agencies to participate, not as a representative sample. Victim interviews were preferred over suspect interviews. The measures of failure did not include a variety of psychological, employment, or quality of life indicators which may be relevant to an assessment of the overall effectiveness of arrest. The experiments did not standardize the delivery of treatments within or between sites and obtained few common measures of what the alternative police responses to domestic violence actually involved. Both official records and victim interview data collection were not always systematic, complete or accurate. The data that were collected and archived do not permit the production of the complete set of originally contemplated multi-site analyses and, of course, the findings and data from Atlanta were never published. Future research would do well to build upon the strengths of the police arrest studies and to avoid, if possible, their design and implementation limitations.

The contemporary policy discussion surrounding the appropriate societal responses to domestic violence includes numerous suggestions for mandating arrest, coordinated legal and social service responses, the use of protection orders, offender treatment programs, intensive responses to high-rate or high-risk situations, and the prosecution and incarceration of offenders. These suggestions do not appear to be derived from, nor tested by, systematic empirical research that approaches the standards proclaimed by the National Academy of Sciences and met by the police arrest studies. The current discussions and policy options appear to be driven more by the personal preferences and ideology of the currently powerful than any real evidence about the safety of victims or behavior of suspects subjected to these plausible but untested approaches.

Decisions about alternative police responses to domestic violence need to be made every day and made without complete knowledge of the actual effectiveness of those responses. Innovation and policymaking cannot and should not wait for research findings, but we should learn from what we are doing. This is true in 1999 as it was in Minneapolis in 1981 and in Omaha, Charlotte, Colorado Springs, Dade County and Milwaukee in 1986. The police arrest studies were possible because a small number of police managers and domestic violence reformers were prepared to invest in a long-term program of rigorous research testing their most cherished beliefs about the most effective police responses to domestic violence, while the rest of the country continued to make decisions based on the best information available. At present, millions of victims and suspects and their families are part of a grand social experiment for which it appears the commitment to and use for knowledge approximates the police family crisis intervention debacle of the 1970s more than the program of systematic social research that was the police arrest studies. Moreover, there appears to be less of a willingness among researchers and policymakers to accept Wilson's challenge to obtain "reliable information as to the consequences of following different approaches." We fear that there is a lesson here.

NOTES

1. Bard provides no details on when or why the 24th precinct was chosen as control.

2. At the time, the National Institute of Justice was called the National Institute of Law Enforcement and Criminal Justice.

3. Gartin's dissertation was chaired by Sherman, making his analysis less than completely independent of the original authors of the Minneapolis experiment. Gartin also analyzed police dispatch data and found that this new measure, in combina-

tion with victim interviews and suspect criminal history data, resulted in no differences between arrest and other treatments (p. 157).

4. For a more detailed discussion of the issue of statistical power in the police arrest studies, see Garner et al., 1995, p. 13-16.

5. With 907 experimental incidents, the findings of no effect in Dade cannot be attributed to a weak design or low statistical power. Pate et al., 1991, also reported statistically significant deterrent effects when failure is defined as a new rearrest.

6. These studies report inconsistent results for three other stakes in conformity variables–race, marriage, and prior criminal record.

7. We did not include the Omaha offender absent study because it did not include arrests; the necessary information to conduct this analysis was not present in the archived data from the Minneapolis study (See Gartin, 1991).

8. For these and other details of our analyses, see Maxwell et al. (Forthcoming, 2000).

REFERENCES

American Bar Association, Project for Standards for Criminal Justice. (1981). *Standards relating to the urban police function.* American Bar Association, Chicago, IL.

Bard, M. (1970). *Training police as specialist in family crisis intervention.* National Institute of Law Enforcement and Criminal Justice. Washington, DC: U.S. Government Printing Office.

Bard, M., & Zacker, J. (1971). The prevention of family violence: Dilemmas of community intervention. *Journal of Marriage and the Family, 33,* 677-82.

Bard, M., & Zacker, J. (1972). *Police family crisis intervention and conflict management: An action research analysis.* New York City: University of New York.

Berk, R.A., & Sherman, L.W. (1988). Police responses to family violence incidences: An analysis of an experimental design with incomplete randomization. *Journal of the American Statistical Association, 83*(401), 70-76.

Berk, R.A., & Sherman L.W. (1993). *Specific deterrent effects of arrest for domestic assault: Minneapolis, 1981-1982.* Computer file. Ann Arbor, MI: Interuniversity Consortium for Political and Social Research.

Berk, R.A., Campbell, A., Klap, R., & Western, B. (1992a). Bayesian analysis of the Colorado Springs spouse assault experiment. *Journal of Criminal Law and Criminology, 83,* 170-200.

Berk, R.A., Campbell, A., Klap, R., & Western, B. (1992b). The deterrent effect of arrest in incidents of domestic violence: A Bayesian analysis of four field experiments. *American Sociological Review, 57,* 698-708.

Black, H., Berk, R.A., Lilly, J., & Rikoski, G. (1991). *Evaluating alternative police response to spouse assault in Colorado Springs: An enhanced replication of the Minneapolis experiment, 1987-1989. Final Report.* Colorado Springs, CO: Colorado Springs Police Department.

Blumstein, A., Cohen, J., & Gooding, W. (1983). Influence of capacity on prison population–A critical review of some recent evidence. *Crime and Delinquency, 29,* 1-51.

Blumstein, A., Cohen, J., & Nagin, D. (Eds.). (1978). *Deterrence and incapacitation:*

Estimating the effects of criminal sanctions on crime rates. Washington, DC: National Academy of Sciences Press.

Blumstein, A., Cohen, J., Roth, J., & Visher, C. (1986). *Criminal careers and 'career criminals'.* Washington, DC: National Academy of Sciences Press.

Boffey, P.M. (1983). Domestic violence: Study favors arrest. *New York Times,* 5 April, C1.

Bork, R.H. (1974). *Fowler v. North Carolina, U.S. Supreme Court number 73-7031.* Brief for the U.S. as amicus curiae; 32-39.

Boruch, R.F., Wortman, P.M., & Cordray, D.S. (1981). *Reanalyzing program evaluations: Policies and practices for secondary analysis of social and educational programs.* San Francisco: Jossey-Bass.

Bryant, F.B., & Wortman, P.M. (1978). Secondary analysis: The case for data archives. *American Psychologist, 33,* 381-387.

Bushman, D.J. (1993). Vote-counting procedures in meta-analysis. In H.M. Cooper & L. Hedges (Eds.), *The handbook of research synthesis* (pp. 194-214). New York: Russell Sage Foundation.

Campbell, D.T., & Stanley, J.C. (1966). *Experimental and quasi-experimental designs for research.* Chicago: Rand McNally College Publishing Company.

Chalk, R., & King, P.A. (Eds.). (1998). *Violence in families: Assessing prevention and treatment programs.* Washington, DC: National Academy Press.

Cohen, J. (1988). *Statistical power for the behavioral sciences* (2nd ed.). Hillsdale, NJ: Lawrence Erlbaum Associates.

Cohn, E., & Farrington, D. (1996). Crime and justice and the criminal justice and criminology literature. *Crime and justice: A review of research, 20,* 265-300. Chicago, IL: University of Chicago Press.

Cook, T.D., & Leviton, L.C. (1980). Reviewing the literature: A comparison of traditional methods with meta-analysis. *Journal of Personality, 48,* 449-472.

Cooper, H.M., & Rosenthal, R. (1979). Statistical versus traditional procedures for summarizing research findings. *Psychological Bulletin, 87,* 442-449.

Cooper, H.M., & Hedges, L. (1993). Research synthesis as a scientific enterprise. In H.M. Cooper & L. Hedges (Eds.), *The handbook of research synthesis* (pp. 3-14). New York: Russell Sage Foundation.

Crowell, N.A., & Burgess, A.W. (Eds.). (1996). *Understanding violence against women.* Washington, DC: National Academy Press.

Dunford, F.W. (1990). System-initiated warrants for suspects of misdemeanor domestic assault: A pilot study. *Justice Quarterly, 7* (4), 631-53.

Dunford, F.W., Huizinga, D., & Elliot, D.S. (1989). *The Omaha domestic violence police experiment. Final Report.* Washington, DC: National Institute of Justice, Department of Justice.

Dunford, F.W., Huizinga, D., & Elliot, D.S. (1990). The role of arrest in domestic assault: The Omaha police experiment. *Criminology, 28* (2), 183-206.

Garner, J., Fagan, J., & Maxwell, C. (1995). Published findings from the spouse assault replication program: A critical review. *Journal of Quantitative Criminology, 11,* 3-28.

Gartin, P.R. (1991). *The individual effects of arrest in domestic violence cases: A reanalysis of the Minneapolis domestic violence experiment. Final Report.* Washington, DC: National Institute of Justice.

Glass, G.V.B. (1976). Primary, secondary, and meta-analysis research. *Educational Researcher, 5*, 3-8.

Hedges, I.V., & Olkin, I. (1980). Vote-counting methods in research synthesis. *Psychological Bulletin, 88*, 359-369.

Hedges, I.V., & Olkin, I. (1982). Analyses, reanalyses, and meta-analyses. *Contemporary Education Review, 1*, 157-165.

Hedges, I.V., & Olkin, I. (1985). *Statistical methods for meta-analysis.* Orlando, FL: Academic Press.

Hirschel, J.D., & Hutchison, I.W. (1992). Female spouse abuse and the police response: The Charlotte, North Carolina experiment. *Journal of Criminal Law and Criminology, 83* (1), 73-119.

Hirschel, J.D., Hutchison, I.W., & Dean, C.W. (1992). The failure of arrest to deter spouse abuse. *Journal of Research in Crime and Delinquency, 29*, 7-33.

Hirschel, J.D., Hutchison, I.W., Dean, C.W., Kelley, J.J., & Pesackis, C.E. (1991). *Charlotte spouse assault replication project. Final Report.* Washington, DC: National Institute of Justice.

Hyman, H. (1972). *Secondary analysis of sample surveys.* New York: Wiley.

International Association of Chiefs of Police. (1967). *Training key 16: Handling disturbance calls.* Gaithersburg, MD: International Association of Chiefs of Police.

Langan, P.A., & Innes, C.A. (1986). *Preventing domestic violence against women.* Washington, DC: U.S. Government Printing Office.

Laub, J., & Sampson, R. (1989). Unraveling families and delinquency: A reanalysis of the Glueck's data. *Criminology, 26*, 355-380.

Lempert, R. (1984). From the editor. *Law & Society Review, 18*(4), 505-13.

Lipton, D., Martinson, R., & Wilks, J. (1975). *The effectiveness of correctional treatment.* New York: Praeger.

Maxwell, C.D. (1998). *The specific deterrent effect of arrest on aggression between intimates and spouses.* Unpublished doctoral dissertation, Rutgers, The State University of New Jersey.

Maxwell, C.D., Garner, J.H., & Fagan, J.F. (forthcoming, 2000), The specific deterrent effect of arrest on aggression against intimates and spouses.

Maxwell, C.D., Garner, J.H., & Fagan, J. (1999). *The impact of arrest on domestic violence*: Comprehensive results from five policy experiments (Video). Washington, DC: National Institute of Justice Research in Progress Series.

Mohr, W.M., & Steblein, J. (1976, January). Mental health workshop for law enforcement. *FBI Law Enforcement Bulletin, 45* (1), 3-8.

National Institute of Justice. (1985). *Replicating an experiment in specific deterrence*: Alternative police responses to spouse assault. Washington, DC: National Institute of Justice.

Pate, A., & Hamilton, E.E. (1992). Formal and informal deterrents to domestic violence. *American Sociological Review, 57*, 691-97.

Pate, A., Hamilton, E., & Annan, S. (1991). *Metro-Dade spouse assault replication project*: Draft final report. Washington, DC: The Police Foundation.

Pence, E. (1998). *The researcher and the activist: Finding common ground.* Paper presented at the Program Evaluation and Family Violence Research Conference. Durham, NH.

Police Foundation. (1977). *Domestic violence and the police: Studies in Detroit and Kansas City.* Washington, DC: The Police Foundation.

Rosenthal, R. (1978). Combining results of independent studies. *Psychological Bulletin, 85,* 185-193.

Sampson, R.J., & Laub, J.H. (1993). *Crime in the making: Pathways and turning points through life.* Cambridge, MA: Harvard University Press.

Sechrest, L., White, S.O., & Brown, E. (Eds.). (1979) *The rehabilitation of criminal offenders: Problems and prospects.* Washington, DC: National Academy of Sciences.

Sherman, L.W. (1992). *Policing domestic violence: Experiments and dilemmas.* New York: Free Press.

Sherman, L.W., & Berk, R.A. (1984a). *The Minneapolis domestic violence experiment.* Washington, DC: Police Foundation.

Sherman, L.W., & Berk, R.A. (1984b). The specific deterrent effects of arrest for domestic assault. *American Sociological Review, 49,* 261-72.

Sherman, L.W., & Cohn, E.G. (1989). The impact of research on legal policy: The Minneapolis Domestic Violence Experiment. *Law and Society Review, 23*(1), 117-144.

Sherman, L.W., Schmidt, J., Rogan, D., Gartin, P.R., Cohn, E.G., Collins, D.J., & Bacich, A.R. (1991). From initial deterrence to long-term escalation: Short custody arrest for poverty ghetto domestic violence. *Criminology, 29* (4), 821-50.

Sherman, L.W., Schmidt, J., Rogan, D., Smith, D., Gartin, P.R., Cohn, E.G., Collins, D.J., & Bacich, A.R. (1992). The variable effects of arrest on crime control: The Milwaukee domestic violence experiment. *Journal of Criminal Law and Criminology, 83,* 137-169.

Sherman, L.W., Smith, D.A., Schmidt, J.D., & Rogan, D.P. (1992). Crime, punishment, and stake in conformity: Legal and informal control of domestic violence. *American Sociological Review, 57,* 680-90.

Sugarman, D. B., & Boney-McCoy, S. (1999). The art of reviewing research. In S.K. Ward & D. Finkelhor (Eds.), *Program Evaluation and Family Violence Research.* New York: The Haworth Press, Inc.

Sullivan, R. (1968, November 24). Violence, like charity, begins at home. *New York Times Magazine,* 59.

U.S. Attorney General's Task Force on Family Violence. (1984). *Attorney General's Task Force on Family Violence.* Washington, DC: U.S. Government Printing Office.

Visher, C.A. (1986). The Rand inmate survey: A reanalysis. In A. Blumstein, J. Cohen, J.A. Roth, & C.A. Visher (Eds.), *Criminal careers and 'career criminals'* (pp. 161-211). Washington, DC: National Academy of Sciences Press.

Wilson, J.Q. (1977). Foreword in Police Foundation, *Domestic violence and the police: Studies in Detroit and Kansas City* (pp. iii-vi). Washington, DC: The Police Foundation.

Wylie, P.B., Basinger, L.F., Heinecke, C.L., & Rueckert, J.A. (1976). *Approach to evaluating a police program of family crisis intervention in six demonstration cities*. Alexandria, VA: Human Resources Research Organization.

Zimring, F. (1978). Policy experiments in general deterrence. In A. Blumstein, J. Cohen & D. Nagin (Eds.), *Deterrence and incapacitation: Estimating the effects of criminal sanctions on crime rates* (pp. 140-186). Washington, DC: National Academy of Sciences.

Zimring, F.E., & Hawkins, G.J. (1971). The legal threat as an instrument of social change. *Journal of Social Issues, 27*(2), 33-48.

Linking Research to Practice:
Challenges and Opportunities

Deborah Daro

SUMMARY. While most agree on the need for empirical evidence in determining best practice standards, little consensus exists on how best to build an effective, ongoing linkage between research and practice. This article examines how one prevention effort has sought to better integrate research and practice through the promotion of diversified research methodologies and structures designed to insure the ongoing exchange of empirical evidence and clinical practice. Healthy Families America (HFA) is a national initiative to develop the infrastructure necessary to sustain a universal support system for all new parents. Initiated in 1992 by the National Committee to Prevent Child Abuse (NCPCA), the program is grounded in a belief that the most effective prevention efforts are those which are shaped by empirical realities and an ongoing commitment to using research to shape program development. The article begins with an overall discussion of HFA's theoretical framework and the role of research in its initial conceptualization. It then reviews emerging research on HFA's home visitation component and how these findings compare to other evaluation efforts examining programs and policies designed to enhance child development and parental capacity. The article concludes with the implications of both the findings and the HFA planning approach on developing empirically sound and clinically effective future prevention initiatives. *[Article copies available for a fee from The Haworth Document Delivery Service: 1-800-342-9678. E-mail address: <getinfo@haworthpressinc.com> Website: <http://www.HaworthPress.com>]*

Address correspondence to: Deborah Daro, PhD, The Chapin Hall Center for Children, University of Chicago, 1313 E. 60th Street, Chicago, IL 60637.

[Haworth co-indexing entry note]: "Linking Research to Practice: Challenges and Opportunities." Daro, Deborah. Co-published simultaneously in *Journal of Aggression, Maltreatment & Trauma* (The Haworth Maltreatment & Trauma Press, an imprint of The Haworth Press, Inc.) Vol. 4, No. 1 (#7), 2000, pp. 115-137; and: *Program Evaluation and Family Violence Research* (ed: Sally K. Ward, and David Finkelhor) The Haworth Maltreatment & Trauma Press, an imprint of The Haworth Press, Inc., 2000, pp. 115-137. Single or multiple copies of this article are available for a fee from The Haworth Document Delivery Service [1-800-342-9678, 9:00 a.m. - 5:00 p.m. (EST). E-mail address: getinfo@haworthpressinc. com].

KEYWORDS. Child maltreatment, home visitation, prevention, ecological theory, program evaluation, parent support, participant outcomes

Science plays a major role in the development of most interventions
to alleviate individual or societal problems. In general, two lines of
inquiry guide the development of program evaluations and other
forms of applied research: does the program make a measurable difference with participants (efficacy) and does a given strategy represent
the best course of action within a given context (effectiveness). Commenting on the relative strengths and weaknesses with each of these
approaches, Seligman (1996) has suggested both strategies suffer from
imperfect and incomplete data and therefore should not be considered
in a hierarchical fashion. Others, however, disagree. The National
Institute of Mental Health (NIMH) (Mrazek & Haggerty, 1994) rates
information from multiple, randomized controlled trials as the highest
grade of evidence, particularly when they are preceded by an extensive examination of the problem's scope or incidence and perceived
risk and protective factors. In contrast, evidence based upon clinical
experience, descriptive studies, prior service delivery programs or
reports of expert committees, strategies commonly employed in effectiveness studies, is rated as having the least utility in determining
whether or not a specific intervention merits replication.

With some notable exceptions (e.g., Olds, Henderson, Chamberlin, &
Tatelbaum, 1986; Olds, Eckenrode, Henderson et al., 1997; Olds et al.,
1998), the majority of family support efforts and other home visitation
strategies often have been replicated without being subjected to solid
conceptual modeling and clinical trials. This is not to say that such
efforts have developed in the absence of empirical thinking. Indeed,
child abuse treatment and prevention efforts as well as a host of family
support and early intervention programs often have emerged from
either an initial incidence study highlighting the broad scope of a
problem or basic theoretical work which emphasized the importance
of early intervention. While this line of research justified the rapid
expansion of a number of promising innovations, many of these so-
called "silver bullets" proved disappointing, often generating as many
problems as they initially were designed to resolve (MacDonald,
1994; Nelson, 1984; Schuerman, Rzepnicki, & Littell, 1994; Zigler &
Styfco, 1993). These new problems led to increased skepticism on the

part of both practitioners and policy makers, further undermining the formation of effective public policy.

This article examines how one prevention effort has sought to better integrate research and practice through the promotion of diversified research methodologies and structures designed to insure the ongoing exchange of empirical evidence and clinical practice. Healthy Families America (HFA) is a national initiative to develop the infrastructure necessary to sustain a universal support system for all new parents. Initiated in 1992 by the National Committee to Prevent Child Abuse (NCPCA), the program is grounded in a belief that the most effective prevention efforts are those which are shaped by empirical realities and an ongoing commitment to using research to shape program development (Mitchel-Bond & Cohn-Donnelly, 1993). The article begins with an overall discussion of HFA's theoretical framework and the role of research in its initial conceptualization. It then reviews emerging research on HFA's home visitation component and how these findings compare to other evaluation efforts examining programs and policies designed to enhance child development and parental capacity. The article concludes with the implications of both the findings and the HFA planning approach on developing empirically sound and clinically effective future prevention initiatives.

HEALTHY FAMILIES AMERICA: A NEW CONTEXT FOR PREVENTION

Building a continuous and reciprocal relationship between research and practice played a central role in the development of Healthy Families America (HFA). Continued high rates of maltreatment, the instability of many prevention programs and the growing public and professional dissatisfaction with child welfare efforts suggested that the conceptual framework governing child abuse prevention efforts contained serious flaws. Initially, the vast majority of work in this field assumed that the diversified causal factors associated with maltreatment required an equally diversified response system. Community service planners were encouraged to adopt a broad continuum of services to prevent child abuse, each of which were viewed as equally necessary and equally efficacious (Cohn, 1986; Daro, 1988; Helfer, 1982). While promoting a variety of services was understandable, even logical, this approach failed to generate programs which explicitly addressed the inevitable interaction among causal agents central in interactional and transactional causal theories of maltreatment and child development (Belsky, 1980; Bronfenbrenner, 1979; Cicchetti & Rizley, 1981; Sampson, 1992). Preventing abuse and neglect was not simply a matter of creating a network of services targeting each individual causal agent. Rather, the real challenge was creating a system that explicitly recognized the integration of these factors in an individual's ability to adequately care for his or her child.

In essence, prevention advocates needed to shift their paradigm from the horizontal to the vertical and recognize that not all prevention efforts were equal in importance or impact. Rather, prevention efforts are best planned and delivered in a more orderly way, beginning with a strong foundation of universal support available at the time a child is born or a woman is pregnant. Subsequent prevention services are then integrated into this base of support, as necessary in response to emerging needs presented by the growing child or the evolving parent-child relationship.

A key component of this universal foundation is developing strategies that alter not only individual parent-child relationships but also community systems of support (U.S. Department of Health and Human Services, 1990, 1991, 1995). As such, HFA's theory of change places equal importance on identifying and impacting both individual and community mechanisms. While conceptually supporting systemic change, the majority of HFA activity over the past six years at both the national and local levels has involved the design and development of intensive home visitation programs. In 1997, an estimated 18,000 families were enrolled in intensive home visitation services offered by almost 270 HFA programs located in 38 states and the District of Columbia. Overall, 30,000 new parents were assessed and provided information on various educational, health and support services (Daro & Winje, 1998).

In addition to altering the conceptual framework for prevention, research was central in the design of the HFA home visitation approach. In crafting these programs, HFA planners drew on the experiences of many in the early childhood and family support fields, particularly those who designed and implemented Hawaii's Healthy Start Program (Breakey & Pratt, 1991). Collectively, these efforts underscored the importance of developing an intervention which embraced, among others, the following principles: direct services to both the parent and the child; multiple and diverse target outcomes; and suffi-cient intensity and duration to assist families at greatest risk (Daro, 1988; Kagan, Powell, Weissbourd, & Zigler, 1987; U.S. Department of Health and Human Services, 1991; Weiss & Jacobs, 1988).

A unique feature of the HFA program development strategy is its commitment to a set of principles or core elements rather than to replication of a single, highly specified model. These critical elements, summarized in Figure 1, cover three key areas of program develop-

FIGURE 1. Critical Elements for HFA Home Visitation Services

Service Initiation

Prevention services need to be initiated prenatally or at the time a baby is born. In order to ensure the efficient allocation of resources, programs need to implement a standardized process of assessing the needs of all new parents in their target community. Services need to be offered on a voluntary basis and use positive, persistent outreach efforts to build family trust in accepting services.

Service Content

Services for those families facing the greatest challenges need to be intensive (at least once a week) with well-defined criteria for increasing or decreasing the service intensity. Services must be made available to families for an extended period (three to five years) in order to achieve lasting behavioral change. Services should be culturally competent such that the staff understands, acknowledges and respects cultural differences among partici-pants; materials used should reflect the cultural, linguistic, racial and ethnic diversity of the population served. Services should be comprehensive, focusing on supporting the parent as well as supporting parent-child interaction and child development. At a minimum, all families should be linked to a medical provider to assure timely immunizations and well-child care. Depending upon the family's needs, they also may be linked to additional services such as school readiness programs; child care; job training programs; financial, food and housing assistance programs; family support centers; substance abuse treatment pro-grams; and domestic violence shelters. Staff should have limited caseloads to assure that home visitors have an adequate amount of time to spend with each family to meet its varying needs and to plan for future activities.

Staff Characteristics

Service providers will be selected based upon their ability to demonstrate a combination of the requisite personal characteristics (e.g., be nonjudgmental, compassionate, possess-ing the ability to establish a trusting relationship, empathic) and knowledge base as repre-sented by a specific academic degree or employment portfolio. All service providers must receive intensive, didactic training specific to their roles within the HFA service structure as defined by the critical elements and related standards of best practice. Program staff should receive ongoing, effective supervision so that they are able to assist families in realizing their service objectives and protect themselves from stress-related burnout.

ment–participant identification and engagement, program content and structure, and program staffing and supervision. In each of these areas, literature reviews were undertaken to identify the most common themes emerging from research and practice and then to apply these themes to HFA program development. The goal in this process was not to identify a single, successful individual program. Rather, this process sought to identify those program design elements that repeatedly emerged as contributing to positive participant outcomes (Daro, in submission). Findings were viewed not merely as validating a given service model but rather as providing program planners with distinct building blocks to use in crafting the best local response. Such an approach represented a new way of using research, one which HFA planners viewed as more integrative and reliable.

Finally, the HFA approach took steps to insure the ongoing communication between research and practice by establishing a Research Network comprised of some 50 academics and public administrators monitoring and evaluating HFA programs within their local communities. Having now completed its fourth operating year, the HFA Research Network provides insights into how simple communication can be transformed into a powerful force for enhanced social policy. As articulated by Robert Kahn, research network development begins by members listening carefully to each other's positions and theoretical orientations in an effort to better understand the issues governing their respective work (Kahn, 1993). Eventually, this "listening" phase transforms into a concerted effort toward "conceptual translation" as each member works to insure that words have shared meaning. In moving through these stages, Network deliberation contributed to the articulation of a common set of goals and increased consensus regarding critical research questions, measurement strategies and risk assessment procedures.

Most recently Network members have moved toward Kahn's final stage of network development, that of active collaboration. Evidence of this transition emerged as Network members developed joint research proposals, co-presented their findings at numerous conferences and co-authored publications. This type of collaboration and integrated activity may offer the HFA initiative its best opportunity to insure the application of empirical knowledge to program and policy development.

CURRENT HFA EVALUATION EFFORTS

Similar to the critical elements developed to guide program implementation, the HFA research team worked with local program managers
and evaluators to establish evaluation guidelines. Among the criteria
considered important for generating useful, programmatic findings were:

1. the provision of formal control or comparison groups;
2. the establishment of a range of outcome measures;
3. the use of multiple methods of data collection to obtain information on all critical outcome measures;
4. the use of subsequent reports of maltreatment only as one of
   many outcome measures of program efficacy;
5. the use, where possible, of standardized outcome measures;
6. the integration of the evaluation's data collection system into the
   program's ongoing participant monitoring system;
7. the completion of multiple post-intake assessments throughout
   the service delivery period; post-program interviews or observations on at least a sample of program recipients;
8. at least one post-program contact with all families who drop out
   of services; and
9. clear documentation of the process undertaken to establish home
   visitation services.

Twenty-nine evaluations assessing 117 HFA programs are currently in
place across the country. Six additional comprehensive evaluations are
being designed to assess aggregate impacts of large state or communi-
ty-wide HFA initiatives being undertaken in California, Florida, Massachusetts, Minnesota, North Carolina and Ohio. Of these efforts, 16
employ either randomized (8) or comparison (8) group study designs
while the remaining 13 studies employ pre-post test designs. While
some of these efforts focus exclusively on assessing the impact of
services on program participants, several also include explicit process
components and environmental or community impact assessments.
Funding levels for these efforts range from a $10,000 total cost for
smaller, pre-post evaluation efforts to almost $4 million for a five-year
randomized trial of the HFA site in San Diego. Two-thirds of the
current evaluation efforts have received at least partial funding from
federal, state or local agencies such as the state department of health,
the state department of social services, the state general fund or the

state Children's Trust Fund. One-third of the studies are fully funded by local or national private foundations. Collectively, these efforts represent an estimated $15 million investment in research efforts throughout the HFA system.

Common outcome measures used in these evaluations include reported rates of child abuse and neglect; maternal and child health (e.g., establishment of a medical home, immunization rates, well-baby visits, maternal health status, etc); parent-child interactions and parental capacity to care for children; the identification and use of informal and formal social supports; and maternal life course choices (e.g., welfare utilization, educational attainment, employment, subsequent pregnancies, etc.). In virtually all cases, evaluators are combining the information from standardized assessment tools, staff assessments and participant feedback to gauge the extent to which intensive home visitation efforts are realizing their stated objectives.

HFA evaluations, like most social service assessments, struggle with issues of long-term funding, sample retention, and measurement limitations (Azar, 1988; Chalk & King, 1998; Howing, Wodarski, Kurtz, & Gaudin, 1989). In addition, most of these evaluations, particularly those utilizing a randomized trial design, are ongoing and, therefore, have not produced definitive findings regarding initial or long-term program impacts. As such, the current pool of evaluative findings may best be understood as offering only preliminary guidance as to the model's effectiveness in reducing maltreatment levels and in achieving other positive gains among participants.

KEY OUTCOME FINDINGS

Consistent with the initiative's theory of change, HFA program evaluations have focused on the ability of intensive home visitation services to reduce the incidence of child abuse and neglect by improving performance on various mediating factors such as health care utilization, parental knowledge and skills, maternal life choice and use of social supports. As summarized below, the ability of HFA programs to achieve these desired outcomes has been mixed. To a certain extent, the absence of significant change may reflect the fact that many of the evaluations are still in progress. In other instances, this mixed performance may highlight real limitations in the utility of home visitation services, underscoring the importance of the dual focus on participant and community level change.

Child Abuse and Neglect

With respect to child abuse and neglect rates, neither of the randomized trials that examined this phenomenon reported a significant difference between the number of treatment and control group families involved in confirmed reports (Daro, McCurdy, & Harding, 1998; Galano & Huntington, 1996). The randomized trial conducted on the Hawaii Healthy Start program, however, reported a significant difference in the total *number* of reports made during the two-year observation period which involved participants in both groups. In this study, a total of six reports, all of which involved "imminent harm" were filed on three families in the treatment group while 13 separate reports, the majority of which involved actual abuse or neglect, were filed on three families in the control group (Daro et al., 1998).

In contrast, two evaluations in Arizona, which compared the performance of HFA recipients to families who qualified for but were not offered the intervention, found statistically significant differences on this measure. In both of the Arizona studies, almost twice as many families in the comparison group (8.5%) than in either of the treatment groups (3.3% and 4.5%) were reported for abuse or neglect during a two-year observation period (Holtzapple, 1998; LeCroy, Ashford, Krysik, & Milligan, 1996).

Methodological and contextual issues may limit the utility of this measure as a meaningful and reliable indicator of HFA effectiveness. First, the limited sample size for many of these evaluations (e.g., under 150) and the low base rate of child abuse reports reduce the ability of evaluations to detect a significant difference on this measure between treatment and control or comparison groups. Although the HFA programs are generally located in communities with child abuse reporting rates four to six times the national average, the odds of any infant being reported are substantially reduced because of their limited contact with those outside their immediate family (Sedlak & Broadhurst, 1996). Further, overburdened child welfare systems are increasingly limiting their interventions to those cases which represent the most egregious parenting (Karski, Gilbert, & Frame, 1997). Consequently, the absence of a child abuse report says little about the overall quality of a child's care or home environment.

The utility of this measure is further complicated by the fact that home visitation, by definition, increases the odds that a parent will be observed mistreating his or her child or that a child will be observed as being at risk of harm due to parental action or inaction. Indeed, the majority of reports documented by the HFA evaluations monitoring this outcome note that the most frequent source of reports on families in the treatment group is their home visitor. Within this context, the findings from the Hawaii study, for example, are particularly encouraging. The approach allows parents to be referred to the system at an earlier point in time, before actual abuse occurs or before a child is harmed. As noted by other prevention and child welfare researchers, this pattern suggests a more efficient and appropriate use of the existing reporting system (Farrow, 1997; Olds & Kitzman, 1993).

Health Care Utilization

Overall, these early evaluations report 90% or more of the children enrolled in HFA services are up-to-date on their immunizations and are keeping appointments for well-baby check-ups. With respect to the two randomized trials that monitored this variable, one (Galano & Huntington, 1996) found a significant difference between the treatment and control group (92% versus 74%). While the Hawaii randomized trial did not denote significant differences between treatment and control, both of these groups reported immunization rates above 93% (Daro et al., 1998). A comparison study in Wisconsin (Keim, 1998) reported that HFA participants were significantly more likely to keep appointments for well-baby visits than those in the comparison group (8.0 versus 7.3 visits during the first year of life). In this same study, women enrolled in the treatment group continued to breast-feed their infants for twice as long as mothers in the comparison group (6.53 months compared to 3.62 months).

The high use of medical services among program participants reflects the emphasis the programs place on identifying a specific "medical home" for all recipients. Looking across the full range of evaluations, the percentage of program recipients securing health care services from a primary care physician ranges from 94% to 100%. Reflecting this access to appropriate medical care, evaluators in Connecticut found that only 8% of the 183 emergency room visits made by the 386 families during their first year of enrollment in the HFA program were judged by staff as "inappropriate" (Black & Steir,

1997). However, a comparison study on this measure in Wisconsin did not find a significant difference in the number of emergency room visits between treatment and comparison families (Keim, 1998).

Focusing only on those families enrolled in services, two evaluations report a substantial increase in the use of prenatal care among current program participants for subsequent pregnancies. For example, in Oregon, 94% of those who became pregnant during program enrollment received early and comprehensive prenatal care, a health care service only 61% of these women utilized during their first pregnancy (Katzev, Pratt, Henderson, & Ozretich, 1998). Similarly, 75% of participants in the Tennessee program received prenatal care for their second pregnancy, more than twice the percentage who obtained such care during their first pregnancy (Kriener-Althen, Myers, & Homer, 1997). The absence of control or comparison group studies which have examined this concept, however, makes it difficult to determine if this type of behavioral change is due to the program's efforts or is common among women experiencing their second pregnancy.

Parental Capacity

Many of these early evaluations are reporting positive changes among participants in terms of their overall potential for maltreatment. Significant differences between HFA recipients and the control group were documented by Daro et al. (1998) in their randomized trial of the Hawaii program on both the HOME Inventory (Caldwell & Bradley, 1984) and two subscales of the NCAST developed by Barnard (1978). Galano and Huntington (1996) reported similar significant findings in their randomized trial of HFA efforts in Virginia. The Hawaii evaluation cited above also reported significant improvements in the participants' overall level of risk as measured by the Child Abuse Potential Inventory (Milner, 1986). The treatment group improved at three times the rate of the control group on this measure (Daro et al., 1998). Similar differences between treatment and comparison groups were documented by comparison studies conducted by the Arizona evaluation team (Holtzapple, 1998; LeCroy et al., 1996). Significant improvements in CAP scores also were documented among HFA participants following one year of services in Connecticut, Tennessee and Iowa (Black & Steir, 1997; Cowen, n.d.; and Kriener-Althen et al., 1997).

Maternal Life Course

A substantial percentage of participants who exhibited difficulties in such areas as education, employment, welfare dependency and domestic violence at the time they enrolled in HFA services showed improvements over time. Comparisons in welfare utilization rates in Arizona between HFA program participants and a comparison group comprised of those who qualified for but were not provided services reported that HFA participants spent 121 fewer days on AFDC, had 200 fewer days on food stamps and 73 fewer days on Medicaid, resulting in significant savings to the state (Holtzapple, 1998). Of the 801 families enrolled in services in Florida, more than half moved to better housing, 189 families decreased their dependency on welfare, and 146 showed greater involvement of the father (Carnahan, 1997). In contrast, the Connecticut evaluation did not find notable declines in the use of public assistance programs among HFA program recipients during the initial service year. While the use of cash assistance by this group declined from 59% to 55%, the use of WIC increased from 77% to 85% and enrollment in Medicaid and food stamps remained unchanged (Black & Steir, 1997).

Social Supports

None of the evaluations completed to date have found significant differences in the use of social supports between treatment and comparison groups. Indeed, a more common finding has been a decrease in the level of social support reported by program participants during the post-intake observation periods (Daro et al., 1998).

HFA FINDINGS IN LIGHT
OF OTHER EARLY INTERVENTION RESEARCH

Expanded research at HFA sites, coupled with other comprehensive assessments involving intensive home visitation models, is expected to have significant impacts on the future structure of home visitation programs, particularly as emphasis is placed on establishing universal systems of support for all new parents. Considering the existing body of research and the types of studies currently underway, HFA-related evaluation findings offer useful data for both refining the HFA model as well as improving the quality and utility of evaluation efforts. A central challenge facing researchers is harnessing this diverse and rapidly expanding body of research in a way that maximizes its utility without overstating trends that, at best, may be preliminary.

Key to achieving this balanced and tempered response is placing any set of findings within the broader context of related evaluative research as well as within each intervention's theoretical framework. Within such a context, the HFA findings mirror the findings of others that have assessed comparable efforts. Mixed results have been produced by large-scale efforts such as the Infant Health and Development Program (IHDP) and the New Chance program (Brooks-Gunn et al., 1994; Quint, Polit, Bos, & Cave, 1994). Similarly, assessments of such well established, highly regarded national family support programs such as Parents As Teachers, HIPPY and MELD illustrate the difficulty in producing consistent findings when programs are offered to different populations and replicated in diverse communities (Baker & Piotrkowski, in submission; Ellwood, 1988; Wagner & Clayton, in submission).

Despite this mixed performance, those seeking to apply evaluative findings to furthering program and policy development need to make these applications selectively and within a specific context. Even inconsistent and seemingly negative findings can be used to clarify specific service components or service delivery elements (Daro, 1993; Dunst, 1995; Ramey & Ramey, 1998). Rather than offering a single, clear model for replication, research on individual prevention programs continues to offer local planners building blocks to construct the most relevant prevention program for a particular population and context. Such a strategy allows one to maximize the utility of a wide range of information, culling from these studies the most common trends. It also allows for the integration of seemingly contradictory findings.

Even evaluation efforts that appear to suggest no value in early intervention efforts can provide policy guidance. For example, the Comprehensive Child Development Program (CCDP), a large scale Federal demonstration effort implemented in the late 1980s, examined the efficacy of case management services in enhancing child development and helping low-income families achieve economic self-sufficiency. Specifically, CCDP relied heavily on an approach in which a case manager was responsible for coordinating the service needs of a group of CCDP families. Case managers provided some services directly (e.g., counseling, life skills training) while, at the same time, organized the provision of other services through individual referrals and brokered arrangements. Services were initiated shortly after birth and were available for up to five years. A total of 24 sites across the country were funded through this initiative. The intervention was subject to a randomized trial, in which 4,410 families were randomly assigned to treatment and control conditions. A wide range of assessment strategies was used to document changes in over 100 different outcome areas for both the adults and children enrolled in services.

As the evaluators of this effort have noted, CCDP's overall outcomes were not impressive (St. Pierre, Layzer, Goodson, & Bernstein, 1997). Very few significant or substantive differences were noted between the treatment and control groups during the five-year study period. While the average program participant improved, comparable improvements occurred among the average control group participant. Specifically, five years after the program began, CCDP had no statistically significant impacts on the economic self-sufficiency of participating mothers nor on their parenting skills; CCDP had no meaningful impacts on the cognitive or social-emotional development of participating children; and CCDP had no important differential effects on subgroups of participants.

Robert Samuelson, a noted columnist for *Newsweek*, used these findings to conclude that so-called government "investment efforts" (e.g., programs which target poor children in the hopes of making them productive in the future) are doomed and that "large federal programs, whatever their benefits, can't undo parental failure" (Samuelson, 1998, p. 45). Without discounting the validity of the trends documented in the CCDP evaluation, a number of equally plausible and far less global conclusions can be suggested, particularly if the CCDP strategy is contrasted with HFA's overall approach.

First, CCDP was a highly structured program in which the federal government determined all aspects of the model. Indeed, significant money was spent in technical assistance efforts to assure that each of the participating programs followed program criteria with respect to staffing, service plan and assessment strategies. Local variation from the model was neither encouraged nor rewarded. In contrast, the HFA framework encourages site managers to adapt the program's 12 critical elements to their specific community and participants. Such flexibility may be essential to producing programs best able to adjust to local participant needs and community service realities.

Second, while CCDP services were long term, they were not necessarily intensive. The idea of "comprehensive services" as implemented in CCDP meant that a great number of services were offered but none of the services may have been provided with sufficient intensity to be effective. The case manager's role was primarily to determine the family's array of service needs and then secure these services through referrals to existing community agencies. The HFA approach, while including referrals to other services, stresses the need for a strong relationship between provider and participant and the provision of intensive home-based services for an extended period of time.

Third, because of the model being used, CCDP's outcomes were contingent upon the quality of current community-based services. As the evaluators of the program point out, it is possible that the services to which participants were referred were not of sufficient quality to achieve the desired outcomes. Hopefully, HFA's base of home visitation services and the initiative's commitment to improving the overall quantity and quality of services available for all new parents will result in more encouraging findings.

Finally, as the evaluation team noted, significant differences were observed in one of the program sites with the following characteristics:

1. a slightly less at-risk target population;
2. location in a state that provided a relatively high level of support for all low-income families (suggesting that the services to which families were referred may have been of higher, more consistent quality);
3. location in a school district and therefore may have appeared less stigmatizing than services provided through other venues; and
4. consistent, committed staff throughout most of the study period.

While other sites with one or more of these characteristics did not enjoy comparable success, this "package" of positive features may have created a more fruitful context for the CCDP model. Indeed, these characteristics reflect several of the elements promoted by the

HFA approach and by others that advocate for the "normalization" of family support (Daro, in submission; Kagan, 1996).

HFA FINDINGS IN LIGHT OF ITS THEORY OF CHANGE

In addition to comparing HFA evaluative findings with other early intervention research, it is equally important to judge the policy relevance of these data within the context of HFA's theory of change. The inconsistency of the findings underscores the importance of not equating HFA with the provision of intensive home visitation services. To fully implement the HFA vision, a broader array of services is needed to adequately meet the diversified level of needs presented by new parents, many of whom are unwilling or unable to adequately use home visits. Related research by HFA Research Network members has found that, despite repeated and aggressive outreach efforts, somewhere between 20% and 30% of those families targeted for service fail to successfully engage (Barrett, 1998; Daro, in submission; Mitchell-Herzfeld, 1999). These retention rates are comparable to other early intervention programs that have targeted similar populations and, therefore, may not indicate a unique HFA performance difficulty (Gueron & Pauly, 1991; Johnson & Walker, 1991; Quint et al., 1994; St. Pierre, Layzer, Goodson, & Bernstein, 1997). They do, however, raise serious questions about the ability of HFA to adequately reach a very targeted population. This shortcoming is further exacerbated by findings that as many as one-quarter of those families screened out of service at the time they give birth, go on to face significant difficulties in caring for their child over time (Daro, in submission).

Appropriately targeting prevention services and building the type of systemic change implied in the HFA vision may require a more complex participant identification process than is currently offered through the HFA initiative. Specifically, greater effort needs to be focused on designing and implementing a mechanism to provide initial support for all new parents. Whether offered in the home or through community-based family support centers, this initial outreach would systematically examine each participant's strengths and challenges in a number of domains such as general parenting and child development knowledge, degree of formal and informal social supports, attitudes toward parenting and personal, emotional well-being. If appropriate and willing, new parents also would be provided opportunities to connect with and provide support to other new parents in their communities.

In all cases, subsequent services would be presented as a continuation of the community's collective willingness to invest in newborns and their parents, not as a targeted intervention to troubled families. This approach may well facilitate the ability of family support services to successfully engage the most at-risk families into more intensive interventions. Families will no longer be asked to accept a new intervention based upon an identified set of limitations but rather to receive or provide additional assistance based upon their specific needs or abilities.

Altering the assessment process in this manner minimizes the methodological problems cited in the research as well as moves HFA practice closer to the stated HFA vision. By expanding the assessment process to include a "touch point" with all new parents, greater opportunity is created for a fuller, more accurate assessment of all a family's needs. Such an expansion increases the likelihood that fewer families in need of directed assistance would go unserved. Further, an assessment which universally considers a family's strengths as well as weaknesses is more reflective of the family support movement and other reforms in child welfare practice (Dunst, 1995; Kagan, 1996; Kagan & Weissbourd, 1994).

More importantly, this revised assessment process moves HFA beyond participant targeting and secondary prevention. Respondents are no longer classified into either being eligible or not eligible for service based upon a single score. Rather, the issue becomes using this assessment to determine the level or degree of future services. Under this conceptualization, all new parents do indeed receive some intervention, although for many this intervention will be minimal (e.g., a single home visit, a "welcome baby" packet, etc.). However, even this minimal level of support for new parents, if systematically delivered, creates an important message regarding the need for and benefits of universal assistance to all parents. Creating an array of service options at the end of the assessment process also allows HFA to explicitly encompass a broader array of services and existing support programs. HFA is no longer simply an intensive home visitation program but rather a universal, integrated family support system.

The importance of creating a more positive context or environment for parents has been a long-standing goal of child abuse prevention.

Indeed, the most powerful theories of explaining human behavior have drawn on the interdependency of the individual, family and social context (Bronfenbrenner, 1979; Cicchetti & Rizley, 1981). Commenting on the positive results from targeted early intervention programs noted by Olds et al. (1998), Earls emphasized this point by speculating on "how much stronger the effects of this early intervention would have been if the program had continued beyond the child's second year of life or if efforts had been made to engage the wider social settings in which the families lived" (1998, p. 1272). Unless individual prevention programs recognize that their ultimate success rests on the ability of communities to collectively support children, true progress in the prevention of child maltreatment and other negative outcomes which plague young children and their families will continue to elude us.

CONCLUSION

Research and policy development is a circular, not linear process. We think. We do. We think some more. We do some more. Research informs practice and practice informs research. Neither one fully controls the evolution of the other. Consequently, we cannot halt program or policy decisions until we have perfect knowledge. Rather, our challenge is to use emerging findings as guideposts, indicating if a given course of action is moving us, however slowly, toward a desired end.

The HFA experience has suggested that achieving a consistent and productive interaction between research and practice is a challenge on several dimensions. First, not all evaluations will support current policy. As such, evaluators are very likely to produce results at odds with what program managers and direct service staff consider "best practice." This mismatch between expectations and outcomes often results in frustration and a sense of betrayal on the part of both researcher and practitioner. To avoid such conflict, evaluators need to secure the opinions of those involved in the management and delivery of the programs they are assessing at every stage of the research process, developing research questions, defining program goals and objectives, and selecting a specific research design and methodology. In turn, those implementing programs must accept the need for constant change, as dictated by empirical evidence.

Second, it is important to realize that no single research project will provide a comprehensive answer to all questions just as a single service intervention will not be well-suited for all families. To improve practice, researchers need to implement multiple research designs, including randomized trials but not exclusively randomized trials; utilize multiple methods of assessment, including standardized measures but not exclusively standardized measures; and learn from multiple standards of evidence, relying on statistically significant findings but not exclusively relying on statistically significant findings. The best policies and programs emerge when we consider the collective lessons from a wide body of research, utilizing diverse theoretical models and methodologies. Research reviews such as those conducted by the National Academy of Sciences (Chalk & King, 1998; Crowell & Burgess, 1996; National Research Council, 1993), inter-disciplinary conferences, and the formation of research networks in which individual researchers pool their knowledge are all strategies to pursue.

Third, researchers need to recognize their findings are simply one part of a complicated and often highly political planning process. Despite the power of evaluation to restructure reality and to "tell a story" regarding program performance, Berk and Rossi (1976) have cautioned that empirical results should never be the sole determining force of policy. "Social science can demystify, but it remains the task of politics to interpret the meaning of this demystification" (Berk & Rossi, 1976, p. 343).

Finally, both researcher and practitioner need to underscore all their efforts with the realization that early intervention with newborns is only one component of a much broader comprehensive system of support. In reflecting on the initial development of Head Start and the current interest in early brain development, Zigler is most eloquent. "It is shocking," he writes, "that so many have chosen to focus on a year or two when the child was a preschooler and have disregarded the many subsequent years of development, exalted a single experience over myriad others, and are now putting their hopes and money on early childhood programs as the solution–not part of a solution, to pervasive social problems" (Zigler, Styfco, & Gilman, 1993, p. 21). As child abuse prevention advocates look toward the next generation of program planning, this example of building systems around a core successful program and then extending its reach to other developmental stages are perhaps the most critical lessons to be gleaned from emerging research.

REFERENCES

Azar, S. (1988). Methodological considerations in treatment outcome research in child maltreatment. In G. Hotaling, D. Finkelhor, J. Kirkpatrick, & M. Straus (Eds.), *Coping with family violence: Research and policy perspectives* (pp. 288-289). Beverly Hills: Sage.

Baker, A., & Piotrkowski, C. (in submission). Research on the home instruction program for preschool youngsters (HIPPY): Understanding variation in parent involvement and assessing program effectiveness. *The Future of Children.*

Barnard, K. (1978). *Nursing Child Assessment Satellite Training Learning Resource Manual.* Seattle, WA: University of Washington.

Barrett, B. (1998, November). *Engagement and retention factors in a home visitation program for families at-risk of child maltreatment.* Paper presented at the Annual Conference of the American Evaluation Association, Chicago, IL.

Belsky, J. (1980). Child maltreatment: An ecological integration. *American Psychologist, 35*, 320-335.

Berk, R., & Rossi, P. (1976). Doing good or worse: Evaluation research politically reexamined. *Social Problems, 26* (3), 337-349.

Black, T., & Steir, M. (1997). *Healthy families Connecticut: Second year evaluation of a home visitation program to prevent child abuse and neglect.* Hartford, CT: Center for Prevention of Child Abuse, Wheeler Clinic.

Breakey, G., & Pratt, B. (1991). Healthy growth for Hawaii's Healthy Start: Toward a systematic statewide approach to the prevention of child abuse and neglect. *Zero to Three,* April, 16-22.

Bronfenbrenner, U. (1979). *The ecology of human development: Experiments by nature and design.* Cambridge, MA: Harvard University Press.

Brooks-Gunn, J., McCaron, C., Casey, P., McCormick, M., Bauer, C., Berngaum, J., Tyson, J., Swanson, M., Bennett, F., Scott, D., Tonascia, J., & Meinert, C. (1994). Early intervention in low birth weight, pre-mature infants: Results through age 5 years from the Infant Health and Development Program. *Journal of the American Medical Association, 272*, 1257-1262.

Caldwell, B., & Bradley, R. (1984). *Home observation for measurement of the environment (revised).* Little Rock: University of Arkansas.

Carnahan, S. (1997). *Second Annual Report of Healthy Families Orange Evaluation Project.* Report prepared for Heart of Florida, United Way and Success by Six. Orlando, FL: Heart of Florida.

Chalk, R., & King, P. (Eds.) (1998). *Violence in families: Assessing prevention and treatment programs.* Washington, DC: National Academy Press.

Cicchetti, D., & Rizley, R. (1981). Developmental perspectives on the etiology, intergenerational transmission, and sequelae of child maltreatment. *New Directions for Child Development, 11*, 31-55.

Cohn, A. (1986). *An approach to preventing child abuse.* Chicago, IL: National Committee to Prevent Child Abuse.

Cowen, P. (n.d.). *Evaluation Report of Healthy Families Iowa HOPES Project 1992-1996.* Funded by the Iowa Department of Public Health and prepared for the Iowa Chapter of the National Committee to Prevent Child Abuse.

Crowell, N., & Burgess, A. (Eds.) (1996). *Understanding violence against women.* National Research Council. Washington, DC: National Academy Press.

Daro, D. (in submission). Child abuse prevention: New directions and challenges. *Journal on Motivation: Proceeding of the 1998 Symposium on Motivation.* University of Nebraska, Department of Psychology.

Daro, D. (1988). *Confronting child abuse.* New York: The Free Press.

Daro, D. (1993). Child maltreatment research: Implications for program design. In D. Cicchetti & S. Toth (Eds.), *Child abuse, child development, and social policy* (pp. 331-367). Norwood, NJ: Ablex Publishing Corporation.

Daro, D., McCurdy, K., & Harding, K. (1998). *The role of home visiting in prevention of child abuse: An evaluation of Healthy Start.* Chicago, IL: National Committee to Prevent Child Abuse.

Daro, D., & Winje, C. (1998). *Healthy families America: Profile of program sites.* Chicago, IL: National Committee to Prevent Child Abuse.

Dunst, C. (1995). *Key characteristics and features of community-based family support program.* Chicago, IL: The Family Resource Coalition.

Earls, F. (1998). Positive effects of prenatal and early childhood interventions. *Journal of the American Medical Association, 280* (14), 1271-1273.

Ellwood, A. (1988). Prove to me that MELD makes a difference. In H. Weiss & F. Jacobs (Eds.), *Evaluating family programs* (pp. 303-314). New York: Aldine.

Farrow, F. (1997). *Child protection: Building community partnerships–getting from here to there.* Cambridge, MA: John F. Kennedy School of Government, Harvard University.

Galano, J., & Huntington, L. (1996). *Year III evaluation of Healthy Start: 1992-1995.* Williamsburg, VA: William and Mary University.

Gueron, J.M., & Pauly, E. (1991). *From welfare to work.* New York: Russell Sage Foundation.

Helfer, R. (1982). A review of the literature on the prevention of child abuse and neglect. *Child Abuse and Neglect, 6,* 251-261.

Holtzapple, E. (1998, July). *Evaluation of Arizona's healthy families pilot programs: Report prepared for the Arizona Auditor General.* Paper presented at the Program Evaluation and Family Violence Research: An International Conference. Durham, NH.

Howing, P., Wodarski, J., Kurtz, P., & Gaudin, J. (1989). Methodological issues in child maltreatment research. *Social Work Research and Abstracts, 25*(3), 3-7.

Johnson, D.L., & Walker, T. (1991). A follow-up evaluation of the Houston Parent-Child Development Center: School performance. *Journal of Early Intervention, 15*(3), 226-236.

Kagan, S. (1996). American's family support movement: A moment of change. In E. Zigler, S. Kagan, & N. Hall (Eds.), *Children, families and government: Preparing for the twenty-first century* (pp. 156-170). New York: Cambridge University Press.

Kagan, S., Powell, D., Weissbourd, B., & Zigler, E. (Eds.) (1987). *America's family support programs.* New Haven, CT: Yale University Press.

Kagan, S., & Weissbourd, B. (1994). *Putting families first: America's family support movement and the challenge of change.* San Francisco, CA: Jossey-Bass.

Kahn, R. (1993). *An experiment in scientific organization: The MacArthur Founda-*

tion program in mental health and human development. Chicago, IL: The Mac-Arthur Foundation.

Karski, R., Gilbert, N., & Frame, L. (1997). Evaluating the emergency response system's screening, assessment and referral of child abuse reports. *CPS Brief, 9*(5), 1-11.

Katzev, A., Pratt, C., Henderson, T., & Ozretich, R. (1998). *Oregon's Healthy Start effort: 1996-1997 status report. Part II: Performance outcomes for children and families.* Report to the Oregon Commission on Children and Families. Corvallis, OR: Oregon State University Family Policy Program.

Keim, A. (1998). *Living in different worlds: The efficacy of an intensive home visitation program on increasing social support and improving parenting competency of first-time mothers.* Unpublished doctoral dissertation, University of Wisconsin at Madison.

Kriener-Althen, K., Myers, G., & Homer, K. (1997). *Healthy Start: Annual Report 1997.* Report prepared for Tennessee Department of Health.

LeCroy, C., Ashford, J., Krysik, J., & Milligan, K. (1996). *Evaluation report for Tucson, Prescott and Casa Grande HFA sites 1992-1994.* Prepared for the Arizona Department of Economic Security. Phoenix, AZ: LAM Associates.

MacDonald, H. (1994). The ideology of family preservation. *The Public Interest, 115* (Spring), 45-60.

Milner, J.S. (1986). *The Child Abuse Potential Inventory: Manual.* Webster, NC: Psytech, Inc.

Mitchel-Bond, L., & Cohn-Donnelly, A. (1993). Healthy Families America: Building a national system. *The APSAC Advisor, 6*(4), 9-10, 27.

Mitchell-Herzfeld, S. (1999, February). *A study of participant retention in New York state's home visiting programs.* Paper presented at the Fifth National Healthy Families America Conference, Chicago, IL.

Mrazek, P., & Haggerty, R. (Eds.) (1994). *Reducing risks for mental disorders: Frontiers for prevention intervention research.* Washington, DC: National Academy Press.

National Research Council (1993). *Understanding child abuse and neglect.* Washington, DC: National Academy Press.

Nelson, B. (1984). *Making an issue of child abuse: Political agenda setting for social problems.* Chicago, IL: University of Chicago Press.

Olds, D., Eckenrode, J., Henderson, C.R. Jr., Kitzman, H., Powers, J., Cole, R., Sidora, K., Morris, P., Pettitt, L., & Luckey, D. (1997). Long-term effects of home visitation on maternal life course, child abuse and neglect and children's arrests: Fifteen-year follow-up of a randomized trial. *Journal of the American Medical Association, 278*(8), 637-643.

Olds, D., Henderson, C., Chamberlin, R., & Tatelbaum, R. (1986). Preventing child abuse and neglect: A randomized trial of nurse home visitation. *Pediatrics, 78*(1), 65-78.

Olds, D., Henderson, C., Cole, R., Eckenrode, J., Kitzman, H., Luckey, D., Pettitt, L., Sidora, K., Morris, P., & Powers, J. (1998). Long-term effects of nurse home visitation on children's criminal and antisocial behavior. *Journal of the American Medical Association, 280*(14), 1238-1244.

Olds, D., & Kitzman, H. (1993). Review of research on home visiting for pregnant women and parents of young children. *The Future of Children, 3*(3), 53-92.

Quint, J.C., Polit, D.F., Bos, H., & Cave, G. (1994). *New chance: Interim findings on a comprehensive program for disadvantaged young mothers and their children.* New York: Manpower Demonstration Research Corporation.

Ramey, C., & Ramey, S. (1998). Early intervention and early experience. *American Psychologist, 53*(2), 109-120.

St. Pierre, R.G., Layzer, J.I., Goodson, B.D., & Bernstein, L.S. (1997). *National impact evaluation of the Comprehensive Child Development Program: Final report.* Cambridge, MA: Abt Associates Inc.

Sampson, R. (1992). Family management and child development: Insights from social disorganization theory. In J. McCord (Ed.), *Advances in criminological theory: Facts, framework and forecasts (Vol. 3)* (pp. 63-93). New Brunswick, NJ: Transaction.

Samuelson, R. (1998). Investing in our children: Sorry, government programs can't undo most of the ill effects of family breakdown. *Newsweek* (February 23), 45.

Schuerman, J., Rzepnicki, T., & Littell, J. (1994). *Putting families first: An experiment in family preservation.* New York: Aldine de Gruyter.

Sedlak, A., & Broadhurst, D. (1996). *Third National Incidence Study of Child Abuse and Neglect (NIS-3): Executive Summary.* Washington, DC: U.S. Department of Health and Human Services, ACYF, NCCAN.

Seligman, M. (1996). Science as an ally of practice. *American Psychologist, 51*(10), 1072-1079.

U.S. Department of Health and Human Services, U.S. Advisory Board on Child Abuse and Neglect. (1990). *Child abuse and neglect: Critical first steps in response to a national emergency.* Washington, DC: U.S. Government Printing Office, August.

U.S. Department of Health and Human Services, U.S. Advisory Board on Child Abuse and Neglect. (1991). *Creating caring communities: Blueprint for an effective federal policy for child abuse and neglect.* Washington, DC: U.S. Government Printing Office.

U.S. Department of Health and Human Services, U.S. Advisory Board on Child Abuse and Neglect. (1995). *The continuing child protection emergency: A challenge to the nation.* Washington, DC: U.S. Government Printing Office.

Wagner, M., & Clayton, S. (in submission). The Parents As Teachers Program: Results from two demonstrations. *The Future of Children.*

Weiss, H., & Jacobs, F. (Eds.) (1988). *Evaluating family programs.* New York: Aldine.

Zigler, E., & Styfco, S. (1993). *Head Start and beyond: A national plan for extended childhood intervention.* New Haven, CT: Yale University Press.

Zigler, E., Styfco, S., & Gilman, E. (1993). The National Head Start program for disadvantaged children. In E. Zigler and S. Styfco (Eds.), *Head Start and beyond: A national plan for extended childhood intervention* (pp. 1-42). New Haven, CT: Yale University Press.

Treatment Research in Child Maltreatment: Clinical and Research Directions

David Kolko

SUMMARY. This article provides a brief overview of key studies evaluating treatment of children who have been sexually (SA) or physically abused (PA), given the availability of research primarily in these areas. Specific research findings related to outcome following intervention will be discussed along with suggestions for future research. Outcome studies in this area have evaluated an array of treatments that vary in conceptual model, format, participants, components, and, to a lesser extent, settings. Selected studies will be reviewed to emphasize the progress achieved in understanding the role of these treatment parameters. In general, there is modest though emerging empirical support for the impact of short-term treatments for child victims and their parents or families, though the studies in these two areas differ in many of these

---

This paper was presented at the 5th Family Research Laboratory, International Conference (July, 1998).

Address correspondence to: David Kolko, PhD, Director, Special Services Unit, Western Psychiatric Institute & Clinic, 3811 O'Hara Street, Pittsburgh, PA 15213.

[Haworth co-indexing entry note]: "Treatment Research in Child Maltreatment: Clinical and Research Directions." Kolko, David. Co-published simultaneously in *Journal of Aggression, Maltreatment & Trauma* (The Haworth Maltreatment & Trauma Press, an imprint of The Haworth Press, Inc.) Vol. 4, No. 1 (#7), 2000, pp. 139-164; and: *Program Evaluation and Family Violence Research* (ed: Sally K. Ward, and David Finkelhor) The Haworth Maltreatment & Trauma Press, an imprint of The Haworth Press, Inc., 2000, pp. 139-164. Single or multiple copies of this article are available for a fee from The Haworth Document Delivery Service [1-800-342-9678, 9:00 a.m. - 5:00 p.m. (EST). E-mail address: getinfo@haworthpressinc.com].

139

treatment parameters and foci. Knowledge gained from research studies conducted in other areas related to child psychotherapy and research recommendations based on this work are presented. This includes several technical and methodological developments that may enhance the scope and rigor of treatment studies in this area. *[Article copies available for a fee from The Haworth Document Delivery Service: 1-800-342-9678. E-mail address: <getinfo@haworthpressinc.com> Website: <http://www.HaworthPress. com>]*

KEYWORDS. Treatment outcome studies, evaluation of treatment, effects of treatment, treatment efficacy studies, interventions for child abuse, child abuse treatment outcome

WHAT WE HAVE LEARNED SO FAR FROM TREATMENT RESEARCH ON CHILD ABUSE

Introduction

Research on the treatment of child abuse has been conducted for more than two decades (see Smith, 1984). Early interventions consisted of the use of primarily behavioral techniques designed to alter the many disciplinary practices of physically abusive parents (e.g., reinforcement, time-out, use of commands). Interventions for sexually abused children soon followed consisting of both individual and group therapies targeting diverse content areas (e.g., self-esteem, sexuality, coping, symptom control). In the last decade, advances have been reported in terms of both the clinical scope (models) and methodological sophistication (analytic methods) of various treatment applications. Accordingly, several treatment outcome studies directed at child sexual abuse (CSA) or child physical abuse (CPA) have documented their efficacy in altering various clinical problems and, in some cases, the maintenance of these improvements. Still, there is wide diversity in the outcomes and rigor of these studies. This article reviews selected characteristics of these studies, including their findings, implications, and limitations, in an effort to highlight the progress we have achieved in documenting the efficacy of treatment for these populations and some potential directions for future clinical-research in the area.

Sexual Abuse

Background. The need for treatment of childhood victimization is gaining empirical support based on studies that document increased psychosocial and developmental problems among abused youth (see Finkelhor, 1995). Several clinical sequelae have been documented in sexually abused (SA) children and adolescents both in the short-term (Letourneau, Saunders, & Kilpatrick, 1996; Putnam & Trickett, 1995) and long-term (Widom & Ames, 1994), including hypersexuality and sexual behavior problems, fear, anxiety and depression, dysfunctional attributions, and social or interpersonal difficulties. Conceptual and therapeutic models have been developed that offer therapeutic directions for the treatment of these and other symptoms among child victims of SA, including post-traumatic stress disorder (PTSD; see Cohen & Mannarino, 1993; Deblinger, McLeer, & Henry, 1990). Many of the details of initial quasi-experimental and more recent experimental studies of treatment outcome have been reviewed elsewhere (see Beutler, Williams, & Zetzer, 1994; Finkelhor & Berliner, 1995). This work underscores the diversity in population characteristics, treatment methods and formats, assessment measures, inclusion of follow-up, and analytic technique found across studies.

Conceptual Model/Treatment Modality. Treatments based on specific conceptual models have been evaluated, especially based on cognitive-behavioral principles which emphasize training in coping skills, attention to cognitive attributional processes, and instruction in social behavior, among other behaviors. Intervention protocols based on cognitive-behavioral treatment (CBT) have been compared to non-directive-supportive treatment (NST) that is not designed to be abuse-specific or abuse-focused in nature. For example, Cohen and Mannarino (1996) found that CBT led to reductions in internalizing symptoms, home problems, and sexual behavior problems after treatment, compared to NST, though there were no differences in externalizing symptoms or social competence. One significant group × time interaction was observed for internalizing symptoms. All six children who were removed from the study were from NST. This study is also noteworthy for its positive design features (e.g., use of therapist crossover design, client satisfaction measures, inclusion of parents and children).

A related study compared an abuse-specific program based on the four traumagenic dynamics attributed to SA (e.g., self-blame/stigmatization, betrayal; see Finkelhor & Browne, 1985) to an unstructured comparison condition (treatment as usual) with young girls and their offending female caretakers (Celano, Hazzard, Webb, & McCall, 1996). Both programs resulted in significant improvements in PTSD, traumagenic beliefs, and general psychosocial functioning, but the abuse-specific program was more effective in increasing abuse-related caretaker support of the child and in reducing caretaker self-blame and expectations of adverse consequences of the SA on the child. Although the absence of follow-up data is a limitation, the study provides modest evidence for the benefits of treatments developed specifically to address the problems of SA victims.

Despite several reports of the application of group therapy, few controlled studies of group treatments have been conducted. A study by Rust and Troupe (1991) found that a multifocus group (play treatment, supportive discussion) combined with individual treatment and parallel parental treatment improved self-esteem and school achievement relative to a non-abused matched comparison group. Improvements in sexual awareness have been found among participants of a psychoeducational information group relative to wait-list controls (Verleur, Hughes, & Dobkin De Rios, 1986). In another study using wait-list controls (McGain & McKinzey, 1995), a similar group that included more extensive discussions of abusive experiences and preventive recommendations was associated with reduced symptom severity scores in several areas (conduct, anxiety). These studies provide some evidence for the efficacy of group treatment, but they are also characterized by experimental limitations, such as the absence of comparisons to credible alternative treatments, multivariate statistical analyses, or follow-up data. In terms of clinical advantages, it is important to recognize that group therapy may serve as a cost-effective alternative to individual or family treatments.

Treatment Format. The studies reviewed thus far have examined a range of treatment formats, such as individual, group, and family treatment. However, only a few studies have examined how outcome varies in response to treatments that reflect different formats. Perez (1988) found no differences between individual and group play treatments, but did find differences between group treatment and no-treatment in self-concept and self-mastery.

Treatment Participants. One important question concerns the impact of treatment directed towards different participants, such as child victims and non-offending parents. Based on an initial study that included both of these participants, with good results (Deblinger et al., 1990), the relative impact of separate and combined child and parent CBT was examined in relation to community treatment (Deblinger, Lippmann, & Steer, 1996). At posttreatment, parent-reported child behavior problem ratings were reduced only in the two conditions involving parents, whereas child-reported symptom ratings were reduced only in the two conditions involving children as participants. Such results may imply that improvements in self-reported symptoms are more likely if informants are included as treatment participants, whereas changes in externalizing symptoms may require caregiver involvement.

Treatment Components and Their Incremental Effects. It seems reasonable to assume that the combination of different treatment components would be more effective than the components alone. A few studies have evaluated the incremental effects of salient treatment components. Berliner and Saunders (1996) examined the impact of structured educational groups for adolescents based on cognitive-behavioral procedures with vs. without an additional component that included a stress inoculation and gradual exposure component designed to minimize fear and anxiety. Both conditions resulted in improvements in anxiety, fear, depression, traumatic effects, sexual behavior, and internalizing symptoms after treatment and through a two-year follow-up, but there were no significant group × time interactions that supported the superiority of the "enhanced group program." Perhaps the findings would have been different had all patients exhibited high levels of fear and anxiety prior to treatment. The authors are credited with having conducted a methodologically sophisticated study that included clear maltreatment inclusion criteria, a large sample, two-year follow-up data, and analyses of clinical significance. Family sessions and treatments have been evaluated in only a few studies. In some instances, family treatment has been integrated with instruction in normal sexual development and abuse-specific discussions to reduce risk status (Bentovim, Van Elberg, & Boston, 1988; Furniss, Bingley-Miller, & Van Elburg, 1988). One study evaluated the incremental benefit of child and family groups to family/network meetings with 4-16 year-old child victims (Hyde, Bentovim, & Monck, 1995) based on a prior descriptive and treatment outcome study (Monck et al., 1994). Family/network meetings were used to address various issues with therapists and community professionals (e.g., communication, protection, marital problems). The treatment groups provided exposure to abuse-specific information relevant to children (e.g., feelings, self-protection) and adults (secrecy, parental response). As noted in the prior study, cases in both conditions reported gains at posttreatment on self-reports (child health, behavior, depression) and maternal reports (self-concept, behavior), but not on measures of child-reported behavior and self-concept, or teacher reports of symptoms. Interestingly, clinician ratings revealed some superiority for the combined condition on specific treatment aims (e.g., child sharing painful feelings and having more positive self-concept, family perception of child's needs). A strength of the study is its incorporation of age-matched groups and inclusion of offenders in services. However, the long assessment interval (up to 12 months) and the absence of treatment integrity data preclude clear interpretation of the results.

Treatment Setting. Thus far, there do not appear to be any studies comparing the impact of treatments administered in contrasting settings, such as outpatient clinics vs. community settings (e.g., homes).

Child Physical Abuse

Background. Treatment of CPA gains support from comparison studies of abused and nonabused samples showing various consequences following CPA, notably, problems with aggression and social or interpersonal behavior, negative parent-child interactions, school problems, and depressive symptoms, among other problems (e.g., Knutson, 1995; Kolko, 1996a; Malinosky-Rummell & Hansen, 1993; National Academy of Sciences, 1993; Widom & Maxfield, 1996). Adolescents who have been physically assaulted also report related mental health problems relative to non-assaulted youth, including heightened depression, violence, and suicidality in a national survey (Swenson, Saunders, & Kilpatrick, 1996). Models of treatment emphasize the role of cognitive-behavioral treatments and associated educational, clinical, and/or support services that teach skills to parents and, to a lesser extent, their children (Graziano & Mills, 1992; Wolfe & Wekerle, 1993), some of which provide special attention to parent-child relationship programming (Urquiza & Bodiford-McNeil, 1996). Such interventions seek both to promote a pro-social repertoire and minimize the psychological sequelae of abusive behavior.

Ecologically-based interventions also advocate for interventions in multiple areas affecting child functioning, including the family and social system (Belsky, 1993) and as conducted in various community settings. Further details of individual studies in this area can be found elsewhere (see Kolko, 1996a; Mannarino & Cohen, 1990; Oates & Bross, 1995; Wolfe, 1994).

Conceptual Model/Treatment Modality. In this area, only a few studies have compared the efficacy of alternative treatment models. In one early study, behaviorally oriented family casework (modeling, reinforcement) and play therapy were examined as methods to alter individual behavior and family interactions (Nicol et al., 1988). Improvements were reported in family coercion, but not positive behavior. The two treatments were generally similar in outcome, although the study is limited by a large attrition rate (44%) and the absence of follow-up data. Further, it is unclear how well the two conditions were monitored for treatment integrity. One of the few recent comparisons of interventions based on alternative models and modalities examined individual child and parent CBT and family therapy (FT) for school-aged children and their parents/guardians (Kolko, 1996b, c). During treatment, the overall levels of parental anger and physical discipline/force were found to be lower in CBT than FT families, though each group showed a reduction on these items from the early to late treatment sessions. In terms of outcome data (Kolko, 1996c), CBT and FT were associated with improvements in child-to-parent violence and child externalizing behavior, parental distress and abuse risk, and family conflict and cohesion, relative to those cases who received routine community service (RCS). At the same time, all three conditions reported numerous improvements across time (e.g., parental anger, parental practices, child fears). In terms of recidivism rates based on official records, there was no statistically significant difference in the percentages of children from the CBT, FT, and RCS groups who were involved in another incident of child maltreatment during follow-up (10%, 12%, and 30%, respectively); in terms of the adults who participated in treatment, one adult each in CBT (5%) and RCS (6%) and three in RCS (30%) had been reported as having maltreated a participating child during follow-up. No differences between CBT and FT were observed on consumer satisfaction or maltreatment risk ratings at termination; unfortunately, such information could not be assessed in RCS. The findings of this evaluation provide additional, albeit qualified, support for the continued development of individual and family treatments involving child victims of physical abuse. Brunk, Henggeler and Whelan (1987) compared Multisystemic Therapy (MST) designed to target problems in various systems affecting the family with behavioral parent training (PT). MST was associated with greater improvements in parent-child relationships, whereas PT was more effective in reducing child behavior problems. No follow-up data were included, however.

Treatment Participants. Systematic research by Fantuzzo has identified the benefit of peer-mediated socialization procedures (Fantuzzo, Stovall, Schachtel, Goins, & Hall, 1987). One study with maltreated preschoolers compared peer- and adult-mediated socialization techniques. The peer-mediated condition, described as resilient peer treatment (RPT), involves using competent peers as treatment agents in the context of special play activities and settings in order to enhance the social competency of withdrawn abused children. The adult-mediate condition involved having a familiar adult (undergraduate volunteer) employ the same play procedures and settings. Peer techniques were found superior to adult initiations in improving the children's social adjustment and peer initiations (Davis & Fantuzzo, 1989; Fantuzzo, Jurecic, Stovall, Hightower, & Goins, 1988). Withdrawn children were found to respond better to peer than adult sessions, whereas aggressive children showed an increase in negative behavior to peers (Davis & Fantuzzo, 1989; Fantuzzo et al., 1987, 1988). The results of RPT have been documented two months following intervention (Fantuzzo et al., 1996). These systematic research studies suggest some important differences among intervention procedures and have documented short-term follow-up gains, but would benefit from further evaluations of long-term follow-up and impact on risk for recidivism.

Treatment Components and Their Incremental Effects. One other cognitive-behavioral treatment study examined the incremental benefit of individualized parent-child sessions beyond the effects of an information group alone (Wolfe, Edwards, Manion, & Koverola, 1988). The study found that the combination condition was associated with several benefits (fewer and less intense child behavior problems, fewer adjustment problems, lowered risk of maltreatment), but not others (e.g., quality of child-rearing environment, children's adaptive abilities).

CLINICAL-RESEARCH DIRECTIONS

This section provides an overview of some research developments based on the aforementioned studies, and outlines several research issues and directions for future work in this area. In general, there are more research studies with a higher level of rigor among studies evaluating treatment in the area of CSA than in CPA. Among those studies with adequate experimental methodologies, however, the level of efficacy is comparable and generally supportive of abuse-specific treatments. Indeed, studies drawing upon CBT as a treatment modality seem to have documented the highest level of efficacy across various measures for both CSA and CPA. At the same time, the targets of or participants in treatment have differed by abuse subtype. Specifically, individual CBT for child victims and adult offenders has more often been conducted in treatment studies in the areas of CSA and CPA, respectively. There are several evaluations of group therapy in the area of CSA, but none in the area of CPA. In contrast, several family-directed interventions have been reported in the treatment of CPA, with only a few studies found in the area of CSA (e.g., Hyde et al., 1995). Thus, we have learned about the impact of different abuse-specific interventions in CSA and CPA. The level of experimental rigor that characterizes existing treatment studies also has varied considerably. Among the many reports of group therapy, few have included adequate experimental methodologies, such as comparison conditions, random assignment, and descriptions of treatment integrity. Thus, such reports are often excluded from summaries of treatment outcome studies, despite the widespread use of group treatment with victims of CSA (see Finkelhor & Berliner, 1995). Likewise, studies or reports of family-centered, in-home services in the area of CPA may suffer from comparable empirical limitations (see Whittaker, Kinney, Tracy, & Booth, 1990). It is especially important to evaluate carefully the efficacy of family-based treatment approaches given that they often incorporate multiple intervention components, which are administered in various community settings (e.g., home, school).

Turning to the effects that have been reported in outcome studies, a summary of the general treatment effects and findings reported by treatment research studies in these two areas is shown in Table 1. In CSA, studies show that treatments have been most effective in reducing internalizing symptoms, with only a few studies reporting reduc-

TABLE 1. Outcomes from Treatment Research Studies

Outcome Domain	Level of Support
Child Sexual Abuse	
Child CBT	
Internalizing	+/+
Sexual Behavior	+
Externalizing	+/-
Parent CBT/Skills Training	
Protection	+
Support	+
Parent-Child Relationship	+
Child Physical Abuse	
Child Programs/CBT	
Child Development and Behavior	+/+
Peer and Social Relations	+/+
Internalizing	+/-
Parent Treatment/Family Therapy	
Parent-Child Interventions and Parenting Skill	+/+
Family Cohesion/Conflict	+

Note: (+) = positive outcomes; (−) = negative outcomes; (+/−) = mixed outcomes

tions in sexual behavior and externalizing symptoms. Fewer effects on parent behavior have been examined. Some of the effects include increased parental support of the child victim. However, virtually none of the studies have reported efficacy data for parent-child relationships or abuse recidivism. In contrast, treatment studies for CPA have generally reported reductions in negative parental behavior and, to some extent, deviant child behavior, with more mixed evidence to suggest improvements in internalizing symptoms. Some studies directed to child victims have found improvements in social behavior. There is also mixed evidence for reductions in treated children's risk for re-abuse. Long-term improvements following treatment have been reported in some studies of CSA and CPA, though many studies have not collected follow-up data (e.g., Brunk et al., 1987; Celano et al.,

1996; Hyde et al., 1995; Whiteman, Fanshel, & Grundy, 1987). There has been considerable diversity in the procedures used to address the clinical concerns of abused children and their families. Certain common therapeutic components and targets described in treatment research studies of CSA and CPA have been identified. For example, abuse-specific or abuse-focused programming emphasizes direct discussion of recent traumatic experiences aided by the use of alternative forms of cue-exposure, such as imagery, drawing, and role-playing. Multiple aspects of the traumatic experience may be reviewed in vivid detail, along with salient emotional (e.g., fear, shame, blame) and cognitive reactions (e.g., helplessness, negative view of self, seeing self as responsible). These methods have been more often used in the treatment of CSA than CPA where the focus has been on parent-child coercion and over-reliance upon punitive methods of control by parents. Some work has emphasized the use of offender apologies, safety plans, and preventive skills.

Some of the clinical-research issues facing the field are shown in Table 2. One of the more contemporary issues facing clinicians and researchers relates to the question as to *when* treatment should be conducted, that is, whether one should treat all abused children or only those cases of abuse exhibiting some type of symptom or adjustment problems. It may be difficult to treat abused children who show signs

TABLE 2. General Practice Considerations

Treatment of the Symptoms versus the Experience Itself
Target/Goal
Abuse Specific
General
Methods to Address View of Oneself/Others
Treating Abuse in Its "Ecological Context"
When, Where, & How to Administer Treatment?
Earlier vs. Later
Settings
Format, Orientation, Sequence
Goals of Service: Child Protection and Welfare

of dysfunction or impairment, especially since most cognitive-behavioral procedures are directed toward reducing specific sequelae, and to justify the resources needed to treat such a large group (see Berliner & Saunders, 1996). However, it is not always possible to determine the specific problems experienced by an abused child or to predict which ones may show symptoms at a later date. Research has found that certain reactions in traumatized children, such as PTSD or social behavior problems, are responsive to CBT interventions (Cohen & Mannarino, 1997; Deblinger et al., 1996; Fantuzzo et al., 1987). Relatedly, we need to know more about how to enhance a child's negative self-perception (e.g., blame, shame, vulnerable, damaged). Comparisons of specific procedures that can promote a more balanced and supportive self-view need to be conducted with victims of CSA and CPA. Finally, few studies have evaluated where it is best to administer treatment. Although there are advantages to working in clinic settings where privacy and safety can be assured, services provided in community settings provide access to more naturalistic cues and participants, and permit greater targeting of the contexts affecting children. Other research directions that require attention in subsequent studies are also noted in Table 3. We need to learn more about ways to motivate both

TABLE 3. Future Directions for Treatment Research

Develop models of impact of abuse
Engagement and related methods to motivate
Address obstacles to clinical treatment trials
Examine moderators and mediators of outcome
Examine maintenance and recidivism over time
Compare alternative treatments
Examine role of parental and family treatment
Promote treatment effectiveness in real-world settings
Study service systems and their impact
Conduct efficacy studies
Access/obstacles
Decision making
Service availability and quality

caregivers and child victims to participate in treatment. Methods of engagement have been studied in other areas and deserve further attention in work with abusive families, especially when many families feel, if not in actuality, coerced into treatment. Comparisons of alternative but equally credible approaches are also warranted, given potential differences in the speed with which treatment exerts its effects or the scope of impact (see Brunk et al., 1987; Deblinger et al., 1996; Kolko, 1996b). This is especially relevant in the case of parental or family treatment. We also know little about how services are delivered in the real world and how well service systems operate on behalf of abusive families. Some recent research suggests that many abused children do not receive treatment, and certain characteristics are most likely to be associated with treatment referral or participation in CSA (e.g., Caucasian victim, legal service involvement, see Haskett, Myers, Pirrello, & Dombalis, 1995; Tingus, Heger, Foy, & Leskin, 1996); and that other characteristics may be related to treatment for families involved in sexual or physical abuse (e.g., victims are Caucasian and low in anxiety, parental abuse history; Kolko, Selelyo, & Brown, 1999). Kolko et al. (1999) also found, based on child and parent reports, that few children had received their own treatment services upon intake into the study, respectively (17.2%, 18.8%), and after the conclusion of an initial service, approximately six months later (13.0%, 17.8%). Several aspects of the CPS service system merit evaluation, including access to and obstacles to service involvement, caseworker decision-making, service availability, and the effectiveness of interventions. One final consideration worth noting is the difficulty of conducting controlled outcome studies with abused populations. Several obstacles exist that require attention before a study can be initiated. These include the implementation of interventions by CPS workers even prior to clinical referral, caseworker dissatisfaction with random assignment given their frequent preference for a specific type of treatment for each referred family, the fact that children or parents may be removed prior to referral for specialized treatment, and the use of different methods of assessment in the CPS and mental health systems. Each of these systems issues may impede the conduct of clinical research on the effects of treatment with abused children and their families.

WHAT HAVE WE LEARNED FROM GENERAL STUDIES OF CHILD/FAMILY PSYCHOTHERAPY?

Treatment Parameters

There is an enormous literature on the effects of child and adolescent psychotherapy covering more than 200 studies reported over the past 46 years (see Weisz, Weiss, & Donenberg, 1992). Using specialized techniques to summarize the effects of these studies, such as meta-analysis, reviews of these studies have articulated the effects of therapy across a range of important treatment parameters. Many of these findings and their implications bear relevance to the research on the treatment of child abuse.

The review reported by Weisz et al. (1992) examined studies that were conducted in primarily two settings, the specialized research laboratory or the traditional clinic. Overall, the studies showed that therapy with children and adolescents was beneficial, but most of these studies were based on samples, clinicians, and procedures, that were not representative of typical clinical settings. Much more modest effects were found, if they were found at all, in the clinic studies that were reported. These studies examined treated samples in comparison to matched normals or therapy dropouts. Thus, the effects of psychotherapy were less positive for the treatment of clinic-referred children being treated by practicing clinicians in routine clinic settings. As noted by Weisz et al. (1992), we lack convincing evidence that the large positive effects of psychotherapy demonstrated in controlled psychotherapy research, and summarized in the meta-analyses, are being "replicated in the clinic and community settings where most real-life interventions actually occur" (p. 1584). Thus, there is a clear need to identify the conditions under which treatments conducted in clinics are most effective.

Related work by Weisz (Weisz, Donenberg, Han, & Kauneckis, 1995) explored possible reasons for these differences by examining various study characteristics. It is of interest that several were not associated with the differential efficacy of research and clinic treatment studies (e.g., age and rigor of studies, severity of clinical problems, training of therapists). However, they did find greater efficacy among studies that draw upon structured (vs. unstructured) interventions and the use of treatment manuals or clinical guidelines. These are some of the few variables that may enhance the impact of child psychotherapy. Of course, there are other potential differences between research-treatment and clinic-based treatment that might account for the greater efficacy of research-treatment. Weisz, Weiss, Han, Granger, and Morton (1995) conducted a meta-analysis of 150 outcome research studies that evaluated the differential impact of various treatment parameters. Behavioral interventions were found to be more effective than non-behavioral treatments and their effects were not found to be any less durable. Further, the effects of treatment were generally greater for adolescents than children, and for females than males, even when controlling for problem type. Paraprofessionals were found to have greater overall effects than professionals or students. Recruited cases were found to show greater improvement than clinic cases, and individual treatment was more effective overall than group treatment. In contrast, there was no difference between the types of problems that were treated (overcontrolled vs. undercontrolled). These findings provide some indication of those aspects of treatment that may be more or less likely to be associated with positive effects. Other analyses revealed that the effects of treatment were greater when there was a match between the target problem and the outcome measure that was used, highlighting the need to try to focus specifically on changing problems that were directly being targeted by the treatment. Treatment effects generally reflected the specific and intended outcomes of treatment, rather than generalized positive effects.

These general findings highlight the need to invest additional research resources in understanding the impact of treatment in traditional clinical practice where cases are complex, treatment techniques are variable, and therapists are highly diverse in level of training, sophistication, and commitment. Studies of service agencies using quasi-experimental designs may facilitate hypothesis-generation and permit the identification of research questions worthy of more formal evaluation. Further, attention to some of the treatment parameters may be expected to enhance the efficacy of treatment outcome and, thus, deserve further consideration in programs serving abused children and youth.

Assessment Models

One other way to enhance the quality of research on treatment outcome and impact is to expand the scope of assessment to include multiple outcomes in several important domains. Hoagwood, Jensen,

Petti, and Burns (1996) described an interactional model of outcomes of mental health care. The model posits five domains that reflect primary outcomes important for the evaluation of treatments administered in diverse settings. The first reflects the severity of symptoms and diagnoses (e.g., fewer PTSD symptoms, less serious depressive or aggressive behavior). The second domain reflects the child's functional status or level of impairment, an area that is not often evaluated in the abuse field (e.g., role efficacy, enhanced social and problem-solving skill). The next domain is concerned with the child or family functioning in its environmental context, such as home, school, and other community settings (e.g., appropriate parenting practices and family support; involvement with deviant peers; school behavior problems). The client's level of consumer satisfaction describes a fourth domain in which information is obtained about the adequacy of treatment (e.g., acceptability, usefulness). The final domain solicits information about service use (e.g., participation rates, use of inpatient services).

Few studies actually evaluate outcomes in all five domains (Jensen, Hoagwood, & Petti, 1996). In fact, only two of 38 studies that met minimal scientific criteria were found by Jensen et al. (1996) to evaluate them. Most studies evaluate symptoms/diagnoses, and a majority of studies evaluate environmental context and functional status. However, few studies evaluate consumer perspectives and even fewer have examined service system use and change. In terms of the outpatient services or settings in which treatments have been applied, studies of family preservation have often evaluated all of these domains but not the perspectives of consumers. A similar situation exists with respect to therapeutic foster care programs. In both cases, assessments of the environment were modestly represented in outcome analyses.

One can appreciate the relevance of each domain to assessing the outcome of treatment in cases of child abuse. For example, most evaluations of outcome include children's symptoms, such as PTSD, depression, aggression and anxiety, and parental or family functioning. However, few studies have evaluated the children's level of impairment, school and peer behavior, consumer satisfaction, and service system involvement. Given the possibility of extended system contact, multiple interventions, and a history of multiple traumas and family adversities, an outcome assessment with both depth and breadth seems warranted.

Context and Ecology

One of the implications of the aforementioned model is the need to evaluate the effects of treatment across settings and in multiple contexts. This is due, in part, because real world settings are where we hope to realize the effects of treatment and because more and more services are being administered in the child's ecology. Indeed, one of the major therapeutic developments in the past decade is the expansion of clinical services in various community settings, such as the child's home, school, and neighborhood, especially in the area of children's conduct problems (CP). An important reason for this development is the fact that contextual problems do contribute to the prediction of child CP, conduct disorder, and delinquency (Loeber, Farrington, Stouthamer-Loeber, & Van Kammen, in press; Loeber, Green, Keenan, & Lahey, 1995; Tolan & McKay, 1996). Indeed, CP has been associated with parent, family, and contextual variables such as living conditions, school setting, and neighborhood (Loeber & Hay, 1997; Patterson, Reid, & Dishion, 1992; Thornberry, 1996). The diverse "context" that supports children's CP has been targeted (Kazdin, 1996; Tolan, Guerra, & Kendall, 1995; Walker et al., 1996) with favorable outcomes in studies that have conducted sessions in the natural environment (see Burns, Farmer, Angold, Costello, & Behar, 1996; Coie, Underwood, & Lochman, 1991; Conduct Problems Prevention Research Group, 1992; Cunningham, Bremner, & Boyle, 1995; Henggeler, Schoenwald, & Pickrel, 1995; Kolko, 1996c). Studies of Multisystemic Therapy (MST) with juvenile offenders have documented improvements in youth behavior and family-system supports using an approach directed towards child, parent, family, and social system factors associated with CP (see Borduin et al., 1995; Henggeler, Melton, & Smith, 1992; Henggeler et al., 1995). All told, there may be several potential benefits to targeting ecological factors in the community, such as the following:

1. Enhance family involvement and the use of community resources (Lourie, Katz-Leavy, & Jacobs, 1986; Stroul & Friedman, 1986).
2. Serve more effectively the needs of multi-problem youth with serious behavioral problems whose long-term dysfunction places them at-high risk for placement and costly multi-system involvement (Epstein, Cullinan, Quinn, & Cumblad, 1995; Greenbaum et al., 1996).

3. Minimize obstacles and enhance cooperation.
4. Maximize the cost-effectiveness of services (e.g., Cunningham, Bremner, & Secord-Gilbert, 1993; Henggeler et al., 1995).

Of course, few studies of the effectiveness of community treatments have been conducted with psychiatrically disturbed or abused children and their families (Jensen, Hoagwood, & Petti, 1996). In the abuse field, a few noteworthy studies of family-based interventions have been conducted in the home and directed towards various systems affecting children (see Brunk, Henggeler, & Whelan, 1987; Lutzker, 1990; Nicol, Smith, Kay, Hall, Barlow, & Williams, 1988; Whittaker, Kinney, Tracy, & Booth, 1990). These interventions have reported improvements in child and parent behavior, although studies have been based on small samples, have been limited in scope, or suffered from other methodological problems. Accordingly, questions as to the utility, disadvantages, and potential costs of these innovative approaches to service delivery in this area remain unanswered. Further, potential drawbacks to community services exist, such as threats to staff safety and welfare, the difficulty of integrating diverse services across settings, and increased costs. Certainly, studies are needed to determine whether the positive findings reported in research settings can be "replicated in the clinic and community settings where most real-life interventions actually occur" (Weisz et al., 1992, p. 1584).

WHAT DO WE NEED TO LEARN NEXT?

The studies reviewed herein highlight some of the developments that have been achieved in addressing the diverse consequences of an abusive experience and in documenting the impact of intervention based on experimentally rigorous methodologies. Further, information based on studies reported from the general child psychotherapy literature provides some insights regarding the types of characteristics believed to be associated with clinical improvement. Based on this collective work, several areas of further program development and evaluation seem warranted. An important question raised earlier concerns who should be treated and, if so, using what treatment strategies. This can be addressed in studies that compare different subgroups of potential clients (e.g., substantiated vs. unsubstantiated cases, child abuse vs. child maltreatment) on measures of clinical symptoms, likelihood of recidivism, and responsiveness to treatment. The heterogeneity in abuse definitions and the types of samples available for study also bear implications for understanding the efficacy of treatment and the follow-up course of the sample. The presence of a more serious abuse history or other psychiatric comorbidities, for example, may be expected to convey a more limited response to treatment.

We also have to learn more about ways to enhance the participation and impact of those settings that influence the level of adjustment and competence of abused children, notably, the family, school, and peer context. Particular challenges to treatment efficacy include addressing school classroom and placement problems, parental dysfunction (e.g., depression, substance abuse), and family violence and disorganization. Details of new procedures designed to target these settings would be an important contribution to enhancing community-based applications.

Another difficulty for the abuse field is the absence of standardized abuse assessments. Studies of abuse often incorporate a wide variety of measures to assess abuse history and abusive behavior. Although no single standard exists to evaluate other children's clinical problems, a few instruments have been evaluated psychometrically and included in several outcome studies. It would be helpful to further refine both case record and interview measures proposed to be useful in documenting children's abuse histories. Examples of these two types of instruments include the Maltreatment Classification System (Barnett, Manly, & Cicchetti 1993) and the Abuse Dimensions Inventory, respectively (Chaffin, Wherry, Newlin, Crutchfield, & Dykman, 1997).

There is also a need to accumulate additional evidence regarding the efficacy of new treatments and the effectiveness of existing ones already found to be effective. Many of the interventions reported in the abuse field have some modest level of efficacy, but are in need of replication. Further investigation of existing treatments could include comparison with a minimal-care condition or an alternative treatment. Ultimately, replication may be the most rigorous form of experimental validation. Additionally, investigators must include measures that capture the magnitude or clinical significance of change following experimental interventions (see Jacobson, 1988). In many instances, interventions may achieve statistical significance but with questionable clinical significance. Better documentation of the impact of treatment on primary measures of child and parent functioning is a high priority for this field.

As intervention programs gain empirical support, tests of the impact of specific procedures become an important next step. Most interventions in the abuse field consist of multiple therapeutic techniques, many of which have not been evaluated independently. By examining the constituents of such packages in next generation studies, we may be able to determine the active ingredients in these programs. Potential ingredients worth evaluating include discussion of the victim's attributions about the experience and its impact, exposure and discussion of the experience, teaching psychological and coping skills, and working with parents and families to provide support, among other procedures. Just what the effective parameters of treatment are in the child abuse field has received limited empirical attention. It may be the case that specific procedures work best under particular conditions, suggesting the need to evaluate treatment moderators and mediators. Recent work by Cohen and Mannarino (1998) indicates that certain variables may influence treatment outcome in conducting CBT with young abused children. Finally, more attention ought to be paid to the ways in which treatments and interventions are applied in existing clinical practice or service delivery systems. The aforementioned evidence suggests that the efficacy of laboratory-based, research treatments exceeds that found in routine clinic practice. Further, most of the existing studies in the abuse field have been conducted in specialized research treatment settings. Therefore, treatment applications are needed in clinic settings in order to understand their limitations and any need for modifications. The ultimate test of an intervention utility reflects its successful application under the real world or naturalistic conditions of existing clinical practice.

CONCLUSION

This review has examined the outcome literature in the areas of child sexual and physical abuse. There is a clear progression from small, single-case studies with limitations in methodology and clinical scope to large studies with adequate group designs, clear conceptual models, and multivariate analytic approaches. Interestingly, the outcomes of both early and recent studies generally support the efficacy of specific interventions for sexually abused children and physically abusive parents or families. Improvements have been documented in various symptom areas following treatment and, in some cases, at follow-up. More recently, studies have documented such improvements among physically abused children and non-offending caregivers of sexually abused children.

For all of these positive outcomes, however, limitations in the empirical underpinnings of these studies highlight the need for developments in treatment conceptualization, analytic technique, and study design, among other areas, in order to better document the overall impact of treatment and the generality of their improvements. Furthermore, studies are needed that replicate and extend recent outcomes in order to support the robustness of these outcomes and to contribute to revisions in treatment procedures as a means to enhance their applicability to different problems. Only through continued advances in technique and methodology will the benefits of treatment for abused children and their families be maximized.

REFERENCE LIST

Barnett, D., Manly, J. T., & Cicchetti, D. (1993). Defining child maltreatment: The interface between policy and research. In D. Cicchetti, & S. L. Toth (Eds), *Child abuse, child development, and social policy* (pp. 7-74). Norwood, NJ: Ablex.

Belsky, J. (1993). Etiology of child maltreatment: A developmental-ecological analysis. *Psychological Bulletin, 114*, 413-434.

Bentovim, A., Van Elberg, A., & Boston, P. (1988). The results of treatment. In A. Bentovim, A. Elton, J. Hildebrand, M. Tranter, & E. Vizard (Eds.), *Child sexual abuse within the family: Assessment and treatment* (pp. 252-268). London: Wright.

Berliner, L., & Saunders, B. (1996). Treating fear and anxiety in sexually abused children: Results of a controlled 2-year follow-up study. *Child Maltreatment, 1*, 294-309.

Beutler, L. E., Williams, R. E., & Zetzer, H. A. (1994). Efficacy of treatment for victims of child sexual abuse. *Sexual Abuse of Children, 4*, 156-175.

Borduin, C. M., Mann, B. J., Cone, L. T., Henggeler, S. W., Fucci, B. R., Balske, D. M., & Williams, R. A. (1995). Multisystemic treatment of serious juvenile offenders: Long-term prevention of criminality and violence. *Journal of Consulting and Clinical Psychology, 63*, 569-578.

Brunk, M., Henggeler, S. W., & Whelan, J. P. (1987). Comparison of multisystemic therapy and parent training in the brief treatment of child abuse and neglect. *Journal of Consulting and Clinical Psychology, 55*, 171-178.

Burns, B. J., Farmer, E. M., Angold, A., Costello, E. J., & Behar, L. (1996). A randomized trial of case management for youths with serious emotional disturbance. *Journal of Clinical Child Psychology, 25*, 476-486.

Celano, M., Hazzard, A., Webb, C., & McCall, C. (1996). Treatment of traumagenic beliefs among sexually abused girls and their mothers: An evaluation study. *Journal of Abnormal Child Psychology, 24*, 1-17.

Chaffin, M., Wherry, J. N., Newlin, C., Crutchfield, A., & Dykman, R. (1997). The abuse dimensions inventory: Initial data on a research measure of abuse severity. *Journal of Interpersonal Violence, 12* (4), 569-589.

Cohen, J. A., & Mannarino, A. P. (1993). A treatment model for sexually abused preschoolers. *Journal of Interpersonal Violence, 8*, 115-131.

Cohen, J. A., & Mannarino, A. P. (1996). A treatment outcome study for sexually abused preschool children. Initial findings. *Journal of the American Academy of Child and Adolescent Psychiatry, 35*, 42-50.

Cohen, J. A., & Mannarino, A. P. (1997). A treatment study for sexually abused preschool children: Outcome during a one-year follow-up. *Journal of the American Academy of Child and Adolescent Psychiatry, 36*, 1228-1235.

Cohen, J. A., & Mannarino, A. P. (1998). Factors that mediate treatment outcome of sexually abused preschool children: Six- and 12-month follow-up. *Journal of the American Academy of Child & Adolescent Psychiatry, 37(1)*, 44-51.

Coie, J. D., Underwood, M., & Lochman, J. E. (1991). Programmatic intervention with aggressive children in the school setting. In D. J. Pepler & K. H. Rubin (Eds.), *The development and treatment of childhood aggression* (pp. 389-407). Hillsdale, NJ: Lawrence Erlbaum Associates.

Conduct Problems Prevention Research Group (1992). A developmental and clinical model for the prevention of conduct disorder. *Development and Psychopathology, 4*, 509-527.

Cunningham, C. E., Bremner, R., & Boyle, M. (1995). Large group community-based parenting programs for families of preschoolers at risk for disruptive behavior disorders: Utilization, cost effectiveness, and outcome. *Journal of Child Psychology and Psychiatry, 36*, 1141-1159.

Cunningham, C. E., Bremner, R., & Secord-Gilbert, M. (1993). Increasing the availability, accessibility, and cost efficacy of services for families of ADHD children: A school-based systems-oriented parenting course. *Canadian Journal of School Psychology, 9*, 1-5.

Davis, S., & Fantuzzo, J. W. (1989). The effects of adult and peer social initiations on social behavior of withdrawn and aggressive maltreated preschool children. *Journal of Family Violence, 4*, 227-248.

Deblinger, E., Lippmann, J., & Steer, R. (1996). Sexually abused children suffering posttraumatic stress symptoms: Initial treatment outcome findings. *Child Maltreatment, 1*, 310-321.

Deblinger, E., McLeer, S. V., & Henry, D. (1990). Cognitive behavioral treatment for sexually abused children suffering post-traumatic stress: Preliminary findings. *Journal of the American Academy of Child and Adolescent Psychiatry, 29*, 747-752.

Fantuzzo, J. W., Jurecic, L., Stovall, A., Hightower, A. D., & Goins, C. (1988). Effects of adult and peer social initiations on the social behavior of withdrawn, maltreated preschool children. *Journal of Consulting and Clinical Psychology, 56*, 34-39.

Fantuzzo, J. W., Stovall, A., Schachtel, D., Goins, C., & Hall, R. (1987). The effects of peer social initiations on the social behavior of withdrawn maltreated preschool children. *Journal of Behavior Therapy and Experimental Psychiatry, 18*, 357-363.

Fantuzzo, J., Sutton-Smith, B., Atkins, M., Meyers, R., Stevenson, H., Coolahan, K., Weiss, A., & Manz, P. (1996). Community-based resilient peer treatment of withdrawn maltreated preschool children. *Journal of Consulting and Clinical Psychology, 64*, 1377-1386.

Finkelhor, D. (1995). The victimization of children: A developmental perspective. *American Journal of Orthopsychiatry, 65*, 177-193.

Finkelhor, D., & Berliner, L. (1995). Research on the treatment of sexually abused children: A review and recommendations. *Journal of the American Academy of Child and Adolescent Psychiatry, 34*, 1408-1423.

Finkelhor, D., & Browne, A. (1985). The traumatic impact of child sexual abuse: A conceptualization. *American Journal of Orthopsychiatry, 55*, 530-541.

Furniss, T., Bingley-Miller, L., & Van Elburg, A. (1988). Goal-oriented group treatment for sexually abused adolescent girls. *British Journal of Psychiatry, 152*, 97-106.

Graziano, A. M., & Mills, J. R. (1992). Treatment for abused children: When is a partial solution acceptable? *Child Abuse & Neglect, 16*, 217-228.

Haskett, M. E., Myers, L. W., Pirrello, V. E., & Dombalis, A. O. (1995). Parenting style as a mediating link between parental emotional health and adjustment of maltreated children. *Behavior Therapy, 26*, 625-642.

Henggeler, S. W., Melton, G. B., & Smith, L. A. (1992). Family preservation using multisystemic therapy: An effective alternative to incarcerating serious juvenile offenders. *Journal of Consulting and Clinical Psychology, 60*, 953-961.

Henggeler, S. W., Schoenwald, S. K., & Pickrel, S. G. (1995). Multisystemic therapy: Bridging the gap between university- and community-based treatment. *Journal of Consulting and Clinical Psychology, 63*, 709-717.

Hoagwood, K., Jensen, P. S., Petti, T., & Burns, B. J. (1996). Outcomes of mental health care for children and adolescents: I. A comprehensive conceptual model. *Journal of the American Academy of Child and Adolescent Psychiatry, 35*, 1055-1063.

Hyde, C., Bentovim, A., & Monck, E. (1995). Some clinical and methodological implications of a treatment outcome study of sexually abused children. *Child Abuse & Neglect, 19*, 1387-1399.

Jacobson, N. S. (1988). Defining clinically significant change. *Behavioral Assessment, 10*, 133-145.

Jensen, P. S., Hoagwood, K., & Petti, T. (1996). Outcomes of mental health care for children and adolescents: II. Literature review and application of a comprehensive model. *Journal of the American Academy of Child and Adolescent Psychiatry, 35*, 1064-1077.

Kazdin, A. E. (1996). Combined and multimodel treatments in child and adolescent psychotherapy: Issues, challenges, and research directions. *Clinical Psychology–Science & Practice, 3*, 69-100.

Knutson, J. F. (1995). Psychological characteristics of maltreated children: Punitive risk factors and consequences. *Annual Review Psychology, 46*, 401-431.

Kolko, D. J. (1996a). Child physical abuse. In J. Briere, L. Berliner, J. A. Bulkley, C.

Jenny, & T. Teid (Eds.), *APSAC Handbook of child maltreatment* (pp. 21-50). Thousand Oaks, CA: Sage.

Kolko, D. J. (1996b). Clinical monitoring of treatment course in child physical abuse: Child and parent reports. *Child Abuse & Neglect, 20,* 23-43.

Kolko, D. J. (1996c). Individual cognitive-behavioral treatment and family therapy for physically abused children and their offending parents: A comparison of clinical outcomes. *Child Maltreatment, 1,* 322-342.

Kolko, D. J., Selelyo, J., & Brown, E. J. (1999). The treatment histories and service involvement of physically and sexually abusive families: Description, correspondence, and correlates. *Child Abuse & Neglect, 23,* 459-476.

Letourneau, E. J., Saunders, B. E., & Kilpatrick, D. G. (1996). In B. E. Saunders (Chair), *Adolescents and abuse: Results from a national survey study.* Paper presented at the Annual Meeting of the San Diego Conference on Responding to Child Maltreatment, San Diego, CA.

Loeber, R., Farrington, D. P., Stouthamer-Loeber, M., & Van Kammen, W. (in press). Antisocial behavior and mental health problems: Explanatory factors in childhood and adolescence. *First volume of the Pittsburgh Youth Study.* Mahwah, NJ: Lawrence Erlbaum.

Loeber, R., Green, S. M., Keenan, K., & Lahey, B. B. (1995). Which boys will fare worse? Early predictors of the onset of conduct disorder in a six-year longitudinal study. *Journal of the American Academy of Child & Adolescent Psychiatry, 34,* 499-509.

Loeber, R., & Hay, D. (1997). Key issues in the development of aggression and violence from childhood to early adulthood. *Annual Reviews in Psychology, 48,* 371-410.

McGain, B., & McKinzey, R. K. (1995). The efficacy of group treatment in sexually abused girls. *Child Abuse & Neglect, 19,* 1157-1169.

Malinosky-Rummell, R., & Hansen, D. J. (1993). Long-term consequences of child physical abuse. *Psychological Bulletin, 114,* 68-79.

Mannarino, A. P., & Cohen, J. A. (1990). Treating the abused child. In R. T. Ammerman, & M. Hersen (Eds.), *Children at risk: An evaluation of factors contributing to child abuse and neglect* (pp. 249-266). New York: Plenum.

Monck, E., Sharland, E., Bentovim, A., Goodall, G., Hyde, C., & Lewin, B. (1994). *Child sexual abuse: A descriptive and treatment outcome study.* London: HMSO.

National Academy of Sciences (1993). *Understanding child abuse and neglect.* Washington, DC: National Academy Press.

Nicol, A. R., Smith, J., Kay, B., Hall, D., Barlow, J., & Williams, B. (1988). A focused casework approach to the treatment of child abuse: A controlled comparison. *Journal of Child Psychology and Psychiatry, 29,* 703-711.

Oates, R. K., & Bross, D. C. (1995). What have we learned about treating child physical abuse? A literature review of the last decade. *Child Abuse & Neglect, 19,* 463-473.

Patterson, G. R., Reid, J. B., & Dishion, T. J. (1992). *Antisocial boys.* Eugene, OR: Castalia.

Putnam, F. W., & Trickett, P. K. (1995). *The developmental consequences of child sexual abuse*. Paper presented at the Conference on Violence Against Children in the Family and the Community, University of Southern California, Los Angeles.

Rust, J. O., & Troupe, P. A. (1991). Relationships of treatment of child sexual abuse with school achievement and self-concept. *Journal of Early Adolescence, 11,* 420-429.

Smith, J. (1984). Non-accidental injury to children. *Behavior Research & Therapy, 22,* 331-347.

Swenson, C. C., Saunders, B. E., & Kilpatrick, D. G. (1996). Physical assault of adolescents: Prevalence, case characteristics, and mental health consequences. In B. E. Saunders (Chair), *Adolescents and abuse: Results from a national survey study*. Paper presented at the Annual Meeting of the San Diego Conference on Responding to Child Maltreatment.

Thornberry, T. P. (1996). Empirical support for interactional theory: A review of the literature. J. D. Hawkins (Ed.), *Delinquency and crime: Current theories* (pp. 198-235). New York: Cambridge University Press.

Tingus, K. D., Heger, A. H., Foy, D. W., & Leskin, G. A. (1996). Factors associated with entry into therapy in children evaluated for sexual abuse. *Child Abuse & Neglect, 20,* 63-68.

Tolan, P. H., Guerra, N. G., & Kendall, P. (1995). A developmental-ecological perspective on antisocial behavior in children and adolescents: Toward a unified risk and intervention framework. *Journal of Consulting and Clinical Psychology, 63,* 579-584.

Tolan, P. H., & McKay, M. M. (1996). Preventing serious antisocial behavior in inner-city children: An empirically based family intervention program. *Family Relations, 45,* 148-155.

Urquiza, A. J., & Bodiford-McNeil, C. (1996). Parent-child interaction therapy: An intensive dyadic intervention for physically abusive families. *Child Maltreatment, 1,* 134-144.

Verleur, D., Hughes, R. E., & Dobkin De Rios, M. D. (1986). Enhancement of self-esteem among female adolescent incest victims: A controlled comparison. *Adolescence, 21,* 843-854.

Walker, H. M., Horner, R. H., Sugai, G., Bullis, M., Sprague, J. R., Bricker, D., & Kaufman, M. J. (1996). Integrated approaches to preventing antisocial behavior patterns among school-age children and youth. *Journal of Emotional and Behavioral Disorders, 4,* 194-209.

Weisz, J. R., Donenberg, G. R., Han, S. S., & Kauneckis, D. (1995). Child and adolescent psychotherapy outcomes in experiments and in clinics: Why the disparity? *Journal of Abnormal Child Psychology, 23,* 83-106.

Weisz, J. R., Weiss, B., & Donenberg, G. R. (1992). The lab versus the clinic: Effects of child and adolescent psychotherapy. *American Psychologist,* 1578-1585.

Weisz, J. R., Weiss, B., Han, S. S., Granger, D. A., & Morton, T. (1995). Effects of psychotherapy with children and adolescents revised: A meta-analysis of treatment outcome studies. *Psychological Bulletin, 117,* 450-468.

Whiteman, M., Fanshel, D., & Grundy, J. F. (1987). Cognitive-behavioral interventions aimed at anger of parents at risk of child abuse. *Social Work,* 469-474.

Whittaker, J., Kinney, J., Tracy, E. M., & Booth, C. (1990). *Reaching high-risk families: Intensive family preservation in human services.* New York: Aldine de Gruyter.

Widom, C. S., & Ames, M. S. (1994). Criminal consequences of childhood sexual victimization. *Child Abuse & Neglect, 18,* 303-318.

Widom, C. S., & Maxfield, M. (1996). A prospective examination of risk for violence among abused and neglected children. In C. F. Ferris & T. Grisso (Eds.), *Understanding aggressive behavior in children. Annals of the New York Academy of Sciences* (pp. 224-237). New York: New York Academy of Sciences.

Wolfe, D. A. (1994). The role of intervention and treatment services in the prevention of child abuse and neglect. In G. B. Melton & F. D. Barry (Eds.), *Protecting children from child abuse and neglect: Foundations for a new national strategy* (pp. 224-303). New York: Guilford Press.

Wolfe, D., Edwards, B., Manion, I., & Koverola, C. (1988). Early intervention for parents at risk for child abuse and neglect: A preliminary report. *Journal of Consulting & Clinical Psychology, 56,* 40-47.

Wolfe, D. A., & Wekerle, C. (1993). Treatment strategies for child physical abuse and neglect: A critical progress report. *Clinical Psychology Review, 13,* 473-500.

Canadian Child Welfare Outcomes Indicator Matrix: An Ecological Approach to Tracking Service Outcomes

Nico Trocmé
Bruce MacLaurin
Barbara Fallon

SUMMARY. The Client Outcomes in Child Welfare (COCW) Project was designed to examine the state of knowledge about outcomes measurement in Canada and initiate a consensus building process for a coordinated strategy in tracking outcomes across Canada. Through interviews with key informants, reviews of the literature and analysis of legislation, policy documents and information systems, the COCW Project identified some of the challenges to outcome measurement that may explain the limited progress made in this field. These include a needs driven service delivery system, competing objectives of child

---

The authors would like to thank Jacqueline Oxman-Martinez, McGill University, and Jacques Moreau, Université de Montréal, for their feedback on an earlier version of this document. Work for this project was conducted under a grant from Human Resources Development Canada (#4587-06-94/94) with additional support from Bell Canada.

Address correspondence to: Nico Trocmé, PhD, Bell Canada Child Welfare Research Unit, Faculty of Social Work, University of Toronto, 246 Bloor Street West, Toronto, Canada M5S 1A1.

[Haworth co-indexing entry note]: "Canadian Child Welfare Outcomes Indicator Matrix: An Ecological Approach to Tracking Service Outcomes." Trocmé, Nico, Bruce MacLaurin, and Barbara Fallon. Co-published simultaneously in *Journal of Aggression, Maltreatment & Trauma* (The Haworth Maltreatment & Trauma Press, an imprint of The Haworth Press, Inc.) Vol. 4, No. 1 (#7), 2000, pp. 165-190; and: *Program Evaluation and Family Violence Research* (ed: Sally K. Ward, and David Finkelhor) The Haworth Maltreatment & Trauma Press, an imprint of The Haworth Press, Inc., 2000, pp. 165-190. Single or multiple copies of this article are available for a fee from The Haworth Document Delivery Service [1-800-342-9678, 9:00 a.m. - 5:00 p.m. (EST). E-mail address: getinfo@haworthpressinc.com].

165

welfare, definitional confusion, and differences between clinical and administrative use of outcomes. The Outcomes Indicator Matrix was developed as a first stage in a strategy that focuses initially on the administrative use of outcomes information, allowing the clinical use of outcomes measures to develop in a more gradual fashion. Indicators were selected in four domains which reflect the breadth of the child welfare mandate in Canadian jurisdictions: child protection, child functioning, permanence and continuity of care for the child, and family and community support. *[Article copies available for a fee from The Haworth Document Delivery Service: 1-800-342-9678. E-mail address: <getinfo@ haworthpressinc.com> Website: <http://www.HaworthPress.com>]*

KEYWORDS. Evaluation, safety, protection, permanence, continuity, support, preservation, child functioning

INTRODUCTION

Remarkably few systematic data are available to support the various extremist positions on child care. In fact most policies and practice decisions are still based primarily on value judgements and assumptions. Until more conclusive data are available . . . it seems likely that the question of what forms of care have what effects on what types of children under what circumstances will continue to be a major issue. (Kammerman & Kahn, 1976, as quoted in Kadushin, 1978)

Limited progress has been made over the last twenty years in child welfare outcome research since Kammerman and Kahn's assessment of the state of knowledge in this area. Despite repeated calls for systematic tracking of outcomes (Magura & Moses, 1986; National Research Council, 1993; Pecora, Whittaker, Maluccio, Barth, & Plotnick, 1992), services to maltreated children and their families continue to be driven primarily by evidence of need irrespective of evidence of service effectiveness. Our article presents findings from a Canadian child welfare outcome development project–the Client Outcomes in Child Welfare (COCW) Project, designed to develop an outcome measurement strategy that could help shift the child welfare system to an outcomes-based approach in developing policy and practice. Following an overview of the COCW Project, we analyze some of the dynamics that have limited the development of outcome measurement in child welfare. These include the needs driven emphasis of child welfare practice, the tensions inherent in the competing mandates of the child welfare system, and the definitional challenges inherent in measuring outcomes in this field. We then outline a multi-dimensional framework, which reflects the complexity of child welfare practice, and present an incremental outcome measurement strategy designed to address some of the obstacles that have impeded previous outcome initiatives.

BACKGROUND

The COCW Project was initiated by the Canadian provincial and territorial directors of child welfare in conjunction with the Canadian Federal Government to support the development of a coordinated approach to assess the effectiveness of child welfare services and policies across Canada. The Project developed in a context of growing public concern about the safety and well-being of children, increasing government requirements for service accountability, and increasing challenges for agencies to develop better targeted and more effective services (Federal Provincial Working Group on Child and Family Services Information, 1994; Gove, 1995).

The COCW Project was designed to meet two primary objectives:

1. to review the existing state of knowledge about outcomes measurement for child welfare in Canada and internationally; and
2. to initiate a consensus-building process among key stakeholders for a coordinated strategy in tracking child welfare outcome information across Canada.

The COCW Project used an iterative process for both information gathering and consensus-building amongst child welfare practitioners and policy makers. In addition to traditional literature and instrument surveys, we examined child welfare statutes, policy documents, and service information systems in each Province and Territory. Key informant interviews, regular consultation with a national advisory committee and the distribution of a newsletter for regular Project updates ensured a dynamic process. An inventory of child welfare outcome initiatives from across Canada was developed. The focal point for the Project was an examination of promising instruments and existing data collection systems, in order to understand the processes and issues arising from the development of outcome initiatives.

Following the first set of consultations, *The First Canadian Roundtable on Child Welfare Outcomes* was convened to present the initial Project findings. The Roundtable brought together key stakeholders, including policy makers, information specialists, senior service providers and researchers to review our initial findings. The Roundtable participants endorsed the outcome development strategy presented at the end of this article in principle, and the matrix of ten key indicators was adopted as a starting point.

As soon as the work for the COCW Project was initiated it became abundantly clear that the lack of progress made in this domain was not due to an absence of interest in moving to outcome-based service delivery. Kammerman and Kahn's call for systematic data collection was echoed in the literature reviewed (Ayoub, Willet, & Robinson, 1992; Magura & Moses, 1986; Pecora, Seelig, Zirps, & Davis, 1996; Ward, 1995), in the key informant interviews, and in many of the government reports we consulted. Close to forty different child welfare outcome measurement projects employing an array of instruments and innovative approaches to tracking client outcomes were identified across Canada (MacLaurin, 1998). In England and Canada the development of the Looking After Children initiative has demonstrated that a comprehensive outcomes focused casework approach can be used to improve planning and decision-making for children in out-of-home care (Kufeldt, Simard, & Vachon, 1994; Ward, 1995). In the United States, in addition to a number of agency and state level initiatives, the American Humane Association and the National Association of Public Child Welfare Administrators had convened six National Roundtables on outcomes in child welfare, and the Federal government had initiated a number of projects including the State Automated Child Welfare Information Systems (Courtney & Collins, 1994).

In contrast to the abundance of outcome initiatives, we found few examples of initiatives that had developed to the point of providing information that had influence on policy and practice decisions. One of the exceptions to this situation has been the rapid development of family preservation research, which moved in less than a decade from simple pre-post studies to multi-site experimental designs (Bath & Haapala, 1994; Blythe, Patterson-Salley, & Jayaratne, 1994; Maluccio & Whittaker, 1997). The mixed results from these studies have been considered by Canadian child welfare policy makers and service providers who have generally taken a cautious approach to developing family preservation programs. Our interviews with policy makers and senior managers and our review of information systems and policy documents, found that outcome data were not being used as a basis for decision-making. Most child welfare information systems in Canada do not have the capacity to report potential outcome information beyond number of investigations and number of children in care.

Given the relatively slow progress in the development of outcome measurement in child welfare, we initially focused our analysis on identifying some of the reasons for this limited progress, and then designed strategies to overcome these. In this article we examine two critical sets of issues that arose from our analyses: the multiple dimensions of child welfare practice and the need for an incremental multi-level approach to address outcome measurement. Strategies for addressing these issues are proposed.

CAPTURING THE MULTIPLE DIMENSIONS
OF CHILD WELFARE PRACTICE

The first challenge in developing any outcomes measurement system is to identify the key objectives from which measurable indicators can be selected. The COCW interviews and document reviews found that there was limited consensus about the objectives of child welfare. This confusion stems in part from a history of providing services on the basis of need with limited consideration of service objectives. Attempts to articulate objectives have also been hindered by the fact that child maltreatment is a multi-dimensional problem requiring intervention at different levels of children's environment.

Needs Driven Services

The urgency of the need to help maltreated children has overshadowed the question of whether interventions are effective. Child welfare policy, legislation and services have focused primarily on detecting and reporting maltreatment and removing children from dangerous situations. Less attention has been paid to long-term outcomes and the effectiveness of interventions (Lindsey, 1994; Parton, 1985; Pecora et al., 1992). Traditionally, funders have not required accountability based on outcomes, but have focused on trying to respond to increasing caseloads. For example, the rapid expansion of family preservation programs in the United States was initially driven by the increase in the number of children entering foster care. Success was primarily measured in terms of placement prevention rather than evidence that children were benefiting from the programs (Littell & Schuerman, 1995; Pelton, 1997).

While funders are now starting to request evidence of program effectiveness, funds for evaluation research are often expected to come out of already stretched program budgets, at the expense of direct services. Evaluation research appears to be an unaffordable luxury for an overburdened child welfare system where responding to need is the driving concern.

The development of an outcome-based approach has been further complicated by the fact that service providers are keenly aware that funding will be determined by the types of outcome that are measured. Service providers, from front-line staff to senior managers, worry that the measures that are selected will not document the impact of the services they provide. The principle of "what gets measured gets done" can be interpreted to mean "what gets measured gets funded" (Grasso & Epstein, 1988; Traglia, Massinga, Pecora, & Paddock, 1996). As a result, the introduction of outcome measures has led some service providers to fear a loss of clinical independence. Government funders, on the other hand, are concerned that the information collected by an outcome tracking system will simply put them under pressure to provide more resources. The process of choosing outcome measures can therefore bring out previously unresolved debates about critical service priorities.

Balancing Competing Objectives

The key informant interviews and reviews of legislation and policy found that there was no consensus about the objectives of child welfare services, and several apparent contradictions. Some informants spoke of the tension between family preservation and child protection. Others focused on the difference between child well-being and child protection. These tensions can be summarized in terms of three overlapping but potentially competing objectives: protecting children from maltreatment; enhancing child well-being; and providing services, when possible, that preserve the child's family and community (see Figure 1).

FIGURE 1. The Balancing Objectives of Child Welfare

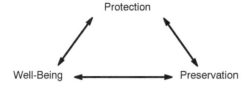

Protection vs. Preservation. The tension between providing protection and supporting children within their family and community is the fundamental challenge of child welfare. While protection is the paramount principle, the child's family and community are the preferred milieu for intervention. Child welfare statutes attempt to balance the intrusive powers accorded to child protection workers by requiring them to provide where possible home-based services. Maintaining the appropriate balance between these two principles is complicated by the fact that it can be difficult to determine when the risk of harm is too great to leave a child at home (Browne, Davies, & Stratton, 1988; Lyons, Doueck, & Wodarski, 1996).

The challenge of balancing protection and family support arose in all our interviews and was a dominant theme in the policy and legislative review. For instance, New Brunswick's legislation requires that children be removed only when "all other measures are inappropriate." Over half of the key informants suggested that family preservation or family functioning were key objectives for child welfare, and many people stressed the importance of maintaining a balance between preserving the family and protecting the child. The emphasis put on providing services in the home has recently come under criticism in a number of jurisdictions as a result of deaths of children known to the child welfare system (Gelles, 1996; Gove, 1995; Ontario Ministry of the Solicitor General, 1997). Changes to child welfare statutes in a number of jurisdictions have been made or are being considered in order to clearly emphasize the primacy of protection over family preservation (Panel of Experts on Child Protection, 1998). In British Columbia, for example, the legislation now states that if there is any conflict between any of the stated principles, "the child's safety and protection will take priority" (Province of British Columbia, 1996, p. 6). In the United States the Adoption and Safe Families Act of 1997 further clarifies the primacy of protection by allowing child protection services to waive the "reasonable efforts" require-ment in the most serious cases of maltreatment (Welte, 1997).

In most provinces, child welfare statutes also stress the importance of community preservation. Ontario's Child and Family Services Act states that services should be "provided in a manner that respects cultural, religious and regional differences" (Sect. 1 e), and sets specific provisions for considering community factors in placing children in out-of-home care, especially for children from native communities. While there appears to be less discussion in the literature about the potential tension between child protection and community preservation, there are circumstances where the child's community may also pose risks to the child. For example, the rapid development of kinship care in some American jurisdictions has raised questions about over-reliance on extended families that may not have the resources to adequately protect some children (Dubowitz, Feigelman, & Zuravin, 1993).

Protection vs. Well-Being. To a lesser extent, the principle of child protection can also be at odds with the principle of enhancing child well-being. This may seem paradoxical. One would assume that a child's well-being requires first and foremost that a child is protected from harm. Indeed, the terms are used interchangeably in some pro-vincial legislation. In Ontario, for example, the "paramount objec-tive" of the Child and Family Services Act is to "promote the best interests, protection and well-being of children" (Sect. 1 a). However, some child welfare critics argue that child welfare policy and legisla-tion have focused far too much on protection and not enough on the broader concepts of child well-being (Lindsey, 1994; Pelton, 1989; Wharf, 1993). Putting too great an emphasis on protection may ex-clude broader family support and community development activities. Some reformers argue that the mandate to protect children has di-verted child welfare from its original purpose, and that child welfare agencies should leave protection to the police and re-focus on child welfare (Lindsey & Regehr, 1993; Wharf, 1993). Others, however, see the tension between protection and well-being as an unavoidable char-acteristic of child welfare (Hutchinson, 1987; Maidman, 1984; McDo-nald, 1994; Savoury & Kufeldt, 1997).

Research on children in foster care shows that the protection offered by removing children from their homes does not necessarily ensure that these children will do better than children who remain at home. Much of the push towards family preservation originated from studies showing that children in care were not doing as well as expected (Fanshel & Shinn, 1978; Klee & Halfon, 1987). Although foster care does not seem to put children at additional risk of doing poorly, it has not yet been proven to improve children's lives (Pecora et al., 1992; Wald, Carlsmith, & Leiderman, 1988). The success of foster care and residential placements must be evaluated in terms of more than just protection.

Well-Being vs. Preservation. A third source of tension arises from trying to achieve a balance between the principle of child well-being while preserving children in their families and communities. While providing services to children in their homes and in their communities is often the best way of enhancing their well-being, some critics argue that family preservation is not always in the child's best interests (Gelles, 1996; Gove, 1995; Lindsey, 1994). Programs designed to keep children at home are criticized when they delay the removal of children from dangerous home environments that show little likelihood of improvement. Taken to extremes, family preservation has been interpreted to mean that an array of home-based interventions must be attempted before a child can be removed. For children who end up being permanently removed, especially young children who could easily be adopted, a more decisive approach may be required (Steinhauer, 1991). The "dual planning" model encouraged in the United States under the Adoption and Safe Families Act of 1997 allows child protection services to commence adoption planning while making continued reunification efforts (Welte, 1997).

The tension between child well-being and community preservation was at the forefront of a recent custody case in British Columbia. Two aboriginal children who had been adopted by non-aboriginal parents contested a decision to have their youngest sibling placed in a native home, rather than in their own home (British Columbia Family Review Board, 1998). The tension between ethno-cultural matching and achieving permanency has become a critical issue in the United States where a growing number of young African American children are in limbo waiting for adoptive placements (Berrick, Needell, Barth, & Jonson-Reid, 1998; Brooks, Barth, Bussiere, & Patterson, 1999).

A Multi-Level Ecological Outcomes Framework

There is no simple way to harmonize these conflicting objectives. Service providers must constantly seek to balance a child's immediate need for protection, a child's long-term need for a nurturing and stable home, the family's potential for growth and the community's capacity to meet a child's needs. Likewise, an effective outcome measurement system must find a balanced way of tracking outcomes associated with each principle. The importance of keeping outcome measurement focused on these complex and at time conflictual sets of objectives reflects the ecological dimensions of child maltreatment. Child maltreatment can only be understood as a complex problem resulting from the interplay of factors at the level of the child, parents, the family's immediate community, and the sociocultural context of parenting (Belsky, 1993; Garbarino & Eckenrode, 1997). While the child welfare system alone cannot be expected to affect all levels of the problem, a narrow focus on the parent-child dimension would fail to account for the important advocacy roles that Canadian child welfare services play.

The greatest challenge in developing an outcomes framework in child welfare is finding a framework that integrates and balances the principles of child protection, child well-being, and child and family support. The selection of specific objectives and related outcome indicators is not a neutral technical exercise but reflects fundamental views about the objectives of child welfare (Fallon & Trocmé, 1998). The rapid expansion of placement prevention programs, for example, was strongly influenced by a focus on placement rates (Pelton, 1997). The current emphasis on risk assessment has been criticized by those who feel that it pushes child welfare agencies away from their traditional child and family support roles towards a system focused primarily on investigation and removal (Pelton, 1989; Wharf, 1993). A unidimensional outcome measurement system that fails to recognize the complex nature of child welfare runs the risk of supporting simplistic cure-all initiatives that fail to meet the diverse needs of maltreated children (Gibbons, 1997; Parker, Ward, Jackson, Aldgate, & Wedge, 1991).

The framework developed by the American Humane Association Outcomes Roundtables provides a good example of a multi-dimensional approach to defining the scope of child welfare. The framework uses four overlapping outcome domains (child safety, child functioning, family functioning, and family preservation) viewed in terms of three levels of intervention (child, family and community).[1] The COCW Project developed a modified Canadian framework that reflects some of the issues that were identified by the Project (see Table 1). We have replaced the domain of family preservation with the more child-focused domain of permanence, shifting the emphasis from the family to the child. We maintained the distinction between safety and child functioning, because it reflects the tension between the principles of protection and well-being. We have added a preservation domain to reflect the importance of maintaining a child's family and community supports. As suggested by the National Advisory Committee for the Project, the framework is mapped onto points of intervention rather than level of intervention.

The rankings in Table 1 (critical, central and secondary) reflect the shifting emphasis on different objectives at different points of intervention. Protection from maltreatment is the critical concern for children served in their homes (investigations and home-based interventions). Investigations focus primarily on protection. The decision to provide ongoing services is based primarily on the assessment of risk of future maltreatment. Child and family functioning play a secondary role at the investigation stage, since family support services are not generally provided at this initial point.[2]

The focus of home-based services includes child well-being, preservation of family and community, child protection. Preservation of family and community draws attention to the fact that interventions at this level are not only directed at parents but also targets the family's environment.[3] Child welfare workers may assist families to secure better and more stable housing. Social support groups are run to help parents develop more effective social support networks in their communities. Increasing attention has also been drawn to the importance of involving natural helping networks, such as relatives or members of a faith community. Most Canadian child welfare statutes require that the community be involved in cases involving aboriginal children.

TABLE 1. Outcome Domains by Point of Intervention

	Investigation	Home-Based Interventions	Out-of-Home Interventions
Protection	Critical	Critical	Central
Well-Being	Central	Critical	Critical
Permanence	Secondary	Central	Critical
Preservation	Central	Critical	Secondary

In out-of-home interventions, the child welfare system takes on a direct parenting responsibility, which requires greater consideration of child well-being as well as a permanent plan to ensure that children are not left in limbo. Although protection continues to be a consideration for children in long-term care, child welfare agencies also have the considerable responsibility of providing children with a stable and nurturing environment where they can be supported to reach their full potential.

In practice, there is considerable overlap between the three main points of intervention described in Table 1. Children in care who will be returning home receive both out-of home services and home-based services. Permanency planning becomes the focus of service the longer a child is in care, but it also plays a role at all points. Even during the initial investigation, it is important to identify potentially chronic situations where decisive early intervention could preclude a protracted series of multiple case-openings and admissions.

All forms of intervention should take into account the child's immediate need for protection, the child's long-term needs for a nurturing and stable home, the family's potential for growth and the communities' capacity to support the child and her family. The multi-dimensional framework developed by the COCW Project underscores the importance of these domains, while recognizing that when families break down, the balance between these objectives can be difficult to achieve.

AN INCREMENTAL MULTI-LEVEL STRATEGY FOR OUTCOMES MEASUREMENT

The second challenge for the Project, was the lack of progress in developing outcomes measurement which cannot be simply attributed to the difficulties inherent in harmonizing competing objectives. The need for multi-dimensional frameworks has been well recognized for a number of years (Dallaire, Chamberland, Cameron, & Hebert, 1995; Fuchs, 1995; Kufeldt, 1999; Maidman, 1984). Problems around the definition of critical terms as well as confusion about the uses and purpose of outcome measurement have made it difficult for practitioners, administrators and researchers to reach consensus on a common framework.

Amorphous Definitions

The tensions inherent in trying to balance the three objectives outlined in the previous section are well known to front-line workers, judges and other decision-makers who need to find the best possible solutions for children and families in difficult circumstances. Outcome evaluation projects are also faced with similar dilemmas when they try to identify the key outcomes that need to be tracked. Many evaluation projects have avoided controversy by making use of vague definitions and confusing taxonomies.

Indeed, most reviewers conclude that the development of child welfare research and evaluation has been seriously hampered by confusion over definitions (Hutchinson, 1994; Starr, Dubowitz, & Bush, 1990; Traglia et al., 1996). Our interviews and reviews found that the tensions between competing objectives were usually understated, and that even when these tensions were apparent, their impact on outcome evaluation was not specified. Key informants often mentioned indicators that were not clearly linked to the objectives that they had identified. As a result, the contradictions between the objectives they stated and the objectives that could be measured using the indicators were obscured. For instance, placement rates ranked second as the most commonly used indicator, but they were the lowest ranked objective. Similarly, protection from maltreatment was ranked high as an objective, however most of the child welfare information systems that we examined were unable to track rates of recurrence of maltreatment.

This definitional vagueness has also been identified as a problem in formal evaluations of child welfare interventions. Rapp and Poertner (1988) observe that because client problems are not clearly described, it is often hard to understand how the outcomes that are evaluated are linked to client needs. Courtney (1993) notes that evaluated child welfare programs are generally so poorly described that even the program objectives are unclear. Furthermore, even when a program is found to be effective, the lack of detailed program description makes it difficult to replicate. This amorphous approach to describing child welfare clients and services has not only led to confusing evaluations but it has also left unresolved the critical issue of specifying the core objectives of the child welfare system.

Multiple Purposes of Outcome Assessment

Further confusion is created by the different ways in which the purpose of outcome measurement is understood. In our review of the literature and of other child welfare outcomes projects, we found that different groups are proposing the assessment of outcomes for different purposes. For some, the purpose of outcomes measurement is to guide intervention in individual cases. Others see it as a quality assurance monitoring device. Still others see outcome assessment as a way to evaluate intervention effectiveness. To confuse matters even further, instruments designed to assess outcomes have at times been used to assess risk, and risk assessment tools have been suggested as outcome measures (Wald & Woolverton, 1990). McCroskey (1997) argues that much of the confusion over outcome measurement rises from a failure to distinguish between the needs of different users (also see Parker et al., 1991). Table 2 illustrates some of the key differences between potential users of outcome information.

Clinically Meaningful Outcomes. The distinction between the use of outcome measurement for clinical purposes and outcome assessment for program evaluation is a critical one (McCroskey, 1997; Unrau & Gabor, 1997). At the clinical level, child welfare workers need to know how well individual clients are doing. Has a child's self-esteem improved? Is a parent better able to control his or her aggressive impulses? Are there more effective community supports in place to help a family? The specific outcomes that interest child welfare workers relate to the treatment plan developed to meet the specific circumstances of the child and family being served. Social workers need to be

TABLE 2. Purpose and Use of Outcome Assessment

Area of Use	Purpose	Level of Analysis	Primary Source of Data	Primary User
Case Management	Track indicators of client progress	Individual clients	Direct client measures	Front-line workers
Program Management	Monitor and evaluate programs	Service population	Systems level indicators	Administrators and government officials
Treatment Outcome Research	Determine intervention effectiveness controlling for confounders	Sampled clients	Direct client measures & systems level indicators	Independent researchers

able to choose from a broad array of clinically significant measures. These measures must be sensitive to small changes that provide meaningful feedback to front-line workers (Grinnell, Williams, & Tutty, 1997). Different sets of measures will be appropriate for different clients. For instance, a depression inventory is appropriate for an adolescent who is showing depressive symptoms but not in a case where lack of infant stimulation is the reason for service.

Tracking clinically meaningful outcomes requires instruments that collect information at the client level, usually through clinician observation or client self-report. A number of instruments are currently being used by child welfare practitioners in Canada, including the Child Well-Being Scales (Magura & Moses, 1986), an adapted version of the Child Behaviour Checklist (Achenbach, 1991), and the Looking After Children instruments (Ward, 1995). While there is increasing clinical interest in using standardized instruments to track individual client outcomes, these measures may not lend themselves as well to the needs of administrators and policy makers.

Outcomes as Management Tools. Administrators and policy makers require different levels and types of information (Rubin & Babbie, 1997). They need aggregate data that lets them know how well a program is serving a client population. They are interested in outcomes that are common to all clients, that reflect program and service goals, and that are meaningful to funders. Administrators and policy makers tend to rely on systems-based indicators that record systems events that serve as proxy measures *for client outcomes.* These range from case reopenings due to new incidents of maltreatment, to number of placement changes for children in out-of-home care. Caution must be used in interpreting systems-based indicators because they are proxy measures that can be influenced by a number of factors.

In some instances, instruments used to assess individual client outcomes can be aggregated across a client population. Using clinical instruments to assess program effectiveness can, however, be problematic. The accuracy of measurements based on clinical judgments made by child welfare workers can be compromised if the measurement instruments are being simultaneously used for other purposes, for example, if a worker's performance evaluation or program funding is tied to improved client outcomes. For program evaluation, systems-based indicators are a more reliable source of data, because they are easily linked to program objectives, can generate meaningful base-lines, and are not vulnerable to reporting bias.

Research Use of Outcome Measures. It is important to separate the evaluation efforts of administrators from those of independent re-searchers, who use more complex research designs that provide better control for measurement bias and for confounding explanations. Whereas administrators are primarily concerned with demonstrating that clients' outcomes have improved, researchers struggle to show that changes can be attributed to the intervention rather than to a co-occurring event or other factors (Gibbs, 1991). By using compari-son group designs, clinical researchers seek to identify client changes that can be attributed to child welfare interventions (Wolfe & Wekerle, 1993). Ecological researchers focus their analyses on the relationship between child welfare indicators such as rates of reported maltreat-ment, and other social indicators such as rates of poverty and unem-ployment (Zuravin, 1989).

In summary, front-line workers, administrators and researchers ap-proach outcome assessment from very different perspectives. Front-line workers need sensitive measures of individual client progress in many different areas. Administrators need a limited number of key indicators that monitor client progress in specific programs in an ag-gregated way. Researchers require sensitive measures applied by inde-pendent evaluators, using well-controlled designs. These different in-formation needs must be considered in developing consensus for a common outcomes framework.

Incremental Multi-Level Outcomes Development Strategy

Our review of some of the more successful outcomes initiatives, such as the clinically driven Looking After Children project in Eng-land and Canada, and the administration driven State Automated Child Welfare Information System in the United States, shows that initia-tives that focus primarily on meeting the needs of either clinicians or administrators are more successful than initiatives that attempt to meet the needs of both groups. On this basis, the COCW Project has devel-oped an incremental multi-level strategy that separates out the needs of clinicians and administrators.

The strategy builds on the types of information systems and instru-ments that are currently being used. Two primary sources of data are available to assess outcomes: direct client measures using worker-managed instruments, and systems-based indicators that reflect the relationship between clients and the service system. Both sources of data have advantages and limitations that depend in part on how well the information is collected and on the level of analysis required by those who will be using the information.

The proposed incremental strategy places the immediate emphasis on making use of systems-based indicators. Systems-based indicators are easily collected and can be standardized, are relatively objective, and are meaningful to multiple stakeholders. Although these indicators are proxy measures that cannot be directly linked to client outcomes, these limitations can be partially overcome by using multiple indicators. A proposed model is discussed in the following section.

A less centralized strategy is recommended for developing clinical assessment and case-management tools. Most of the Canadian outcomes projects identified by the COCW review are developing clinical outcome measurement systems. Better information sharing between projects will enrich them without losing the momentum set by each project. An outcomes-based case-management model requires a strategy that nurtures the commitment of front-line workers who may need to significantly shift their approaches from case planning to assessment and case-planning (see Traglia et al., 1996, for a good overview of this issue).

The proposed strategy also draws attention to the need to coordinate, track, and disseminate independent research initiatives more systematically. Clinical outcome studies using well-controlled designs are an essential component of an effective outcomes framework. Although these studies are expensive, they provide essential information on evaluation that is not otherwise available. Well-developed programs should be subjected to this level of empirical scrutiny.

Ecological research should also be used to examine the relationship between child welfare indicators and other population level statistics. Community "report card" projects fall into this category of research. More effective use of child welfare indicators will help to ensure a more accurate portrayal of child welfare services in studies and community initiatives examining indicators across service sectors.

Multi-Level Outcomes Indicator Matrix

An index of ten systems-based indicators associated with the four dimensions of protection, well-being, permanence and preservation was developed by the COCW Project and received strong support at *The First Canadian Roundtable on Child Welfare Outcomes* (see Table 3). While the complex and multi-level services provided by the Canadian child welfare systems cannot be reduced to a simple list of ten indicators, the Index is an initial step in an incremental outcomes development strategy. The feasibility of adapting the matrix to provincial information management systems is being considered in several provinces.

Child Protection. Child protection is the paramount consideration for child welfare services, and should be monitored at all points of intervention. Two key child protection indicators are included in the index: *recurrence of maltreatment,* and *child injury and death* (an indication of severity of maltreatment).

Maltreatment is rarely an isolated incident, and rates of recurrence are estimated to range between 30% and 50% (Wald & Woolverton,

TABLE 3. Child Welfare Outcomes Indicator Matrix

DOMAIN	INDICATOR	INTAKE AND INVESTIGATION	HOME-BASED SERVICES	OUT-OF-HOME SERVICES
PROTECTION	RECURRENCE OF ABUSE	✔	✔	✔
	CHILD INJURY & DEATH	✔	✔	
WELL-BEING	COGNITIVE FUNCTIONING		✔	✔
	CHILD'S BEHAVIOR		✔	✔
PERMANENCE	PLACEMENT RATE	✔	✔	
	PLACEMENT DISRUPTION			✔
	TIME TO ACHIEVE PERMANENCE		✔	✔
PRESERVATION	HOUSING STABILITY	✔	✔	
	PARENTING CAPACITY	✔	✔	
	ETHNO-CULTURAL PLACEMENT MATCHING			✔

1990). *Recurrence of maltreatment* is more easily measured when cases are reopened for investigation of a new alleged incident. There is significant variation in jurisdictions on how new incidents on open caseload are investigated and recorded. Substantiated case reopening is recommended as the more conservative and reliable indicator for recurrence of maltreatment.

Child injury is designed to provide a crude measure of the severity of recurring maltreatment. In Ontario, 2% of substantiated or suspected maltreatment cases involved major physical injury, and 8.6% of cases involved minor physical injury (Trocmé, McPhee, Tam, & Hay, 1994). While emotional and developmental harm are, in practice, the most significant negative outcomes for maltreated children, the public's attention to serious injury and death requires the systematic collection of physical harm data.

Child Well-Being. Although child well-being does not lend itself well to tracking by child welfare information systems, two proxy indicators have been identified. These measures are *cognitive functioning* and *child behavior.*

School performance is the simplest indicator of *cognitive functioning* as children who have suffered maltreatment experience multiple and significant challenges in school (Trocmé & Caunce, 1995). Age-to-grade ratio is an effective measure of school performance for children receiving home-based services, while graduation rates are recommended as a measure of school performance for older youth in care.

Children who have suffered child maltreatment are at a higher risk for behavioral problems at home and in school, delinquency and criminal activity (Widom, 1989). Positive *child behavior* and a decrease in behavioral problems are indicators of improved child well-being. Child behavior sub-scales of several standardized Risk Assessment tools can provide one effective measure of behavior change over time. For children twelve years of age and older, young offender charge rates under the Young Offender's Act of Canada can provide a proxy measure of serious behavioral problems in the community. While bias in reporting and charging practices must be considered in interpreting youth crime statistics, this is an indicator that professionals and the community are concerned about.

Permanence. Permanence can be measured by a number of different systems-based indicators. The three indicators selected for this index are *placement rates, placement disruption, and time to achieve permanence.*

Out-of-home care is necessary for children who cannot be adequately protected at home or who have needs that cannot be met at home. *Placement* has been used as an outcome indicator for child welfare programs designed to prevent children at risk of placement from entering care. It is also used as a community health indicator since high per capita placement rates are powerful indicators of poor overall well-being of children and families in communities. However, since placement is an intervention designed to protect children, placement data should be used as service trend information only in conjunction with child safety and well-being data.

Placement disruption is more readily interpreted as a measure of continuity and permanence. Children may experience an average of three-four moves during the time they spend out of home (Cooper, Peterson, & Meier, 1987), and these changes have an impact on the child's sense of permanence and belonging (Steinhauer, 1991). This indicator is easily monitored on information systems.

Time to achieve permanence is a critical indicator for the effectiveness of child welfare services. Rates of reunification and adoption were key outcome indicators to measure the effectiveness of permanency planning during the 1980s. The use of rate of reunification/ adoption as an indicator of permanence requires an examination of additional indicators (e.g., recurrence of maltreatment, placement breakdown), as estimates of placement breakdown are generally about 30% for family reunification programs (Fein & Staff, 1993).

Preservation. Three indicators of preservation have been selected including parenting capacity, number of family moves, and ethno-cultural placement matching.

Risk assessment instruments may provide a potential source of direct information about *parenting capacity.* As these instruments are becoming standard measures in many jurisdictions, it may be possible to extract a subset of measures related to family functioning (Garbe, 1999). Family influences that may be measured include stress, social supports, living conditions, and family violence.

Housing stability is a serious problem for many families receiving child welfare services (Cohen-Schlanger, Fitzpatrick, Hulchanski, & Raphael, 1995; Zuravin, 1986). Housing instability is an indicator of the high cost and poor quality of housing for these families. Housing instability also leads to loss of peer and social support networks for children and parents and multiple school changes for children. While child welfare services are not responsible for providing housing, child welfare social workers actively advocate for better and more stable housing for their clients.

A final indicator of preservation is *ethno-cultural placement matching*. Significant numbers of children from at-risk communities in Toronto–in particular children from aboriginal and West Indian communities–are placed in settings that do not match their original community (Trocmé, 1990; also see Shireman & Johnson, 1997, in the United States). This indicator is strongly influenced by the availability of community specific placements, and is therefore an interesting proxy indicator of the extent to which an agency or office has managed to develop good working relationships with these communities. This is a critical indicator that should be balanced by a child's need for permanence.

CONCLUSIONS

Our suggested approach separates the outcomes development strategies used in research, case management and child welfare administration. The interplay between the three strategies will also play a significant role in ensuring that outcomes are comprehensively assessed. The links between systems-based indicators and direct client measures will become better defined as each source of data is strengthened. For example, the rapid development of risk assessment tools could soon provide measures of case severity that could be easily aggregated for program evaluation. Moreover, front-line workers are far more likely to commit to outcomes-oriented case-management instruments if managers have already made the shift to outcomes-based management.

Research, case management, and program management strategies must be developed within a common overall outcomes framework. Although the appeal of the proposed multi-level strategy is that it allows clinicians, program administrators, policy makers and researchers to develop outcome measurement systems that best suit their needs, the danger is that these initiatives will lead to approaches that are not complementary and cannot eventually be integrated. The ecological perspective, which informs the proposed model, provides such a framework. The relatively simple set of indicators proposed in this article provide a feasible model for an outcomes measurement system consistent with an ecological perspective. However, it is only by tying the selection of indicators into such a framework that the natural drift to simpler uni-dimensional indicators can be avoided.

NOTES

1. British researchers have focused on three domains: (1) protection, (2) child physical, emotional and intellectual development, and (3) family functioning (Farmer, 1997).

2. The amount of service provided at the investigation phase varies from jurisdiction to jurisdiction. While some crisis support services are provided at the investigation phase, these are not the primary focus of investigations.

3. The importance of this community dimension was one of the critical themes arising from the COCW Roundtable consultation.

REFERENCES

Achenbach, T.M. (1991). *Manual for the youth self-report and 1991 profile*. Burlington, VT: University of Vermont Department of Psychiatry.

Ayoub, C.C., Willet, J.B., & Robinson, D.S. (1992). Families at risk of child maltreatment: Entry level characteristics and growth in family functioning during treatment. *Child Abuse and Neglect, 16*, 495-511.

Bath, H., & Haapala, D. (1994). Family preservation services: What does the outcome research really tell us? *Social Service Review, 68* (3), 386-404.

Belsky, J. (1993). Etiology of child maltreatment: A developmental-ecological analysis. *Psychological Bulletin, 114* (3), 413-434.

Berrick, J.D., Needell, B., Barth, R., & Jonson-Reid, M. (1998). *The tender years: Toward developmentally sensitive child welfare services for very young children*. New York: Oxford University Press.

Blythe, B.J., Patterson-Salley, M., & Jayaratne, S. (1994). A review of intensive family preservation services research. *Social Work Research, 18* (4), 213-224.

British Columbia Family Review Board. (1998). Ruling for the Metis association case.

Brooks, D., Barth, R., Bussiere, A., & Patterson, G. (1999). Adoption and race: Implementing the multi-ethnic placement act and the interethnic adoption provisions. *Social Work, 44* (2), 167-178.

Browne, K., Davies, C., & Stratton, P. (Eds.). (1988). *Early prediction and prevention of child abuse*. Chichester, UK: John Wiley & Sons.

Cohen-Schlanger, M., Fitzpatrick, A., Hulchanski, J.D., & Raphael, D. (1995). Housing as a factor in admissions of children to temporary care: A survey. *Child Welfare, 74* (3), 547-562.

Cooper, C.S., Peterson, N.L., & Meier, J.H. (1987). Variables associated with disrupted placement in a select sample of abused and neglected children. *Child Abuse and Neglect, 11*, 75-86.

Courtney, M. (1993). Standardized outcome evaluation of child welfare services out of home care: Problems and possibilities. *Children and Youth Services Review, 15*, 349-369.

Courtney, M.E., & Collins, R.C. (1994). New challenges and opportunities in child welfare outcomes and information technologies. *Child Welfare, 23*(5), 359-378.

Dallaire, N., Chamberland, C., Cameron, S., & Hebert, J. (1995). Social prevention: A study of projects in an urban environment. In J. Hudson & B. Galaway (Eds.), *Child welfare in Canada: Research and policy implications* (pp. 123-139). Toronto: Thompson Educational Publishing, Inc.

Dubowitz, H., Feigelman, S., & Zuravin, S. (1993). A profile of kinship care. *Child Welfare, 27*(2), 153-170.

Fallon, B., & Trocmé, N. (1998). A survey of the child welfare outcomes literature. In J. Thompson & B. Fallon (Eds.), *The first Canadian roundtable on child welfare outcomes* (pp. 65-84). Toronto: Bell Canada Child Welfare Research Unit.

Fanshel, D. & Shinn, E. (1978). *Children in foster care: A longitudinal investigation.* New York: Columbia University Press.

Farmer, E. (1997). Protection and child welfare: Striking a balance. In N. Parton (Ed.), *Child protection and family support: Tensions, contradictions, and possibilities* (pp. 146-164). London: Routledge.

Federal Provincial Working Group on Child and Family Services Information (1994). *Child welfare in Canada.* Ottawa: National Clearinghouse on Family Violence.

Fein, E., & Staff, I. (1993). Last best chance: Findings from a reunification services program. *Child Welfare, 72*(1), 25-40.

Fuchs, D. (1995). Preserving and strengthening families and protecting children: Social network intervention, a balanced approach to the prevention of child maltreatment. In J. Hudson & B. Galaway (Eds.), *Child welfare in Canada: Research and policy implications* (pp. 113-122). Toronto: Thompson Educational Publishing, Inc.

Garbarino, J., & Eckenrode, J. (1997). *Understanding abusive families.* San Francisco: Jossey-Bass Publishers.

Garbe, D. (1999). *Family functioning outcomes: Measurement potential of the Ontario risk assessment instrument.* Toronto: University of Toronto.

Gelles, R. (1996). *The book of David: How preserving families can cost children's lives.* New York: Basic Books.

Gibbons, J. (1997). Relating outcomes to objectives in child protection policy. In N. Parton (Ed.), *Child protection and family support: Tensions, contradictions, and possibilities* (pp. 78-91). London: Routledge.

Gibbs, L.E. (1991). *Scientific reasoning for social workers: Bridging the gap between research and practice.* New York: Macmillan Publishing Company.

Gove, T.J. (1995). *Report of the Gove inquiry into child protection in British Columbia: Volume I, Matthew's story.* Victoria, BC: British Columbia Ministry of Community and Social Services.

Grasso, A.J., & Epstein, I. (1988). Management by measurement: Organizational dilemmas and opportunities. *Administration in Social Work, 11*(3-4), 89-100.

Grinnell, R., Williams, M., & Tutty, L. (1997). Case-level evaluation. In R. Grinnell (Ed.), *Social work research & evaluation: Quantitative and qualitative approaches* (p. 640). Itasca, IL: F.E. Peacock Publishers, Inc.

Hutchinson, E. (1987). Use of authority in direct social work practice with mandated clients. *Social Service Review, 61*, 581-598.

Hutchinson, E. (1994). Child maltreatment: Can it be defined? In R. Barth, J.D. Berrick, & N. Gilbert (Eds.), *Child welfare research review* (pp. 5-27). New York: Columbia University Press.

Kadushin, A. (1978). Children in foster families and institutions. In H. Maas (Ed.), *Social service research: Reviews of studies* (pp. 90-150). Washington: NASW Press.

Kammerman, S., & Kahn, A. (1976). *Social services in the United States: Policies and programs.* Philadelphia: Temple University Press.

Klee, L., & Halfon, N. (1987). Mental health care for foster children in California. *Child Abuse and Neglect, 11*, 63-74.

Kufeldt, K. (1999). Challenges of research with youth and children. In B. Fallon & J. Thompson (Eds.), *Roundtable proceedings: The first Canadian roundtable on child welfare outcomes* (pp. 158-168). Toronto: Bell Canada Child Welfare Research Unit.

Kufeldt, K. et al. (1994). *Looking after children in Canada: How effectively does child welfare meet the needs of children?* Proposal Submitted to National Welfare Grants, Social Development and Education Group, Human Resources Development, Canada.

Lindsey, D. (1994). *The welfare of children.* London, UK: Oxford University Press.

Lindsey, D., & Regehr, C. (1993). Protecting severely abused children: Clarifying the roles of criminal justice and child welfare. *American Journal of Orthopsychiatry, 63*, 509.

Littell, J.H., & Schuerman, J.R. (1995). *A synthesis of research on family preservation and family reunification programs.* Chicago: National Evaluation of Family Preservation Services for the Office of the Assistant Secretary for Planning and Evaluation, Department of Health and Human Services.

Lyons, P., Doueck, H.J., & Wodarski, J.S. (1996). Risk assessment for child protective services: A review of the empirical literature on instrument performance. *Social Work Research, 20*(3), 143-155.

MacLaurin, B. (1998). *An inventory of Canadian child welfare outcome initiatives.* Toronto: University of Toronto

Magura, S., & Moses, B. (1986). *Outcome measures for child welfare services: Theory and applications.* Washington, DC: Child Welfare League of America.

Maidman, F. (Ed.) (1984). *Child welfare: A source book of knowledge and practice.* New York: Child Welfare League of America.

Maluccio, A.N., & Whittaker, J.K. (1997). Learning from the "family preservation" initiative. *Children and Youth Services Review, 19*(1/2), 5-16.

McCroskey, J. (1997). Outcomes measurement for family and children's services: Incremental steps on multiple levels. In G.J. Mullen & J.L. Magnabisco (Eds.),

Outcome measurement in the human services (pp. 189-195). Washington, DC: NASW Press.

McDonald, T. (1994). Should the police have greater authority in investigating cases of suspected child abuse? No. In E. Gambrill & T. Stein (Eds.), *Controversial issues in child welfare* (pp. 85-90). Boston: Allyn & Bacon.

National Research Council (1993). *Understanding child abuse and neglect.* Washington, DC: National Academy Press.

Ontario Ministry of the Solicitor General (1997). Verdict of the coroner's jury regarding Shanay Johnson.

Panel of Experts on Child Protection (1998). *Protecting vulnerable children.* Toronto, Ontario: Ministry of Community and Social Services.

Parker, R., Ward, H., Jackson, S., Aldgate, J., & Wedge, P. (Eds.) (1991). *Looking after children: Assessing outcomes in child care.* London, UK: The Department of Health.

Parton, N. (1985). *The politics of child abuse.* London, UK: MacMillan.

Pecora, P., Seelig, W., Zirps, F., & Davis, S. (Eds.) (1996). *Quality improvement and evaluation in child and family services.* Washington, DC: CWLA Press.

Pecora, P., Whittaker, J., Maluccio, A., Barth, R.D., & Plotnick, R.D. (1992). *The child welfare challenge: Policy practice and research.* New York: Aldine de Gruyter.

Pelton, L. (1989). *For reasons of poverty: A critical analysis of the child welfare system in the United States.* New York, NY: Praeger.

Pelton, L. (1997). Child welfare policy and practice: The myth of family preservation. *American Journal of Orthopsychiatry, 67*(4), 545-553.

Province of British Columbia (1996). Child, family and community service act (Revised statutes of British Columbia), chapter 46. Updated to October 31, 1977. Victoria, B.C.: Queens Printer.

Rapp, C.A., & Poertner, J. (1988). Moving clients center stage through the use of client outcomes. *Administration in Social Work, 111*(3-4), 23-39.

Rubin, A., & Babbie, E. (1997). Program-level evaluation. In R. Grinnell (Ed.), *Social work research & evaluation: Quantitative and qualitative approaches* (pp. 560-587). Itasca, IL: F.E. Peacock Publishers, Inc.

Savoury, G., & Kufeldt, K. (1997). Protecting children versus supporting families. *The Social Worker, 65*(3), 146-153.

Shireman, J.F., & Johnson, P.R. (1997). A longitudinal study of black adoptions. *Social Work, 31,* 172-176.

Starr, R.H., Dubowitz, H., & Bush, B.A. (1990). The epidemiology of child maltreatment. In R. Ammerman & M. Hersen (Eds.), *Children at risk: An evaluation of factors contributing to child abuse and neglect* (pp. 23-53). New York: Plenum Press.

Steinhauer, P.D. (1991). *The least detrimental alternative: A systematic guide to case planning and decision making for children in care.* Toronto: University of Toronto Press.

Traglia, J., Massinga, R., Pecora, P., & Paddock, G. (1996). Implementing an outcome-oriented approach to case planning and service improvement. In P. Pecora, W. Seelig, F. Zirps & S. Davis (Eds.), *Quality improvement and evaluation in child and family services* (pp. 75-98). Washington, DC: Child Welfare League of America.

Trocmé, N. (1990). *Child welfare services for visible minorities: A review of the literature.* Toronto: Harambee Child & Family Services & Children Aid Society of Metropolitan Toronto.

Trocmé, N., & Caunce, C. (1995). Educational needs of abused and neglected children: A review of the literature. *Early Childhood Development and Care*, 106, 91-100.

Trocmé, N., McPhee, D., Tam, K.K., & Hay, T. (1994). *Ontario incidence study of reported child abuse and neglect.* Toronto: Institute for the Prevention of Child Abuse.

Unrau, Y., & Gabor, P. (1997). Program-level evaluation. In R. Grinnell (Ed.), *Social work research & evaluation: Quantitative and qualitative approaches* (pp. 588-604). Itasca, IL: F.E. Peacock Publishers, Inc.

Wald, M., Carlsmith, J., & Leiderman, P. (1988). *Protecting abused & neglected children.* Stanford, CA: Stanford University Press.

Wald, M., & Woolverton, M. (1990). Risk assessment: The Emperor's new clothes? *Child Welfare*, 69(6), 483-511.

Ward, H. (1995). *Looking after children: Research into practice.* London, UK: The Department of Health on Assessing Outcomes in Child Care.

Welte, C. (1997). *New federal law seeks to promote adoptions, shorten foster care stays*: CASAnet.

Wharf, B. (Ed.) (1993). *Rethinking child welfare in Canada.* Toronto, ON: McClelland & Stewart.

Widom, C.S. (1989). Child abuse, neglect, and violent criminal behavior. *Criminology*, 27(2), 251-271.

Wolfe, D., & Wekerle, C. (1993). Treatment strategies for child physical abuse and neglect: A critical progress report. *Clinical Psychology Review*, *13*, 473-500.

Zuravin, S. J. (1986). Residential density and urban child maltreatment. *Journal of Family Violence*, *1*(4), 307-322.

Zuravin, S. (1989). The ecology of child abuse and neglect: Review of the literature and presentation of data. *Violence and Victims*, *4*(2), 101-120.

EVALUATING INTERVENTIONS IN SPECIFIC INSTITUTIONAL SETTINGS

Evaluating Interventions for Children Exposed to Family Violence

Sandra A. Graham-Bermann

SUMMARY. This paper presents a critical overview of the state of evaluation research with regard to intervention programs for children who witness family violence. The range and types of programs include universal preventive interventions as well as targeted interventions designed to prevent problems for at-risk children who have observed and experienced violence in their families. While few programs have been assessed to date, a summary of what appear to be the best ways to intervene in the prevention of and aftermath of family violence with children is offered, followed by ten suggestions for improving research in this area. *[Article copies available for a fee from The Haworth Document Delivery Service: 1-800-342-9678. E-mail address: <getinfo@haworthpressinc. com> Website: <http://www.HaworthPress.com>]*

Address correspondence to: Sandra A. Graham-Bermann, University of Michigan, Department of Psychology, 525 E. University Avenue, Ann Arbor, MI 48109-1109.

[Haworth co-indexing entry note]: "Evaluating Interventions for Children Exposed to Family Violence." Graham-Bermann, Sandra A. Co-published simultaneously in *Journal of Aggression, Maltreatment & Trauma* (The Haworth Maltreatment & Trauma Press, an imprint of The Haworth Press, Inc.) Vol. 4, No. 1 (#7), 2000, pp. 191-215; and: *Program Evaluation and Family Violence Research* (ed: Sally K. Ward, and David Finkelhor) The Haworth Maltreatment & Trauma Press, an imprint of The Haworth Press, Inc., 2000, pp. 191-215. Single or multiple copies of this article are available for a fee from The Haworth Document Delivery Service [1-800-342-9678, 9:00 a.m. - 5:00 p.m. (EST). E-mail address: getinfo@ haworthpressinc.com].

KEYWORDS. Prevention, groupwork, woman abuse, battering, witnessing violence, child psychopathology, clinical, trauma, practice

Most of what is known in the field of domestic violence intervention is focused on assessing the efficacy of programs aimed at deterrence (arrest) and/or treatment of batterers (National Research Council, 1998). Very little, however, is known about effective ways of helping victims (e.g., women) exposed to this form of family violence, and certainly still less is known about how best to intervene on behalf of children who have been witness to violence in the home. Since so many children are witness to and at-risk for violence exposure [estimated at more than 10 million children each year (Straus, 1994)], such knowledge would seem vital. The explicit purpose of this paper is the critical review of the present state of social science knowledge about the efficacy of intervention programs for children who are at-risk because of exposure to domestic violence. It is hoped this review will call attention to the need for the creation of more such programs, and beyond that, provide a template for both designing and evaluating the effectiveness of these programs.

The inherent ethical imperative for properly evaluating the intervention work we do is reason enough to pursue this agenda. That we happen to live in an era of managed care and third party payments, with its requirements for hard data on treatments presumed to be "state of the art," serves to further fuel the impetus for this review. However, as will soon become apparent, the research literature on the efficacy of intervention programs for children who are at-risk because of their exposure to domestic violence is now in its early infancy. Compared to other kinds of treatment programs for children at-risk for other reasons (say, parental substance abuse), the track record for interventions aimed at children of battered women is both short and sparsely populated (to date, fewer than a dozen studies can be cited).

We begin this paper by first considering the existing programs with respect to their range and type. Briefly, borrowing from public health terminology, preventive programs may be categorized as universal, selective, and indicated (Gordon, 1983). They can be further classified in ways that differentiate from each other with regard to their specificity (age, culture, type of violence). By definition, universal intervention programs are offered to a broad category of eligible people (e.g., children) for whom they may prove beneficial. Selective preventive programs are designed for those with an above-average risk for developing problems (e.g., children who have been exposed to violence, children living in dangerous neighborhoods). Indicated prevention is offered to those identified as the most likely to develop problems (e.g., children of battered women who are aggressive in school, those who have no social support, those with a depressed mother). Most of the programs reviewed here have selected children at some level of risk for developing problems associated with their prior exposure to family violence.

EXISTING RESEARCH ON INTERVENTIONS WITH CHILDREN OF BATTERED WOMEN

While many shelters and communities now offer either education, support, or intervention programs for children and battered women, there is, as noted earlier, little empirical evidence based on systematic research that these interventions provide help to the children they purport to serve. Furthermore, delineation of which children are best treated by which types of programs has yet to be considered. Of the few studies that have been undertaken to assess treatment success, most are limited in the types of outcomes being evaluated and otherwise plagued with design and method problems, e.g., most studies do not have comparison groups and offer no theory of change.

Only programs that have been systematically evaluated are included in this review. The evaluations take a range of approaches, from qualitative study and clinical case report, to empirically tested, controlled studies with large sample sizes. Evaluated programs were identified through a series of efforts, including searches in psychology, social work, the medical and sociology literatures, and through inquiry with a number of experts who have evaluated interventions for children exposed to family violence. While the presentation of programs is not intended to be exhaustive or to represent a meta-analysis, the programs are representative of the sorts of interventions that are available and have been assessed to date.

The evaluation efforts of three types of programs are reviewed here. Two of the programs may be categorized as universal preventive. That is, the prevention program is instituted prior to the child's possible exposure to domestic violence, such that the child is protected from, or inoculated against, the occurrence of unwanted events or outcomes. In this terminology programs designed to prevent the abuse of women (mothers) may be considered primary interventions. Reducing intimate partner violence against the mother protects the child from witnessing the violence and experiencing negative sequelae (e.g., posttraumatic stress). However, universal prevention programs in the area of domestic violence rarely evaluate their beneficial effects for children who, but for the intervention, may be at-risk for witnessing.

In fact, most programs are designed for children after the violence has already taken place. These programs are, by definition, either selective or indicated interventions, depending on the level of risk to the child. However, at the present time, very few programs are either designed for children with a particular level of symptoms, or screen their participants prior to program entry. Thus, the largest group of intervention programs to be reviewed here may be classed as selective preventive interventions. A total of six such programs will be discussed. These interventions serve to reduce the negative effects on the child of his/her witnessing the violence against the mother (i.e., many such programs aim to reduce the risk of developing negative outcomes early on in the course of a child's reaction to violence).

Finally, a third group of interventions are understood as indicated or targeted preventive. These are interventions for children considered to be the most at-risk for suffering negative sequelae to the trauma of violence exposure. Their risk may be expressed in terms of symptoms (e.g., depressed, anxious), characterological deficits (e.g., impulsive, hyperactive), or interpersonal problems (e.g., socially withdrawn, relationship violence) for which focused treatments are sought. However, only one of the intervention programs to be reviewed is of the indicated preventive kind.

Two Primary Prevention Programs and Their Outcomes

Two school-wide educational programs on violence prevention for all children, were selected to exemplify primary prevention for children in the area of domestic violence. There are many such programs in schools today. "My Family and Me: Violence Free" was developed as part of the Minnesota School Curriculum Project by Stavrou-Peterson and Gamache (1988). Here, both those children exposed to domestic violence and those who have not experienced this form of family abuse are considered to benefit from information and activities designed to reduce violence in families in the future. The primary goal of this program is to inoculate all children in a school setting against the negative effects of many types of violence, including domestic violence.

This broadband program was tested with 238 children in kindergarten through third grade and 176 children in grades 4-6. Each class participated in two 50-minute sessions per week for six weeks. The program sessions were held in class and activities were designed to (a) build problem-solving skills, assertiveness training, (b) enhance feelings of self-worth, (c) develop personal safety skills, and (d) improve the school's response to students affected by family violence. Pre- and post-intervention tests were administered for attitudes towards violence and knowledge change. At the end of the six weeks, students showed significant knowledge change, and positive attitude change (Stavrou-Peterson & Gamache, 1988). Teachers gave the program positive evaluations as well.

Another universal, preventive intervention is "ASAP: A School-Based Anti-Violence Program" by Sudermann, Jaffe, and Hastings (1993). This program was designed for classroom administration with elementary through high school students. Once again, the goals were broad-based, namely: (a) To create a whole-school, nonviolent atmosphere, (b) to develop awareness of many forms of violence, and (c) to incorporate discussion into the curriculum. More specifically, the intervention program targets the prevention and reduction of dating violence, the amelioration of the effects of domestic violence on children, as well as diminishing the interpersonal violence more generally in the school setting and in society at large.

The program was evaluated by Sudermann, Jaffe, and Scheike (1996). Pre- and post-test evaluations of all children who participated in the intervention were used. Unfortunately, data for this primary prevention program are only partially reported, with early results suggesting that the program was successful in improving students' awareness of violence and its consequences.

One of the problems of preventive intervention research is that its goals are generally long term, while efforts to assess program efficacy often employ assessments at the close of the intervention. In order to truly assess the success of the stated goals of these preventive programs, long-term, longitudinal assessments are needed to follow the course and quality of children's interpersonal relationships well after, perhaps years after, program participation. As yet, there is no prospective study of the impact of domestic violence on children later in life (i.e., adulthood)–whether the outcomes assessed are emotional or social adjustment, violence in intimate relationships, school success, delinquency rates, and/or employment success.

Prevention Programs for Identified At-Risk Children

Some prevention programs are aimed at populations at-risk for negative outcome associated with exposure to a deleterious and, in this case, violent event. Given the chronic nature of the trauma and stress related to ongoing violence in woman-abusing families (as well as the number of women and children who present with symptoms of traumatic exposure), the children of battered women are most often, and most appropriately, treated with interventions specifically designed to address their experiences (Graham-Bermann & Levendosky, 1998; Rossman, 1998; Wolfe & Jaffe, in press).

It is clear that most children who witness woman abuse are in need of intervention services (Graham-Bermann, 1998a; Jaffe, Wolfe, & Wilson, 1990). Yet, while all children exposed to the abuse of their mothers may be at-risk for problems in adjustment, we know that approximately half (about 50-60% in most studies) develop symptoms in the clinical range (Davis & Carlson, 1987; Jouriles, McDonald, Norwood, & Ezell, in press). These symptoms include heightened levels of internalizing problems, such as depression and anxiety (Graham-Bermann, 1996; Hughes & Luke, 1998), and externalizing problems of aggression and conduct disorders (Davies & Cummings, 1998; Jaffe et al., 1990). The other, lower-risk children are those who have experienced domestic violence but do not present with problems at the clinical level (Hughes, Graham-Bermann, & Gruber, in press). Still, at this time, intervention programs with children of domestic violence tend to be of a one-size-fits-all nature (Graham-Bermann, 1999).

Sub-populations of children differentially at-risk and differentially protected have yet to be tracked into adulthood. This is because the majority of studies of children exposed to domestic violence employ cross-sectional designs; and, consequently, we know little about the longitudinal course of the development of associated symptoms (Rossman, in press). Hence, it is difficult to judge who may be in need of preventive services or if different kinds of prevention should be, or can be, tailored to the specific needs of subgroups of children at-risk.

While the statistics given above represent children's levels of psychopathology at the time of evaluation, this does not rule out the possibility that some children may develop serious adjustment problems in the future (e.g., so-called "sleeper effects"). Similarly, many children exposed to violence may initially present with adjustment reactions that abate over time (Graham-Bermann & Levendosky, 1998). Nonetheless, most programs do not screen for specific clinical problems in an effort to either rule in, or rule out, a child's eligibility for an intervention program.

Further, we have just begun to distinguish the levels of symptomatology of those children assessed while living in battered women's shelters, from those residing in the community (Graham-Bermann & Edleson, in press). Children living in the community who participate in clinical treatment programs form yet a third population or category whose symptom profiles may differ from sheltered and nontreated community children. In one study comparing rates of traumatic stress symptoms of nonsheltered children of battered women whose mothers did and did not seek out child-based intervention, those in the clinical treatment sample had three times the rate of post-traumatic stress disorder as did the nontreated children (DeVoe & Graham-Bermann, 1997).

Selective Intervention Programs for Children of Batterers

Program for Sheltered Children. One of the first treatment groups for children of battered women was developed by Hughes (1982). This program served children and their mothers living in battered women's shelters and was aimed at fostering parenting skills, building children's self-esteem, reducing anxiety, and improving coping behavior along with altering attitudes toward family violence. Both individual and group modalities were offered.

As with most of the children's programs that are described here, the educational aspects of this program rely on the principles of cognitive theory in assisting children in the development of new ways of thinking about families, of understanding the unacceptability of violence, and about new ways of solving interpersonal problems. Cognitive-behavioral therapies focus on reframing the child's understanding by adding new information and changing existing cognitive scripts (Kendall, 1985).

Evaluation of the treatment groups was undertaken by Hughes and

Barard (1983). Questionnaires measuring self-esteem, anxiety and attitudes toward domestic violence were completed by 12 children both before and after their shelter stay. Mothers completed the parent version of the Child Behavior Checklist (Achenbach, 1991). Children were 3.5 to 11 years old and had lived in the shelter for more than ten days before their participation in the study.

While differences were not found in children's problem behaviors, the mothers did report less anxiety as a result of their child's participation in the program. No changes were found in parenting skills. At the time, no control group was used and no follow-up assessment of the stability of these changes was undertaken. Thus, it is difficult to have confidence in these results. Nonetheless, this was the first published evaluation of an intervention designed expressly for children in families with domestic violence.

Conjoint Program for Sibling Pairs. Another interesting program was designed by Frey-Angel (1989) to address concerns of 3-7 year-old children exposed to family violence and their older sibling. Here sibling pairs were seen in a group setting. The goals of the groups were to learn new coping skills, alternatives to violence, nonviolent emotional expression, and to stop the intergenerational transmission of violence. However, only clinical case examples are provided on outcomes with the report that positive changes in behavior were seen. The lack of follow-up or comparison group leaves this program essentially untested. While the cases are compelling, empirical support is needed to establish this program's efficacy.

Child Witnesses of Wife Abuse Program. In 1986, Wilson, Cameron, Jaffe, and Wolfe, undertook a preliminary evaluation of the "Child Witnesses of Wife Abuse" program. This psychoeducational program emphasizes knowledge about family violence and incorporates exercises designed to help the child build social skills. The goals of the program include raising children's self-esteem while teaching positive conflict resolution strategies, changing attitudes regarding responsibility for violence, and changing attitudes about domestic violence. This ten week intervention program was designed for children in crisis, ages 8-13, whose mothers were living in shelters for battered women. Each session was 90 minutes in length and there were six to nine children in each group. Both male and female group leaders were used.

Jaffe and colleagues report preliminary evidence suggesting that the program was successful and that children changed their attitudes about violence as a result of their participation in the program (Jaffe, Wilson, & Wolfe, 1986, 1988; Wilson, Cameron, Jaffe, & Wolfe, 1989). However, there was no comparison group and little in the way of follow-up to ascertain whether findings were stable over time, were the result of participation in the intervention program, or of subsequent life experiences (e.g., parent leaving the batterer, or move to a new home environment).

Wagar and Rodway (1995) tested the efficacy of the Jaffe et al. program with 38 children ages 8-13, this time employing a comparison group. Sixteen children received the intervention while 22 were in a control or no treatment group. Children were referred by clinical and social service agencies. Pre- and post-treatment evaluations included the conflict tactics scale, as well as parent and child interviews. A significant design improvement in this study was that subjects were randomly assigned to the two comparison groups. However, group leaders doubled as researchers in administering all measures as well as the treatment to the children.

While the study is flawed by small sample size, unequal group sizes, and lack of systematic follow-up assessments, Wagar and Rodway did report significant positive effects of the program on children's attitudes and responses to anger, and on reduction in children's self-blame for the violence between the parents. No significant differences were found for improved knowledge of safety, nor for enhanced coping through the utilization of social support. These preliminary findings show that intervention can help to change children's attitudes concerning family violence. The use of a training manual is a strength in that leaders of different groups can rely on the same model to guide each group session.

Groupwork with Child Witnesses to Domestic Violence. The focus of a ten-week program by Peled and Davis (1995) was (a) to foster a safe and positive arena to help children break the secret of violence in the family, (b) to learn self-protection, (c) to increase self-esteem, and (d) to change attitudes about violence. An optional closing family session abuse program was offered where children, siblings, parents, and the group leader discussed the issues covered in the group together and made recommendations for further treatment, if needed. In addition, a voluntary parenting group for parents was available with the goals of providing both education and support.

An evaluation study of this program (Peled & Edleson, 1992; Peled, Jaffe, & Edleson, 1995) relied on qualitative methodology to assess change and change-inducing processes in their treatment program for 4-12 year-old children of battered women. Inclusion criteria were having a custodial parent in a structured domestic abuse program and the child's having witnessed the abuse. Children unable to separate from their mothers, those with inappropriate attention spans (e.g., those who were too active or too passive), and those not able to interact socially were excluded from the group treatment program. Thirty children were treated in eight groups. These children, 16 mothers, five fathers, and nine group leaders provided information post-treatment. Group leaders conducted the qualitative interviews following the last intervention session. There were no control groups and no outcome data of follow-up evaluations were reported.

The strengths of this study include presentation of a model for treating the children, a treatment manual, and observation of all ten weeks' participation for one group. In addition, group leaders' and mothers' views about the efficacy of the program were solicited. Here, triangulation of data is a strength and speaks to the need for multiple method approaches to work in this area. The study was designed to evaluate both intended and unintended outcomes. The authors found many intended outcomes, e.g., all children discussed the secret in the group, as well as several unintended outcomes, e.g., mothers wanted their children to talk with them about the violence while the children presumed that group confidentiality precluded this possibility. Other findings were that children increased their knowledge of domestic violence, changed attitudes, and had more emotional disclosure about violence events.

Among the reasons given for selecting the qualitative method are the nonspecific and general goals of the program, and the obtrusive quality of many standardized measurements with children. The authors took a grounded theory approach as well as an exploratory approach, as they felt that, at this point in time, "there is little information about the results of intervention programs and their dynamics" (Peled & Edleson, 1992, p. 329).

This approach highlights questions about whether there are appropriate ways of selecting clear, even if limited, program goals, and obtaining information from children that does not include directly asking about the violence, e.g., asking mothers and the child's teachers to evaluate the child's behavior, asking mothers to report on the violence history of the family. In addition, some studies reviewed here use trained clinicians to interview children, thus attempting to reduce the risk of re-traumatization to the child.

Further, some qualitative studies incorporate mechanisms for establishing the validity and reliability of findings. These may include provision of research feedback to the original participants by the researchers in the form of focus groups. This method affords participants the opportunity to give researchers feedback about the research procedures and findings. It may also help in establishing reliabilities for given themes and coding categories. Qualitative comments and feedback regarding themes or categories may be compared with standardized measures of constructs for a subgroup of subjects. Perhaps future intervention program evaluations could incorporate qualitative features (capture program efficacy in participants' own words) as well as the use of standardized procedures for measuring key constructs.

The Storybook Club. A ten-session, weekly program designed to teach problem-solving, conflict resolution, and safety skills to 5-7 year-old children of battered women was evaluated by Tutty and Wagar (1994). Based on the assumption that children learned the responses of either aggression or withdrawal from their parents, they were considered to be at-risk for becoming either perpetrators or victims of violence. The program took place at the YMCA in one Canadian city. Program goals ranged from the general to the specific and included (a) cutting short the intergenerational transmission of violence, (b) teaching alternative problem-solving practices, (c) developing safety skills, and (d) challenging gender roles. The program relied on repetition of story themes presented through both reading and drama and thus, takes a social learning theory perspective on what is needed to create change.

Six groups of children and their mothers were assessed in their homes before and following the intervention program. Most of the mothers (89%) were separated and most of the children (95%) were exposed to conflict between their estranged parents at the time of participation. Mothers and the children's teachers were asked to report on areas of both problems and strengths. Parenting stress, children's anxiety and self-esteem were measured. Within-group interviews also took place with the children, and mothers received feedback at the end of the program. Tutty and Wagar reported that the program was deemed helpful by parents and the children, but give only anecdotal evidence of its success. Attrition rates were reported as more than half, many children had irregular attendance, and only a few parents entered a concurrent support group. There was no follow-up evaluation.

Cox (1995) studied the same program for 13 children ages 5-7 from low-income families and found a significant reduction in anxiety for these children following the intervention. More boys than girls participated. Given the small sample, high attrition and nonattendance rates, and reliance on anecdotal evidence, we can conclude little about whether this program is effective.

Child Witnesses Program. Ragg, Sultana, and Miller (1998) have evaluated a program for 143 school-age children who were witnesses to domestic violence. The goals of the program were to provide social support and social skills training to reduce aggression and enhance the child's adaptive behavior. While the delivery of the treatment protocol was flexible, with group members deciding on the specific focus in a given week, treatment component areas covered included establishing group rapport, challenging assumptions, anger control, assuming responsibility, and problem solving, among others.

Ragg et al. (1998) relied on drop-out subjects as a comparison group and had a pre- and post-test design. Drop-out subjects did not differ significantly on major dependent variables at the beginning of the study, yet they did receive at least some of the intervention program. Thus, these subjects were not entirely independent of the first group. It should be noted that in other treatment evaluation studies (see Stanton & Shadish, 1997), drop-out subjects were considered to be treatment failures, and not appropriate for use as a comparison group. The sample population was better reported in the Ragg et al. study, than in other studies, including statistics on minority status (89% Caucasian), education, and income of participants.

Analyses for the treatment group (n = 70) revealed significant changes in child behavior (CBCL) from before and to after the intervention. Decreases in rates of delinquency were found for both boys and girls as a result of their participation in the program. A greater decrease in externalizing behavioral problems was found for those in the treatment versus the drop-out condition.

Inclusion of a random assignment to groups design and a follow-up evaluation would have aided in presenting a more compelling case that the changes seen were due to participation in the program. Even though the focus of each particular session is unclear here, and the amount of treatment received by drop-out subjects is a possible confound, this program appears to have been successful in at least the short-term reduction of aggression and antisocial behavior.

The Family Follow-Up Study. Sullivan and Davidson (1998) tested the effects of an advocacy intervention program for abused women and their children. Both a longitudinal design and multi-method strategies were used to measure family violence, injury, problems such as depression and aggression, knowledge of family violence, other risk factors and school achievement. The sixteen-week experimental group program included advocacy for mothers and children, weekly paraprofessional assistance, and both a mentoring relationship with a college student and ten-week support and education group for children only. A comparison group received no specific services.

In all, the sample consisted of 85 children ages 7-11 and their mothers. Pre- and post-intervention assessments were made with an eight-month follow-up evaluation. Contact with the family was high, with trained students working an average of nine hours per week with each family. Families received advocacy in the areas of issues for the children, obtaining goods and services, legal issues, employment, education, social support, child care, housing and transportation.

No statistically significant differences were found for 74 child subjects' data when comparing the experimental with the comparison group across all three time points. However, the experimental program was successful in reducing level of depression and in enhancing self-esteem for the mothers. A reduction in abuse to the child and increase in mother's social support and satisfaction with the program were sustained at the eight-month follow-up (Sullivan & Davidson, 1998). As the authors suggested, perhaps a larger sample size would have resulted in more substantial findings, as several child-related outcomes approached the level of significance, specifically, change in internalizing problems and child self-competence.

The advocacy program for the mothers was most effective, whereas the support, mentoring, and education programs provided to the children did not appear to significantly change their levels of problem behaviors, either at home or in the school setting. Compliance was high in this study, as all children attended every session of the intervention. The authors credit the children's attendance to having the mentor provide transportation to each session. Further, there was a low rate of subject attrition from the end of the intervention to the follow-up interviews (approximately 5%).

The Kids' Club: A Preventive Intervention Program for Children of Battered Women. The program developed by Graham-Bermann (1992) was designed to reduce the impact of domestic violence and to reduce the risk of repeated violence for children. This intervention targeted children's knowledge about family violence, their attitudes and beliefs about families and family violence, their emotional adjustment, and their social behavior in the small group setting. The ten-week program was based on the theoretical assumptions that children learn deleterious patterns of behavior as a result of observing violence, that many children are traumatized by their experiences, and that their internalized schemas for social interaction and expectations for themselves and others are affected by the violence in their families.

A parenting program was designed to empower mothers to discuss the impact of the violence on various areas of the child's development, to build parenting competence, to provide a safe place to discuss parenting fears and worries, and to build self-esteem for the mother in the context of a supportive group (Graham-Bermann & Levendosky, 1994). Thus, the mothers' ten-week intervention was aimed at improving their parenting skills, as well as enhancing the social and emotional adjustment of the women (and, by extension, their children).

Three groups of 6- to 12-year-old children exposed to high levels of domestic violence were compared. They were randomly assigned to participate in the child-only intervention format (n = 62), the child-plus-mother intervention format (n = 61), or to a comparison group of children who received no treatment for ten weeks (but were offered treatment following this delay) (n = 58). Treated children received the ten-week social-cognitive intervention. Children in the child-plus-mother group had mothers who also participated in the support and empowerment group for battered women. For this present study, a sample size of approximately 60 children in each group was required to produce reliable evidence of significant change. This was a sample of women currently living in the community and not a sheltered sample, as is found in most other studies of children of battered women. Forty-eight percent of the children and 43% of mothers were minority families; most of these were African-American.

It was important to include multiple vantage points and multiple, standardized measures in assessing key constructs. To that end, four sources of information (child, mother, teacher, group leader) were tapped in assessing the child in the cognitive domain (knowledge of family violence, safety plan, expected family and gender roles), social behavior in the group and in school, as well as self-rated social competence, and the child's level of behavioral and emotional adjustment (inclusive of depression, post-traumatic stress, internalizing and externalizing symptoms). In addition to pre- and post-intervention assessment, evaluations of behavior and progress in the groups were obtained on five occasions at specified intervals (after sessions one, three, five, seven, and ten) from two independent group leaders for each child and mother who participated in the intervention program. Similarly, two group leaders evaluated the mothers' knowledge of the impact of domestic violence on the child, as well as changes in parenting skills. All three groups were assessed again at eight months post-intervention.

Attrition of the sample was reported in two forms. The first was counting the number of families who did not elect to participate in the study after the first interview. Of the 221 children originally interviewed, 18.1% did not return for a second interview. The majority of these were families assigned to the delayed treatment condition. For those 123 who participated in the interventions, the rate of attrition from the time two interview to the eight month follow-up interview was low–only 5.7% of those who entered the ten-week intervention were not interviewed a third time. Four families dropped out of the child-only group and one family from the child-and-mother group. Thus, there was a significant difference in attrition for those who received treatment compared to those in the delayed treatment group. Stanton and Shadish (1997) recommend that both forms of attrition be reported as no-change treatment failures and should not be used as a comparison group.

Change from baseline was assessed in the cognitive, social, and emotional/behavioral domains (Graham-Bermann, 1998b). For the cognitive domain, the intervention program was designed to help children to discuss what they like and don't like about families and to teach children facts about what "most" families are like. This information is crucial in helping the child to develop an alternative image of the ways in which problems are resolved in other families and of the possibilities of their own families in the future. The children's responses to these questions showed that several areas of knowledge about domestic violence in families had changed for those in the treatment groups versus those not receiving the intervention. For example, the nontreatment group did not change in their understanding that most families do not engage in violent fighting. However, the children in the child-only and in the child-plus-mother treatment groups did show statistically significant change in their opinion on this question. That is, they were less likely to endorse family fighting as occurring in most families at the second interview. Change also was found in favor of the intervention groups in the areas of reducing self-blame for family violence, enhanced coping with a safety plan, and other ways of solving differences.

Change in social skill was assessed with a number of indices of behavior, attitudes, knowledge, and skill in interpersonal relationships. Problems found in social interaction with peers during childhood have been predictive of difficulty in social relationships with others in adulthood. The intervention program relied on the clinical skills of the group leaders to enhance and to facilitate social interaction among children in the group. Therefore, the study of children's social behavior in the group may be one vital area in which to measure progress in the development of social skills. Significant, positive change from the first to the final session was found in many areas of the child's emotional functioning in the group, e.g., children became less anxious during the sessions. However, the child's level of anger increased from the beginning to the end of the intervention. This was not unexpected as the intervention was designed to help children identify feelings in general, and feelings in relation to family violence, in particular.

Further, children were significantly more able to participate in group activities, to be connected to others, and to be included by others in play after the intervention, as compared to their abilities when the groups began. Children's skill in entering the peer group, joining others in play, and empathy with others increased significantly from the first to the final session. The groups were less successful in helping children to curb their frustrations and impulsive behavior.

Interestingly, improvement was found in internalizing behavioral symptoms for children in all three groups (the CBCL, parent and teacher forms were used). Similarly, all groups changed in their total behavioral symptoms scores over the ten weeks. However, problems in aggression and conduct disorder (externalizing symptoms) were the most significantly reduced for the children in the child-plus-mother treatment group. It is not surprising that children whose mothers also received intervention could begin to change in this area, as the parenting support program was directly focused on improving the mothers' parenting skills, inclusive of limit-setting and implementing effective discipline strategies.

It is important to note that the change was greater in all three areas for those in the child-plus-mother group and was smallest for those in the nontreatment group. Thus, the intervention was successful in reducing children's behavioral problems over the ten-week evaluation period, even though some problems naturally abated over time. Therefore, intervention that includes the mother was deemed optimal. Further analyses will determine the stability of these changes.

Indicated or Targeted Preventive Intervention Program

Jouriles et al. (1998) evaluated a program designed to break the cycle of violence for battered women whose children were deemed to have problems with aggressive behavior. This program relies on social learning theory in providing different models of parenting and in reinforcing other, nonviolent, conflict resolution strategies with children. Here, aggressive behavior is considered to be learned through the processes of modeling and identification with the aggressor. Jouriles and colleagues studied the ways in which aggressive behaviors were reinforced and maintained in children exposed to family violence (Jouriles, Murphy, & O'Leary, 1989; Jouriles & Norwood, 1995). This intergenerational transmission hypothesis relies on the premise that violence is learned in the family of origin and, unless treated, is repeated in the next generation (Straus, Gelles, & Steinmetz, 1980). The goal of treatment is to interrupt the intergenerational transmission of violence.

This intervention was provided to 4- to 9-year-old children and their mothers departing from shelters for battered women. Unlike some of the other programs described here, this is the only program specifically targeted for mothers of children with aggressive behavior problems. Thus, the focus of the intervention is with the mother and the weekly sessions take place in the home setting. Trained therapists provide the parenting sessions for the mother. Children receive a mentor who gives support and serves as a role model for the mother.

The design of the evaluation study included random assignment of families to either the intervention or a comparison condition. Preliminary results are available and indicate that for 18 families (10 in the treatment condition), externalizing behavior problems in the child were reduced and parenting skill enhanced for the intervention group as compared to the nontreatment group at eight months following the intervention. Several design features are notable here, including the random assignment to groups and follow-up assessment. This evaluation is ongoing and additional data are needed in order to confirm these promising, initial results. Still, while the initial reported sample size is small, this program appears to have been successful in reducing aggression in children. Perhaps the success of this program is due to its having a narrow focus, being clearly delineated, and relying on a proven theory.

Conclusion of Outcomes and Program Strengths

Universal programs offered in the schools that have clearly defined and measurable goals have been successful in raising students' awareness of interpersonal violence and in changing their attitudes toward the acceptability of violence as a means of resolving conflicts. To date, short-term change has been documented.

Most of the selective intervention programs offered to children exposed to family violence have a group format and rely on both education and psychotherapeutic processes in affecting change. The goals common to most of the children's programs reviewed here include building social skills (particularly those focused on interpersonal problem solving), enhancing self-esteem, reducing anxiety, and increasing knowledge (thereby reducing anxiety) about violence in general and family violence in particular. Authors of several programs have included specific sessions to address safety planning and to improve the child's coping with violence (Graham-Bermann, 1997; Hughes, 1982; Tutty & Wagar, 1994), naming the problem or breaking the secret (Graham-Bermann, 1997; Peled & Edleson, 1992), and a focus on recognizing and redefining gender roles (Graham-Bermann, 1997; Tutty & Wagar, 1994).

Among the selected programs described here, the treatment method of group intervention was most commonly used for children, and several programs offered parenting support or education for the mothers. A child mentor was provided in two programs (Jouriles et al., 1998; Sullivan & Davidson, 1998) and a mother's advocate was an integral part of the Sullivan and Davidson (1998) program. It should be noted that while their children participated in programs without a specific parenting component, many of the mothers received a number of different services in either shelters or in the community (e.g., support groups for battered women).

Significant change in child behavior was found in two programs that included a parenting skills component (Graham-Bermann, 1997; Jouriles et al., 1998). Programs with a strong parenting focus were deemed the most successful. Not withstanding the methodological problems cited above, a variety of preliminary results can be identified from reports on evaluations of the child-centered group intervention programs. These include success in changing children's attitudes about violence (most programs), change in child social behavior (Frey-Angel, 1989; Graham-Bermann, 1997; Ragg et al., 1998), emotional disclosure (Graham-Bermann, 1997; Peled & Edleson, 1992), reduction in anxiety (most programs), and an increase in self-esteem and reduced self blame (Graham-Bermann, 1997; Wilson et al., 1989).

SPECIFIC SUGGESTIONS
FOR IMPROVING RESEARCH IN THIS AREA

Since the state of research in this area is in the beginning stages, there is ample room for improvement in a number of domains ranging from the elements of design in program evaluation, to measures employed, to reporters used in obtaining data, and to the ways in which pre- and post-intervention data are compared. Where to begin?

1. At the least, studies of the efficacy of intervention programs designed for children exposed to woman abuse should employ a design that utilizes pre-evaluation and post-evaluation measures. Ideally, beyond this fundamental requirement, long-term follow-up is desirable as it would provide information on enduring effects of the intervention, and, perhaps some understanding of factors that serve to erode program gains and benefits.

2. Similarly, it is essential to have comparison groups to adequately discern the amount of benefit, or extent of change, for those receiving the intervention protocol. Comparison groups can include those who do not receive any intervention as well as those who receive different interventions, or lesser dosages of interventions that are designed to impact the same treatment issue. Here, outcome effects as indexed in levels of change achieved may be compared for children who receive

different numbers of sessions and/or those who receive various forms of a treatment. This design would provide information about the ingredients for change–be it the amount of intervention or its various permutations.

3. It is imperative that future studies of the efficacy of intervention programs rely on triangulation of data sources–i.e., on a broader number of reporters and, where possible, on evaluators who are independent from the intervention itself. For example, while group leaders may evaluate children's behavior in group sessions, they should not be employed as evaluators of children's experience outside of the group, and, preferably, more than one reporter should be used to evaluate each child within the group. Similarly, reporters in addition to the mother should be relied upon for gathering basic data about the extent of children's violence exposure. Such "other" informants can include the children themselves, teachers, other family members, as well as archival data and official documentation (e.g., police reports, arrest records, protective services documentation, and medical records).

4. It is necessary to include a description of the theoretical underpinnings of the intervention program and to base the goals of the program on a theory of ways in which children are affected by exposure to violence. For the researcher, understanding the theoretical assumptions of the program is essential to creating hypotheses that test theories of change. Selection of the appropriate measures for assessing change is dependent on these theories of the ways children are affected and should be matched with complementary theories about the ways in which the program is designed to stimulate change in children (e.g., ideas about behavioral or attitudinal change should be matched by intervention strategies that are age-appropriate and developmentally informed).

5. Assessments must go beyond simply documenting pre- and post-intervention change in knowledge and behavior. Here it is important to include the assessment of multiple stressors and risks to the child in evaluation research. Change in the child may be directly (or indirectly) affected by the presence or change of many factors in the child's life in addition to the violence exposure. Some of the many other factors that may stimulate either positive change or regression in the child are whether mother leaves the abuser, how much contact the child has with the offending parent, the amount of social stress to which the family is exposed, mother's mental health and coping skills, among a

host of other salient variables. By including more sophisticated models in designing interventions and evaluations, knowledge of what is needed for change can be identified. For instance, by studying the role of parenting and its effects for children exposed to domestic violence, one could make suggestions for adding a parenting component to programs initially designed to target the child alone.

6. Research is needed to identify which populations and which target programs are best for early and later interventions. There is a need for creating and improving screening measures or protocols for children exposed to domestic violence. Little information is available to distinguish those effects noticed in the immediate aftermath of family violence from the effects on children with longer histories or chronic abuse. With this information, interventions can be tailored to the needs of the individual child. Indeed, it may be useful to have individual programs that rely on methods for trauma reduction immediately following exposure to severe violence, but group interventions for children exposed to violence when the trauma is not acute. Similarly, it would be more helpful and cost-effective if prevention programs were specifically designed for those most at-risk for developing symptoms in reaction to violence exposure (i.e., for the non-resilient, non-protected percentage of children at-risk).

7. While the state of research in this area is in its initial stages, and as more programs are developed that rely on research findings, it is imperative that programs be designed and studied in culturally sensitive and appropriate ways. To that end, assessments should be done with nonbiased measures and take cultural variation and specification into account. Several ideas for culturally sensitive evaluation come to mind. Comparative analyses with subjects from a variety of cultural groups can rely on analyses of variance from within-group norms rather than between-groups comparisons (such as is often done in comparisons of different ethnic groups). By using within-group variation an individual is assessed relative to others with similar backgrounds, expectations, and experiences. The use of focus groups for evaluation, grounded theory, and qualitative assessments is a method sensitive to capturing these salient characteristics of programs or experiences.

8. In order to foster comparison across studies, it is important to include effect sizes of both significant and nonsignificant findings. It is crucial for researchers to discover and to report the areas of limita-

tion of intervention programs, in order to better develop knowledge of the kinds of problems that can be effectively used for specific populations.

9. Another way of approaching the development of intervention programs is to study success; that is, to identify those children who do not appear to be affected by the violence in order to learn what will help those who were affected. To this end, studies of resiliency in children exposed to domestic violence might explore the essential characteristics of the family, of the child, or of the resources available to the child and the family in order to further distinguish what resources children need in order to be protected from the development of negative outcomes.

Perhaps with all of this information we can design better screening, more accurate assessments, and refined interventions so they can be tailored to the specific needs of children who witness the abuse of their mothers.

REFERENCES

Achenbach, T. M. (1991). *Manual for the child behavior checklist: 4-18 and 1991 profile.* Burlington: Department of Psychiatry, University of Vermont.

Cox, G. M. (1995). *Changes in self esteem and anxiety in children in a group program for witnesses of wife assault.* Unpublished master's thesis, School of Social Work, University of Calgary, Calgary, Alberta, Canada.

Davies, P. T., & Cummings, E. M. (1998). Exploring children's emotional security as a mediator of the link between marital relations and child adjustment. *Child Development, 69* (1), 124-139.

Davis, L. V., & Carlson, B. E. (1987). Observation of spouse abuse: What happens to the children? *Journal of Interpersonal Violence, 2,* 278-291.

DeVoe, E., & Graham-Bermann, S. A. (1997). *Predictors of posttraumatic stress symptoms in battered women and their children.* Poster presented at the Second International Conference on Children Exposed to Family Violence, London, Ontario, Canada.

Frey-Angel, J. (1989). Treating children in violent families: A sibling group approach. *Social Work with Groups, 12* (1), 95-107.

Gordon, R. (1983). An operational classification of disease prevention. *Public Health Reports, 98,* 107-109.

Graham-Bermann, S. A. (1992). *The Kids' Club: A preventive intervention program for children of battered women.* Department of Psychology, University of Michigan.

Graham-Bermann, S. A. (1996). Family worries: The assessment of interpersonal anxiety in children from violent and nonviolent families. *Journal of Clinical Child Psychology, 25* (3), 280-287.

Graham-Bermann, S. A. (1998a). Preventing domestic violence. In H. Friedman (Ed.), *Encyclopedia of mental health* (pp. 1-16). San Diego: Academic Press, Vol. 1.

Graham-Bermann, S. A. (1998b). The impact of woman abuse on children's social development. In G. W. Holden, R. Geffner, & E. N. Jouriles (Eds.), *Children exposed to marital violence: Theory, research, and applied issues* (pp. 21-54). Washington, DC: APA Books.

Graham-Bermann, S. A. (1997). *Intervention in domestic violence* (Final Report). Ann Arbor, MI: University of Michigan.

Graham-Bermann, S. A. (1999). *Violence in the lives of American children: Epidemiology, impact, and intervention studies.* Washington, DC: Office of Juvenile Justice and Delinquency Prevention, United States Department of Justice.

Graham-Bermann, S. A., & Edleson, J. L. (Eds.) (accepted for publication). *Intimate violence in the lives of children: The future of research, intervention, and social policy.* Washington, DC: APA Books.

Graham-Bermann, S. A., & Levendosky, A. A. (1994). *The Moms' Group: A parenting support and intervention program for battered women who are mothers.* University of Michigan.

Graham-Bermann, S. A., & Levendosky, A. A. (1998). Traumatic stress symptoms in children of battered women. *Journal of Interpersonal Violence, 14* (1), 111-128.

Hughes, H. (1982). Brief interventions with children in a battered women's shelter: A model program. *Family Relations, 31,* 495-502.

Hughes, H., & Barad, S. (1983). Psychological functioning of children in a battered women's shelter: A preliminary investigation. *American Journal of Orthopsychiatry, 53* (3), 525-531.

Hughes, H., & Luke, D. A. (1998). Heterogeneity in adjustment among children of battered women. In G. W. Holden, R. Geffner, & E. N. Jouriles (Eds.), *Children exposed to marital violence: Theory, research, and applied issues* (pp. 185-221). Washington, DC: American Psychological Association.

Hughes, H. M., Graham-Bermann, S. A., & Gruber, G. (in press). In S. A. Graham-Bermann & J. Edleson (Eds.), *Children and family violence: The future of research, intervention, and policy.* Washington, DC: APA Books.

Jaffe, P. G., & Sudermann, M. (1990). Child witnesses of woman abuse: Research and community responses. In S. M. Smith & M. A. Straus (Eds.), *Understanding partner violence* (pp. 213-222). Minneapolis, MN: National Council on Family Relations.

Jaffe, P. G., Wilson, S. K., & Wolfe, D. A. (1986). Promoting changes in attitudes and understanding of conflict resolution among child witnesses of family violence. *Canadian Journal of Behavioral Sciences, 18,* 356-366.

Jaffe, P. G., Wilson, S. K., & Wolfe, D. A. (1988). Specific assessment and intervention strategies for children exposed to wife battering: Preliminary empirical investigations. *Canadian Journal of Community Mental Health, 7,* 157-163.

Jaffe, P. G., Wolfe, D. A., & Wilson, S. K. (1990). *Children of battered women.* Newbury Park, CA: Sage.

Jouriles, E. N., McDonald, R., Norwood, W., & Ezell, E. (in press). Documenting the prevalence of children's exposure to domestic violence: Issues and controversies.

In S. A. Graham-Bermann & J. Edleson (Eds.), *Children and family violence: The future of research, intervention, and policy.* Washington, DC: APA Books.

Jouriles, E. N., McDonald, R., Stephens, N., Norwood, W., Spiller, L. C., & Ware, H. S. (1998). Breaking the cycle of violence: Helping families departing from battered women's shelters. In G. W. Holden, R. Geffner, & E. N. Jouriles (Eds.), *Children exposed to marital violence: Theory, research, and applied issues* (pp. 337-370). Washington, DC: American Psychological Association.

Jouriles, E. N., Murphy, C. M., & O'Leary, K. D. (1989). Interpersonal aggression, marital discord, and child problems. *Journal of Abnormal Child Psychology, 57,* 453-55.

Jouriles, E. N., & Norwood, W. D. (1995). Physical aggression toward boys and girls in families characterized by the battering of women. *Journal of Family Psychology, 9,* 69-78.

Kendall, P. C. (1985). Toward a cognitive-behavioral model of child psychopathology and a critique of related interventions. *Journal of Abnormal Child Psychology, 13,* 357-372.

National Research Council (1998). *Violence in families: Assessing prevention and treatment programs.* Washington, DC: National Academy of Sciences.

Peled, E., & Davis, D. (1995). *Groupwork with children of battered women.* Thousand Oaks, CA: Sage Publications, Inc.

Peled, E., & Edleson, J. (1992). Multiple perspectives on groupwork with children of battered women. *Violence and Victims, 7,* 327-346.

Peled, E., Jaffe, P. G., & Edleson, J. (1995). *Ending the cycle of violence: Community responses to children of battered women.* Thousand Oaks, CA: Sage Publications, Inc.

Ragg, D. M., Sultana, M., & Miller, D. (July, 1998). *Decreasing aggression in child witnesses of domestic violence.* Presentation at Program Evaluation and Family Violence Research Conference, University of New Hampshire, Durham, NH.

Rossman, B. B. R. (in press). Long term effects of children's exposure to domestic violence. In S. A. Graham-Bermann & J. Edleson (Eds.), *Children and family violence: The future of research, intervention, and policy.* Washington, DC: APA Books.

Rossman, B. B. R. (1998). Descarte's error and posttraumatic stress disorder: Cognition and emotion in children who are exposed to parental violence. In G. W. Holden, R. Geffner, & E. N. Jouriles (Eds.), *Children exposed to marital violence: Theory, research, and applied issues* (pp. 223-256). Washington, DC: American Psychological Association.

Stanton, M. D., & Shadish, W. R. (1997). Outcome, attrition, and family-couples treatment for drug abusers: A meta-analysis and review of controlled, comparative studies. *Psychological Bulletin, 122* (2), 170-191.

Stavrou-Peterson, K., & Gamache, D. (1988). *My family and me: Violence free.* St. Paul: Minnesota Coalition for Battered Women.

Straus, M. A. (1994). Children as witnesses to marital violence: A risk factor for lifelong problems among a nationally representative sample of American men and women. In D. F. Schwartz (Ed.) *Children and Violence: Report of the Twenty*

Third Ross Roundtable on Critical Approaches to Common Pediatric Problems (pp. 98-109). Columbus, OH: Ross Laboratories.

Straus, M. A., Gelles, R., & Steinmetz, S. (1980). *Behind closed doors: Violence in the American family.* Garden City, NY: Anchor.

Sudermann, M., Jaffe, P., & Hastings, E. (1993). *A school-based anti-violence program.* London, Ontario, Canada: London Family Court Clinic.

Sudermann, M., Jaffe, P., & Scheike, E. (1996). *A.S.A.P.: A school-based anti-violence program.* London, Ontario: London Family Court Clinic.

Sullivan, C., & Davidson, W. (1998). *Preliminary findings from the family follow-up study.* Lansing, MI: Michigan State University.

Tutty, L. M., & Wagar, J. (1994). The evolution of a group for young children who have witnessed family violence. *Social Work with Groups, 17* (1/2), 89-104.

Wagar, J. M., & Rodway, M. R. (1995). An evaluation of a group treatment approach for children who have witnessed wife abuse. *Journal of Family Violence, 10,* 295-306.

Wilson, S., Cameron, S., Jaffe, P., & Wolfe, D. (1989). Children exposed to wife abuse: An intervention model. *Social Casework, 70,* 180-192.

Wolfe, D. A., & Jaffe, P. (in press). Prevention of domestic violence: Emerging initiatives. In S. A. Graham-Bermann & J. Edleson (Eds.), *Children and family violence: The future of research, intervention, and policy.* Washington, DC: APA Books.

Strategies for Evaluating
Dating Violence Prevention Programs

Anna-Lee Pittman
David A. Wolfe
Christine Wekerle

SUMMARY. Adolescence represents an important opportunity to inform youth about healthy, non-violent relationships as they begin to form their own intimate relationships. There are many methodological and practical challenges to conducting educational efforts directed at adolescents, and even greater difficulties in evaluating such efforts. This paper discusses some of the known findings concerning predictors of abusive dating relationships and the research challenges of dating violence prevention, such as identifying and recruiting youth for participation. We identify current dating violence prevention programs that have an evaluation component, with an emphasis on program content and evaluation strategies. The paper concludes with a discussion of the Youth Relationships Project, a program designed to encourage healthy, non-violent relationships among youth who were raised in abusive

The authors would like to thank D. Lynn Hawkins for her work in compiling information for this article. This work was funded in part by a grant from the National Health Research and Development Program (Health Canada). The Ontario Mental Health Foundation contributed to this article through a Senior Research Fellowship (Wolfe) and New Investigator Fellowship (Wekerle).

Address correspondence to: Anna-Lee Pittman, MA, Project Manager, Youth Relationships Project, Department of Psychology, University of Western Ontario, London, Ontario, Canada, N6A 5C2 (E-mail: http://yoda.sscl.uwo.ca:80/psychology/faculty/project/yr-project.html).

[Haworth co-indexing entry note]: "Strategies for Evaluating Dating Violence Prevention Programs." Pittman, Anna-Lee, David A. Wolfe, and Christine Wekerle. Co-published simultaneously in *Journal of Aggression, Maltreatment & Trauma* (The Haworth Maltreatment & Trauma Press, an imprint of The Haworth Press, Inc.) Vol. 4, No. 1 (#7), 2000, pp. 217-238; and: *Program Evaluation and Family Violence Research* (ed: Sally K. Ward, and David Finkelhor) The Haworth Maltreatment & Trauma Press, an imprint of The Haworth Press, Inc., 2000, pp. 217-238. Single or multiple copies of this article are available for a fee from The Haworth Document Delivery Service [1-800-342-9678, 9:00 a.m. - 5:00 p.m. (EST). E-mail address: getinfo@haworthpressinc.com].

environments. Benefits and limitations of research and evaluation strategies are discussed. *[Article copies available for a fee from The Haworth Document Delivery Service: 1-800-342-9678. E-mail address: <getinfo@ haworthpressinc.com> Website: <http://www.HaworthPress.com>]*

KEYWORDS. Teen relationships, child maltreatment, adolescent relationships, abusive relationships

Adolescence is a critical point in the development of intimate relationships, which is why educating youth about relationships and nonviolent conflict resolution skills holds promise as a viable prevention strategy (Pittman, Wolfe, & Wekerle, 1998). The goal of dating violence prevention programs is to educate teens about the dynamics of abusive behavior (e.g., abuse of power and control), and to expose them to alternative conflict resolution strategies. This goal is approached by helping them develop healthy, non-abusive relationships, especially for those at greater risk due to a history of maltreatment, poor attachment, lack of positive role models (Wolfe et al., 1997) and similar risk factors described above. There are relatively few dating violence prevention programs currently in operation, and even fewer that have been carefully evaluated (see Wekerle & Wolfe, 1999, for review). As with other high-risk behaviors such as sexual activity and alcohol or drug use, those prevention programs that have been developed often lack careful evaluation strategies (Rindskopf & Saxe, 1998; Sellers, Taylor, & Esbensen, 1998; Tolan & Brown, 1998). This paper discusses the challenges of longitudinal and intervention research with adolescents, and reviews current strategies to evaluate dating violence prevention programs.

Teen dating relationships have received greater scientific interest lately because they contain many of the elements of abuse and violence that are well-known among marital couples. Emotional and physical abuse among teen dating partners, for example, are estimated to be as widespread and frequent as in adult relationships (Marx, Van Wie, & Gross, 1996; Sudermann & Jaffe, 1993). Abusive teen relationships, moreover, resemble adult patterns and cycles of violence (Walker, 1989): a building of tension, an explosion of anger, and a honeymoon period of "making up." Disturbingly, youths involved in an abusive dating relationship may come to accept abusive behavior as a normal part of intimate relationships (O'Leary, Malone, & Tyree, 1994), which underscores the importance of early prevention.

Dating violence is worrisome not only because of its link to woman abuse in adulthood, but also because of its alarming frequency and potential harm. In a study of 707 high school students (14-17 years of age), 39.3% of the respondents reported being a perpetrator of dating violence, and 38.2% reported being a victim in a dating context (Malik, Sorenson, & Aneshensel, 1997). Such incidents involve a wide range of abusive behaviors, from relatively minor (cursing or swearing, threatening), to moderate (slapping, pinching, choking), to severe (punch, force sex, threaten with a weapon) (Malik et al., 1997; Smith & Williams, 1992). For these reasons, the formative years during which adolescents begin to date may represent a critical point in the development of abusive versus healthy intimate relationships.

PREDICTORS OF DATING VIOLENCE

Explanations for the development of abusive behavior toward intimate partners, based on developmental psychopathology and social learning theories, have received empirical support with adult samples (Malamuth, Sockloskie, Koss, & Tanaka, 1991; O'Leary et al., 1994) and have relevance to adolescent partnerships as well. For example, violence in adolescent dating relationships may be partially understood in terms of relationship models derived from early experiences of child maltreatment (Sroufe, 1989). Being exposed as a child to abusive and violent relationship models increases the chances of repeating such patterns as one forms affective ties with peers and dating partners (Carlson, 1990). In maltreating families, violence and intimidation are seen as viable strategies for maintaining relationships and resolving conflicts; therefore, these experiences may set the stage for future victim and victimizer roles in close relationships (Cicchetti & Howes, 1991; Crittenden & Ainsworth, 1989). As they reach school-age and adolescence, these children behave more aggressively with peers (Dodge, Bates, & Pettit, 1990; Parker & Herrera, 1996), and are more likely to become abusive toward dating partners (Wolfe, Wekerle, Reitzel-Jaffe, & Lefebvre, 1998).

Studies aimed at understanding who is at risk of becoming a victim or perpetrator of dating aggression during adolescence have examined a number of factors, including alcohol/drug use, relationship conflict, relationship satisfaction, socioeconomic status, level of commitment, history of maltreatment, attachment, justification for violence, and exposure to community violence (Malik et al., 1997; O'Keefe, 1997, 1998; Smith & Williams, 1992; Wekerle & Wolfe, 1998a). Male aggression toward a dating partner is linked to a history of maltreatment (Wekerle & Wolfe, 1998b), lower socioeconomic status (O'Keefe, 1998), and greater exposure to community violence (Malik et al., 1997; O'Keefe, 1998). Female victimization has been associated with a history of maltreatment (O'Keefe, 1998; Wekerle & Wolfe, 1998b) and greater exposure to community violence (Malik et al., 1997). Justification or acceptance of dating violence is found to be a strong predictor for both males' and females' dating violence perpetration (O'Keefe, 1997). Similarly, experiencing maltreatment in the family of origin was a substantial risk factor among both non-clinical, community samples of high school students (Wekerle & Wolfe, 1998b; Wolfe, Wekerle, Reitzel-Jaffe et al., 1998) and university males (Reitzel-Jaffe & Wolfe, submitted), as well as samples of children from protective services agencies with documented maltreatment histories (Wolfe & McGee, 1994).

Unlike adult relationship violence, in which men are more commonly the perpetrators of abuse, females report the same or more abusive acts as males in this age group (Gray & Foshee, 1997). However, males are more often the perpetrators of more severe violence and abuse than girls (Foo & Margolin, 1995). It is important, then, to consider the needs of males and females as both victims and perpetrators of abusive behaviors in relationships when planning intervention approaches, since communication, anger management, safety and help-seeking skills will benefit males and females alike (Foshee, 1996; Wolfe et al., 1996).

RESEARCH CHALLENGES
IN DATING VIOLENCE PREVENTION

Definitions

The study and prevention of dating violence is challenged not only by its relative infancy, but also by the private, personal nature of such acts and the lack of awareness of their harm. Child abuse and marital violence studies have benefited from considerable efforts to improve operational definitions for research purposes over two decades, whereas dating violence studies among adolescents have not. Moreover, the dynamics of teen relationships require consideration of the context and norms for abusive acts. For example, abusive acts among adults in intimate relationships (such as pushing, punching, and name calling) may be used to maintain power and control in the relationship, whereas these same behaviors shown among teen dating partners are commonly used to gain attention or to express interest in another (Shapiro, Baumeister, & Kessler, 1991). Similarly, the concept of mutual violence among adolescents is a new and controversial issue that merits investigation (Gray & Foshee, 1997). A mutually violent relationship is one where the individual both sustains violence and initiates violence within the dating relationship. Findings indicate that for individuals in mutually violent relationships, the reported amount and severity of violence received is about equal to the reported amount and severity of violence initiated (Gray & Foshee, 1997).

Some studies of dating violence focus on physical abuse tactics (Foo & Margolin, 1995; Tontodonato & Crew, 1992), others look at physical and psychological aggression (Capaldi & Crosby, 1997), while others examine physical, sexual and emotional abuse (Wolfe, Wekerle, & Reitzel-Jaffe et al., 1998). We define relationship violence and abuse to mean any attempt to control or dominate another person physically, sexually, or emotionally, causing some level of harm (Wekerle & Wolfe, 1999). Although arbitrary, this definition and criterion establishes a reasonable basis for studying dating relationships (McDonald & McKinney, 1994).

Finally, defining what is meant by a "dating relationship" also poses problems for establishing a standard of comparison across studies. Dating relationships among adolescents may be described in various ways, from single dates to long-term relationships, with no consensus as to the minimum amount of time that two people see each other that constitutes a relationship. When asking teens to report on a dating relationship, they may experience difficulty since they are often not familiar with the terms used by researchers, such as dating relationships or partners. Focus groups with teens permit a better understanding of how they define dating relationships, and what terms should be used when asked to evaluate a relationship. They respond with terms such as "dating," "going out," and "seeing each other"; when a commitment has been made to a relationship, the statement "we're together" seems to be an understood concept among peers.

For our research purposes, therefore, dating is defined as a relationship (which may or may not be exclusive) where the couple has been seeing each other for at least one month, using the terminology identified by teens in focus groups.

Recruiting and Following Participants

While longitudinal research is desirable for program evaluation, it is also a challenge when dealing with youth. Obtaining a random sample of youths for an unfamiliar program is difficult, due in part to the reluctance of community agents to refer to a program that has a control-group component (Tolan & Brown, 1998). High costs related to the need for a large subject pool sometimes make it necessary to develop multi-site interventions to ensure an adequate sample size. Needless to say, recruiting school boards, social service agencies, teachers, social workers, parents, peers and youth, as well as soliciting their cooperation through all of the data collection points over the course of several years, can be a monumental task (Capaldi, Chamberlain, Fetrow, & Wilson, 1997). Furthermore, some youth may not perceive the need to participate because they do not experience symptoms of distress or concern, or do not see relationship abuse or violence as an issue for them.

Another difficulty in longitudinal research with this population is the ability to maintain contact with youths for necessary data collection to determine success of preventing abuse. Several procedures have been shown to be useful (Gregory, Lohr, & Gilchrist, 1992): (a) flexibility in meeting times; (b) selecting locations that suit the participant; (c) an escalating payment for participation; and (d) a follow-up schedule for phone contact. A familiar research assistant should contact participants throughout the follow-up, which should occur on a frequent basis. Some participants may live in group homes or foster homes and change residences frequently; thus it is important to complete contact forms at the beginning of the study, providing a list of names, addresses, and phone numbers of people who would be able to provide information about their whereabouts if necessary.

Research assistants must also be as flexible as possible with youth regarding meeting times and locations for meetings such as the youth's home, social service agency, public library, etc. Again, this requires a great deal of coordination and organization, as well as significant community support, such as obtaining interview room space on short notice. Understandably, teens will frequently agree to meet with research assistants only if it is convenient and the location is nonthreatening (this is especially true when youth are asked to invite peers and dating partners to participate in a videotaped interaction or interview; see below).

The success of obtaining other informants for the study, especially peers and dating partners, also depends on the youths' willingness to participate and their understanding of their roles. Asking the teen to invite a same-sex peer to participate in the study greatly increases their likelihood and comfort of inviting a dating partner to participate in the research aspect of the program (Capaldi et al., 1997). Youth are less likely to ask a dating partner to participate if they themselves are unsure of what the process involves. Finally, it is important to emphasize the positive aspects of the program and research (i.e., developing healthy relationships) to youth and other informants since peers and dating partners are less likely to agree to participate if they believe that the focus of the assessment will be on violence or abuse.

Assessment Strategies

As noted, one of the greatest difficulties inherent in measuring the success of dating violence prevention programs concerns the very nature of adolescent dating relationships. Adolescent relationships are often brief in duration, although intense in terms of frequency of contact (Feiring, 1996), which makes measuring the presence or absence, let alone the reduction, of abusive behaviors difficult. In a recent study of students in grades 9-12 in Ontario secondary schools, we found that 85% had begun dating, 43% were currently dating at the time of the study, and the average longest relationship reported was 34 weeks. This pattern limits the window of opportunity for measuring change in behaviors in actual dating relationships. The dating relationships are often too brief in nature to assess significant changes, healthy or unhealthy.

There are few standardized evaluation instruments available to measure dating violence or abuse, or to assess attitudes and beliefs regarding relationship abuse. Questionnaires such as the Inventory of Knowledge and Attitudes (Lavoie, Vezina, Piche, & Boivin, 1995) and Attitudes about Dating Index (Margolin & Foo, 1992) have been developed to measure attitudes and beliefs about sex roles, woman abuse, and similar issues. A common approach to assessing attitudes about dating aggression involves rating the acceptance or justification of dating violence (Avery-Leaf, Cascardi, O'Leary, & Cano, 1997; Foo & Margolin, 1995; Gray & Foshee, 1997; Malik et al., 1997; Smith & Williams, 1992; Tontodonato & Crew, 1992).

The Conflict Tactics Scale (CTS; Straus, 1979), which is a standard measure of abuse in adult relationships, has been used with adolescents to provide an index of the frequency and forms of response to conflict (Avery-Leaf et al., 1997; Capaldi & Crosby, 1997; Foo & Margolin, 1995). However, tactics used in adult relationships do not always represent the same harm or intentions as those of adolescent relationships. Name calling and swearing are seen as abusive acts among adults, but must be assessed carefully among adolescents for context. Often these tactics relate more to immaturity or attention seeking, especially in relation to physical acts such as poking, pushing, punching that lack an intention to harm. Therefore, we developed the Conflict in Relationships Questionnaire (CIRQ; Wolfe et al., submitted) specifically for an adolescent population. Items on the CIRQ ask about negative conflict resolution (e.g., physical, sexual, and emotional abuse) as well as positive communication methods (asking advice, discussing the issue calmly). Teens are asked to report on their experiences both as an offender and as a victim, similar to the CTS. A confirmatory factor analysis of the abuse items represented one latent factor, labelled abusive conflict resolution tactics ($\chi^2 = 80$, GFI = .95; alpha = .82) (Wolfe, Wekerle, Scott, Grasley, & Pittman, 1998). Test-retest reliability over 2 weeks is very good ($r = .84$). Like all self-report instruments relating to violence and abusive behavior, the CIRQ may not be a comprehensive measure of a couple's interaction or an individual's behavior in context. Thus, observational data are useful adjuncts to evaluate the degree of abusiveness between dating partners, using structured clinical procedures (e.g., Capaldi & Crosby, 1997).

Use of Multiple Informants

Once participants have become familiar with prosocial behaviors and attitudes, they have a greater awareness of which behaviors and actions would be deemed socially desirable to endorse in a questionnaire or interview regarding conflict tactics, etc., which makes their self-report information less reliable. Attempts have been made to use informants such as teachers, parents, peers, and dating partners, with limited success. Parents and teachers, for example, are reluctant to assess behaviors that may be occurring in intimate dating relationships, since they seldom witness these behaviors directly. Peers, who are often seen as confidantes, may be protective of their friends and unwilling to endorse or report on negative or abusive behaviors. Dating partners, on the other hand, can be a valuable source of information regarding problem solving skills and conflict tactics used in dating relationships, even though dating couples disagree as to their experiences as victims or perpetrators. Hanley and O'Neill (1997), for example, examined the reporting of received and inflicted aggression from 52 dating couples from a university population, using the CTS. Couples were originally categorized as being violent (33%) if *either* partner reported using or experiencing any of the nine physically violent acts on the CTS in the past 12 months. However, only 19% met the criterion when classification was based on *both* members reporting violence.

In sum, implementing and evaluating a community prevention program is difficult and challenging, and is largely unaided by well-established measures and procedures. Obstacles and challenges include inadequate resources for implementation and evaluation, lack of support or hesitancy of community agencies or social service workers to refer to an unknown or experimental program, and a lack of standardized instruments (Tolan & Brown, 1998). These challenges notwithstanding, there is a strong need for dating violence prevention programs (Avery-Leaf et al., 1997) and a necessity to provide comprehensive evaluations of the programs being developed to determine what is successful and what shows potential for success. Evaluations of several promising dating violence prevention programs are described below.

EVALUATIONS OF DATING VIOLENCE PREVENTION PROGRAMS

Research methods for evaluating treatment and prevention programs should involve, at a minimum, a pre-post intervention design, random assignment to a control or treatment condition, and follow-up measurements over an extended time period. These minimal criteria, however, have seldom been met (Wekerle & Wolfe, 1999), due to the above-noted difficulties and challenges in addressing this topic. Generally, the criteria for determining effectiveness or success for these programs rely on measurement of changes in behaviors, attitudes, and skills that are related to the expression of violence or abuse, rather than actual violent acts themselves, due to limited opportunities to assess such behaviors. Programs that have documented evaluation outcomes have relied on self-report data (Avery-Leaf et al., 1997) and brief follow-ups (Jaffe, Sudermann, & Reitzel, 1992; Lavoie et al., 1995), with one study measuring observed behavior change (Hammond & Yung, 1991). Dating violence prevention programs are often implemented within the school curriculum and applied to a universal audience or groups selected by curriculum subject, such as health class.

Table 1 provides a detailed description of current dating violence prevention programs with evaluation designs, the method used to deliver the programs, the skills, attitudes, behaviors that were targeted in the program, and the results of the evaluation for the programs. As shown, a common goal for dating violence prevention programs is the modification of attitudes and knowledge regarding relationship violence. Each program described in Table 1 has identified this as a target, except for the PACT program that was not designed specifically for prevention of relationship violence. Two programs, the Safe Dates Project (Foshee et al., 1996) and the Youth Relationships Project (Wolfe et al., 1996), have also chosen to focus on conflict resolution skills and the development of healthy relationships. Finally, help-seeking skills are targeted in two of the programs, to aid youth in locating resources for themselves or peers. With the exception of the Youth Relationships Project (YRP), these programs are implemented in schools during class time or as part of a curriculum. The programs vary in length from two sessions to an entire semester. The following section discusses the YRP in greater detail to illustrate several evaluation components.

The Youth Relationships Project

The YRP is an 18-session community-based prevention program that was developed for males and females between the ages of 14 and 17 years. The program has three main components: (1) education about woman abuse, violence, sexual assault and date rape; (2) conflict resolution and communication skills development; and (3) social

TABLE 1. Dating Violence Prevention Programs for Adolescents

Program Description	Method	Target(s)	Results & Comments
Avery-Leaf et al., 1997. Universal program of dating violence prevention. Five-session curriculum for implementation in high school health classes. Facilitators: Health teachers attend an 8-hour training seminar one-week prior to program implementation.	Design: 2-groups (1 control) pre/post design, random assignment of class to intervention/control. Participants: 193 students (106 males & 87 females) enrolled in health classes (grades 9 to 12) at an urban American high school. Predominantly white (79.8%); lower-middle socio-economic levels. Intervention: Skill-based with themes of power and control, and gender inequality. Aim to challenge societal acceptance of violence, and promote healthy dating relationships, effective "help-seeking" and conflict resolution.	Attitudinal justification of violence (self-report; analogue measure).	1) Improvement in attitudes for intervention group only at post-test. 2) "Floor-effect" noted in that 50% to 66% of students at pre-test did not justify the use of "slapping," "pushing," or "punching" under any circumstances.
Jaffe et al., 1992. Universal program of dating violence and woman abuse prevention. Single-session (minimum of 150 minutes) curriculum for flexible implementation in high-schools. Program also aims to provide information and training to teachers and administrators. Facilitators: Community service providers who lead classroom discussion attend a half-day training seminar and follow-up at 6-weeks.	Design: Intervention group only design (no control group). Stratified sampling by grade and program from 4 schools. Pre/post and follow-up at 6 weeks. Participants: 737 students (379 males & 358 females) in grades 9 to 12 from four high-schools in a mid-size city. Predominantly white. Intervention: A) Group Component: 90 minute presentation. Objectives include: defining abuse, addressing myths regarding wife assault, problems with gender-role stereotypes. Focus on protection skills and informing students about existing community resources for those in violent relationships. B) Class Component: 60 minute open format discussion as follow-up to group component. C) 2 schools implemented the above curriculum (half-day).	a) Attitudes, knowledge and behavioral intentions regarding relationship violence (self-report study-designed questionnaire).	1) At post-test, the majority of students (males & females) showed positive improvements in knowledge, attitudes and behavioral intentions, except for a small group of males who showed negative changes in attitudes, particularly for excuses regarding date rape.
Lavoie et al., 1995. Universal program of dating violence prevention. Two-session (minimum of 120-150 minutes) curriculum for flexible implementation in any high school classroom. Facilitators: Community service provider and volunteer trained by project staff.	Design: Comparative intervention design, 2-group, pre/post, 1-month follow-up. Schools randomly assigned to either short or long form. Participants: 517 10th grade students (295 females & 222 males) at suburban area Canadian high schools. Demographics unclear. Intervention: A) Short-form (N = 279): duration of 120-150 minutes over two classroom sessions. Discussion on themes of dominance and control, individual rights, ownership of responsibility, protection skills, and myths regarding dating violence. B) Long-form (N = 238): same as above plus an activity-based component with a movie about dating violence and a "letter" writing exercise (to a victim and a perpetrator).	a) Attitudes regarding violence & knowledge of relationship myths (study-designed questionnaire).	1) Improvement at post-test in attitudes for both males & females. 2) Improvement at post-test in knowledge, with students receiving the short-form showing the greatest improvement.

TABLE 1 (continued)

Program Description	Method	Target(s)	Results & Comments
Positive Adolescents Choices Training (Hammond & Yung, 1991). Interpersonal violence prevention program for African American youth: not limited to dating relationships. PACT is a school based structured program using a cognitive-behavioral approach for social-skills training. Implementation requires one semester of special classes for referred students. <u>Facilitators</u>: Doctoral graduate students in clinical psychology.	<u>Design</u>: 1 group (no control group), multiple assessment design. <u>Participants</u>: 28 students, aged 12 to 15, at an urban American middle-school. Predominantly African American (93%); lower-socioeconomic levels. <u>Intervention</u>; Small group format for 7 to 10 students. Process-oriented, interactive, activity and skill-based. For each target skill, desired behaviors are modelled through culturally sensitive videotaped vignettes. The participants practice observed behaviors through role-play and psychodrama. Activities are videotaped for participants to receive additional reinforcement for appropriate behaviors.	a) Social skills including: giving and receiving positive & negative feed-back, problem-solving, negotiation skills, and handling peer pressure (facilitator, teacher & youth ratings).	1) Of the 28 students who began training, only 15 (53%) completed the entire program: average attendance was 80.4%. 2) Improvements across all targeted skills (with an average gain of 27.4%), as rated by teachers and facilitators. 3) Participants self-rated improvement in all targeted social skills, except problem-solving. Greatest self-rated improvement in the skill of giving & receiving positive feedback. 4) Participants were less likely at post-program to be involved in violence-related behavior at school, as compared to non-participants.
The Safe Dates Project (Foshee et al., 1996). Universal and secondary prevention of dating violence among youth program.	<u>Design</u>: (School level) Intervention/control experimental design. Stratified sampling by grade from 14 schools (7 treatment and 7 control) random assignment of school to condition. Pre/post, follow-up 1-month, and 1-year post-program. <u>Participants</u>: 1965 8th and 9th grade students (975 males and 990 females) from rural area. Predominantly Caucasian (79.5%). <u>Intervention</u>: School intervention: Process-oriented, semi-structured, discussion and activity based. Discussion themes: relationship myths, power and control, defining healthy and abusive relationships, individual rights, ownership of responsibility, gender stereotyping, anger management, effective communication, conflict resolution and help-seeking for self or others in violent relationships (i.e., promoting the special services for youth provided at the community level). Activities include: role-playing exercises, student plays and poster contest.	a) Attitudes regarding dating violence norms and gender stereotypes (self-report). b) Conflict resolution skills (self-report). c) Help-seeking behaviors (self-report).	1) 1700 students completed post-test questionnaires. 2) Students in the intervention group reported less perpetration (sexual and nonsexual) than students in the control group. 3) No differences between control and intervention groups in reported victimization. 4) Students in the intervention group were less accepting of dating violence norms and gender stereotypes; reported using more constructive communication skills, and were more aware of community services.

Program Description	Method	Target(s)	Results & Comments
Youth Relationships Project (Wolfe et al., 1996). Universal and secondary prevention of dating violence. 18 session curriculum (each session 120 minutes) currently implemented as a weekly after school program. <u>Facilitators:</u> Community service providers who attend a two-day (12 hour) training seminar. All sessions led by one female and one male facilitator.	<u>Design:</u> Experimental design: Youth randomly assigned to either intervention or control group. Multiple assessments across intervention, follow-up to 2.5 years post-program. <u>Participants:</u> Study 1: Nonselected youth. Universal delivery of program to high-school youth (N = 90), age 14 to 16 (Wolfe et al., 1997). Study 2: Selected at-risk youth. YRP delivered to child protective custody youth (N = 58: 30 intervention, 28 control), age 14 to 16 with a history of maltreatment (Wekerle & Wolfe, 1998a). <u>Intervention:</u> Process-oriented, semi-structured, interactive, youth-focused action-learning strategy (activity and skill-based). Themes: power and control; myths about abuse; defining abuse; personal power & safety; individual rights; ownership of responsibility, and societal influences (e.g., sexism, gender socialization and media influences). Skill development: how to build healthy relationships; recognizing and responding to abuse in interpersonal relationships; communication and conflict resolution skills. Social action and help-seeking through visiting a social-service agency; developing and implementing a social-action project.	a) Negative attitudes regarding woman abuse. b) Negative and violent behavior in dating relationships. c) Communication and conflict-resolution skills. d) Help-seeking and social action skills.	<u>Study 1:</u> Intervention group showed positive improvement in attitudes and knowledge regarding dating relationships as compared to control group at post-test. <u>Study 2a;</u> Growth curves used to compare individuals in the intervention and control groups. A clinical rather than statistical trend ($p < .20$) was found for the intervention group in terms of a greater decline in the use of coercive tactics with a dating partner. <u>Study 2b;</u> A within-subject growth analysis found improvement over time for intervention group participants in terms of their motivation, interest and understanding of the program content, as rated by facilitators across the 18 weeks.

action. Table 2 provides a listing of program sections and weekly sessions. A male and female facilitate each group, and model positive relationship skills such as power sharing and positive communication. The program is interactive in nature, incorporating a number of activities, exercises, and role plays to help strengthen awareness and develop skills. Information is presented through discussion, guest speakers, videos, and print material. The social action component of the program involves learning how to locate and use community resources when in need. In addition, youth brainstorm and implement a social action project designed to promote awareness about woman abuse and dating violence, and raise funds for a local social service agency. Social action projects have included a march to city hall, mall displays, car washes, and creation of videos and posters.

TABLE 2. The Youth Relationships Project: Program Sections and Weekly Sessions[1]

SECTION A: VIOLENCE IN CLOSE RELATIONSHIPS: IT'S ALL ABOUT POWER

Session 1– Introduction to Group

Session 2– Power in Relationships: Explosions and Assertions

Session 3– Defining Relationship Violence: Power Abuses

SECTION B: BREAKING THE CYCLE OF VIOLENCE: WHAT WE CAN CHOOSE TO DO AND WHAT WE CAN CHOOSE NOT TO DO

Session 4– Defining Powerful Relationships: Equality, Empathy, and Emotional Expressiveness

Session 5– Defining Power Relationships: Assertiveness Instead of Aggressiveness

Session 6– Date Rape: Being Clear, Being Safe

SESSION C: THE CONTEXTS OF RELATIONSHIP VIOLENCE

Session 7– Date Rape and Learning How to Handle Dating Pressure

Session 8– Gender Socialization and Societal Pressure

Session 9– Choosing Partners and Sex-Role Stereotypes

Session 10– Sexism

Session 11– Media and Sexism

SECTION D: MAKING A DIFFERENCE: WORKING TOWARDS BREAKING THE CYCLE OF VIOLENCE

Session 12– Confronting Sexism and Violence Against Women

Session 13– Getting to Know Community Helpers for Relationship Violence

Session 14– Getting Out and About in the Community: Social Service Agencies

Session 15– Getting Out and About in the Community: Social Service Agencies

Session 16– Getting Out and About in the Community: Social Action to End Relationship Violence

Session 17– Getting Out and About in the Community: Social Action to End Relationship Violence

Session 18– Celebration!

[1]From the table of contents of the Youth Relationships Project Manual (Wolfe et al., 1996).

The YRP is designed specifically for youth who may be at greater risk for abuse in dating relationships because of prior maltreatment experiences, which is a risk factor for subsequent relationship violence (Wekerle & Wolfe, 1998a). Thus, youth are usually referred by Child Protective Services in conjunction with services related to their prior history of child maltreatment. Self-reported childhood maltreatment is measured using the Childhood Trauma Questionnaire (Bernstein & Fink, 1997). Table 3 presents a breakdown of the maltreatment experiences of a sample of 150 youth referred to the program (numbers add up to greater than 100% due to overlap). As shown, severe emotional

TABLE 3. Maltreatment Experiences of YRP Youth During Childhood

Amount of abuse	% reporting emotional abuse	% reporting physical abuse	% reporting sexual abuse	% reporting emotional neglect
None[1]	25	32.1		
Low	21.4	12.1	54.3	12.1
Moderate	15	15	22.9	8.6
Severe	38.6	40.7	22.9	79.3

Note: Based on responses to the Childhood Trauma Questionnaire (Bernstein & Fink, 1997).
[1]None reflects scores below the t-score cut off.

abuse, physical abuse, and emotional neglect are the most commonly reported forms of maltreatment, with a high percentage also reporting significant levels of low to moderate sexual abuse in their backgrounds. When beginning the YRP program, youth are either currently living with one or more family members (35%), in foster care (35%), in group homes (20%) or in some other arrangement including dating partner, parents of dating partner, other friend or self (10%).

Evaluation Design

The YRP is currently in its fourth year of a six-year evaluation. We have chosen to incorporate a true experimental design of random assignment by subject to a control or treatment condition. This is a multi-method evaluation including the use of questionnaires, interviews, videotaped observations, and audiotape coding. We also use a number of informants: self, dating partner, social worker, parent, same sex peer and group facilitators. Participants are assessed pre-, mid-, and post-group, as well as in a detailed follow-up schedule. Same-sex peers and dating partners who are willing to participate complete questionnaires regarding their relationships with the youth, and a videotaped interaction. Social workers from Child Protective Services complete forms regarding history of maltreatment and social competence. Parents (when available and possible) rate youth's social competence.

An outcome evaluation is being used to evaluate the following objectives regarding the YRP: (1) to evaluate growth in cognitive awareness of the foundations of abusive behavior and attitudes and beliefs about relationship violence, following a psychoeducational program designed to promote healthy, non-abusive relationships among high-risk male and female youths; (2) to evaluate growth in skills needed to help adolescents build healthy relationships, to recognize and respond to abuse in their own relationships and in relationships of their peers, and to increase competency through community involvement and social action; (3) to maintain expected gains over time, and evaluate whether (and if so, when) violence occurs, as well as the risk of violence occurring in each follow-up period spanning two years.

The follow-up protocol involves an intensive measurement strategy. Each youth from the treatment and control conditions agree to participate in the research program for a period of 2 1/2 years. During this time, teens are contacted by a research assistant on a monthly basis to update their address and similar information, and to determine if they are in a current dating relationship. Once a youth has been dating the same person for a one-month period, he or she is asked to invite that person to participate in the assessment aspect of the study. As long as the relationship continues, the youth and dating partner are asked to meet every other month with a research assistant to complete questionnaires, participate in an interview, and take part in a videotaped interaction. The interaction consists of a 10-minute discussion about things that they may disagree about in their relationship, with a goal of trying to find solutions for the problem. Although analysis of videotape interactions to measure abuse in adult relationships is fairly common (Jacobson et al., 1994), this method is fairly recent in studies of university (Follette & Alexander, 1992) and adolescent couples (Capaldi & Crosby, 1997). Videotape data captures correspondence or convergence between observed and reported aggression, communication, and conflict solving tactics. The videotapes provide data regarding skills that were developed in group, and the degree to which they are being used in the actual dating relationship. The purpose of the interview with the youth is to collect descriptive data about the current dating relationship, and to assess anger management strategies, the presence or absence of relationship abuse, and help-seeking behavior.

Process Evaluation

Facilitators evaluate the participants of the YRP program for level of interest and understanding shown. Group co-facilitators use a descriptive rating form to evaluate each participant's involvement and change in the program each week, using a 7-point scale (1 = lowest level of attainment; 7 = highest level of attainment). The four principle categories are: (1) the extent to which the participant made statements of prosocial support to another member; (2) the degree to which the participant attended to the material; (3) expression of negative attitudes and beliefs about relationship violence; and (4) cognitive understanding of the material. Interrater consistency is achieved through independent ratings by co-facilitators, followed by comparison and discussion of differences. Preliminary analyses of initial groups (N = 30) across the 18 weeks of the program indicated growth in several areas indicative of group process, such as self-expression skills, involvement and participation, listening, and interest and support given and received (Wekerle & Wolfe, 1998a).

Selection and Training of Facilitators

A common strategy for program evaluation involves assessed changes in attitudes and behaviors of the target subjects; however, the results may be misleading if knowledge of the delivery of the program is uncertain. Treatment fidelity is particularly important for programs such as the YRP, since it is offered in the community by persons experienced in service, but not research, procedures. Group facilitators are chosen on the basis of their experience with youth, and typically involve social workers and other community professionals. There are several qualities that we consider necessary for group facilitators: a good understanding and working knowledge of the causes and effects of woman abuse; an ability to work well in partnership with the co-facilitator, the teens in the group, and the project staff; ownership of one's social and personal power in the group and in the broader social context; a strong sense of personal safety skills, limits and boundaries; awareness of ways in which both verbal and nonverbal behaviors communicate messages to teenagers; and a willingness to give youth power and control in a group setting.

Facilitators are required to participate in a 2-day training seminar, whereby they are presented with the goals and philosophy of the YRP, tips and strategies about how to deal with issues and behaviors that may arise in group, and opportunities to practice implementing the exercises in the manual. In addition to the YRP program manual, a facilitator training manual has been developed. Exercises and information presented in the training seminar are included in this manual, which is made available to all participants.

To ensure that facilitators are delivering the YRP program in a uniform manner according to the goals and expectations of the YRP, sessions of the program are audiotaped. Permission is obtained from youth at the beginning of the program to tape each session for the purpose of evaluating the program delivery and content. Research assistants monitor the group process and provide support and assistance to the facilitators as needed. Research assistants evaluate the activities being conducted for comprehension and protocol (comprehension is defined as the extent to which the exercise is explained so that the teens comprehend the task; protocol is defined as the extent to which the facilitators follow the manual protocol). Coding sheets provide valuable information about the amount of the program that is delivered (i.e., any activities that may have been omitted or modified), and how well it has been delivered.

The YRP manual outlines the goals at the beginning of each session. Research assistants and facilitators independently evaluate how well they feel the goals have been met for each session. Representative data for three groups indicate that treatment fidelity by the facilitators are moderately high for comprehension ($r = .53-.78$), protocol ($r = .54-.70$), global impressions ($r = .92-.94$), and objectives ($r = .59-.71$). Overall fidelity assessment indicates treatment fidelity by facilitators ranges from .67 to .77 (Lavallee, 1996). Finally, youth are given the opportunity to evaluate the facilitators, structure and content of the program. Every 2nd week they complete brief questionnaires regarding how much they feel they have learned in the past couple of sessions in relation to specific content, such as the causes and effects of violence in relationships, and ways to communicate with another person more effectively. Opportunities to rate the program delivery and facilitators' styles are also anonymously provided.

FUTURE DIRECTIONS

Because dating violence research is relatively undeveloped, there are a number of definitions and terms to define and measures that need to be standardized for adolescent populations. Strategies that incorporate multi-method assessments and multiple informants will provide a clearer picture of dating relationships. Interviews that examine the context of violence in the relationship will further expand our understanding of its impact on adolescents and its significance for dating relationships. Research suggests that prevalence of violence in adolescent dating relationships underscores a need for these prevention programs, and that these programs should include both males and females (Gray & Foshee, 1997). Effective strategies are required to educate youth regarding the need for these programs to facilitate better voluntary participation. Since dating relationships among adolescents are not clearly defined and understood, it is difficult to determine when primary or secondary prevention programs are required, and who will benefit most.

Despite the limitations outlined, there are many positive advances being made to better understand adolescent dating violence. The development of new measures designed specifically for adolescents, and an increased number of prevention programs available for implementation and evaluation, provide an excellent opportunity for ongoing research that has the potential of breaking the cycle of violence in relationships.

REFERENCES

Avery-Leaf, S., Cascardi, M., O'Leary, K. D., & Cano, A. (1997). Efficacy of a dating violence prevention program on attitudes justifying aggression. *Journal of Adolescent Health, 21*, 11-17.

Bernstein, D. P., & Fink, L. (1997). Validity of the Childhood Trauma Questionnaire in an adolescent psychiatric population. *Journal of the American Academy of Child and Adolescent Psychiatry, 36* (3) 340-348.

Capaldi, D., Chamberlain, P., Fetrow, R., & Wilson, J. (1997). Conducting ecologically valid prevention research: Recruiting and retaining a "whole village" in multi method, multi agent studies. *American Journal of Community Psychology, 25* (4) 471-492.

Capaldi, D., & Crosby, L. (1997). Observed and reported psychological and physical aggression in young, at-risk couples. *Social Development, 6* (2) 184-206.

Carlson, B. E. (1990). Adolescent observers of marital violence. *Journal of Family Violence, 5*, 285-299.

Cicchetti, D., & Howes, P. W. (1991). Developmental psychopathology in the context of the family: Illustrations from the study of child maltreatment. *Canadian Journal of Behavioral Science, 23*, 257-281.

Crittenden, P. M., & Ainsworth, M. D. S. (1989). Child maltreatment and attachment theory. In D. Cicchetti & V. Carlson (Eds.), *Child maltreatment: Theory and research on the causes and consequences of child abuse and neglect* (pp. 432-463). Cambridge: Cambridge University Press.

Dodge, K. A., Bates, J. E., & Pettit, G. S. (1990). Mechanisms in the cycle of violence. *Science, 250*, 1678-1682.

Feiring, C. (1996). Concept of romance in 15 year old adolescents. *Journal of Research on Adolescence, 6* (2) 181-200.

Follette, V. M., & Alexander, P. C. (1992). Dating violence: Current and historical correlates. *Behavioral Assessment, 14*, 39-52.

Foo, L., & Margolin, G. (1995). A multivariate investigation of dating aggression. *Journal of Family Violence, 10*, 351-377.

Foshee, V. A. (1996). Gender differences in adolescent dating abuse prevalence, types, and injuries. *Health Education Research, 11*, 275-286.

Foshee, V. A., Linder, G. F., Bauman, K. E., Langwick, S. A., Arriaga, X. B., Heath, J. L., McMahon, P. M., & Bangdiwala, S. (1996). The Safe Dates Project: Theoretical basis, evaluation design, and selected baseline findings. *American Journal of Preventive Medicine, 12*, 39-47.

Gray, H. M., & Foshee, V. (1997). Adolescent dating violence: Differences between one-sided and mutually violent profiles. *Journal of Interpersonal Violence, 12*, 126-141.

Gregory, M. M., Lohr, M. J., & Gilchrist, L. D. (1992). Methods for tracking pregnant and parenting adolescents. *Evaluation Review, 17*, 69-81.

Hammond, W. R., & Yung, B. R. (1991). Preventing violence in at-risk African-American youth. *Journal of Health Care for Poor Underserved, 2*, 359-373.

Hanley, M. J., & O'Neill, P. (1997). Violence and commitment: A study of dating couples. *Journal of Interpersonal Violence, 12* (5) 685-703.

Jacobson, N. S., Gottman, J. M., Waltz, J., Rushe, R., Babcock, J., & Holtzworth-Munroe, A. (1994). Affect, verbal content, and psychophysiology in the arguments of couples with a violent husband. *Journal of Consulting and Clinical Psychology, 62*, 982-988.

Jaffe, P. J., Sudermann, M., & Reitzel, D. (1992). Working with children and adolescents to end the cycle of violence: A social learning approach to intervention and prevention programs. In R. DeV. Peters, R. J. McMahon, & V. L. Quinsey (Eds.), *Aggression and violence throughout the life span* (pp. 83-99). Newbury Park, CA: Sage.

Lavallee, J. (1996). *Co-facilitator adherence to protocol: A comprehensive approach to treatment fidelity.* Unpublished manuscript. Available from D. Wolfe, Dept. of Psychology, University of Western Ontario, London, Canada, N6A 5C2.

Lavoie, F., Vezina, L., Piche, C., & Boivin, M. (1995). Evaluation of a prevention program for violence in teen dating relationships. *Journal of Interpersonal Violence, 10*, 516-524.

Malamuth, N. M., Sockloskie, R. J., Koss, M. P., & Tanaka, J. S. (1991). Characteristics of aggressors against women: Testing a model using a national sample of college students. *Journal of Consulting and Clinical Psychology, 59*, 670-681.

Malik, S., Sorenson, S., & Aneshensel, C. (1997). Community and dating violence among adolescents: Perpetration and victimization. *Journal of Adolescent Health, 21*, 291-302.

Margolin, G., & Foo, L. (1992). *The Attitudes about Dating Scale.* Unpublished manuscript, Dept. of Psychology, University of Southern California.

Marx, B. P., Van Wie, V., & Gross, A. M. (1996). Date rape risk factors: A review and methodological critique of the literature. *Aggression and Violent Behavior, 1*, 27-45.

McDonald, D. L., & McKinney, J. P. (1994). Steady dating and self-esteem in high school students. *Journal of Adolescence, 17*, 557-564.

O'Keefe, M. (1997). Predictors of dating violence among high school students. *Journal of Interpersonal Violence, 12* (4) 546-568.

O'Keefe, M. (1998). Factors mediating the link between witnessing interparental violence and dating violence. *Journal of Family Violence, 13* (1) 39-57.

O'Leary, K. D., Malone, J., & Tyree, A. (1994). Physical aggression in early marriage: Prerelationship and relationship effects. *Journal of Consulting and Clinical Psychology, 62,* 594-602.

Parker, J. G., & Herrera, C. (1996). Interpersonal processes in friendship: A comparison of abused and nonabused children's experiences. *Journal of Consulting and Clinical Psychology, 32,* 1023-1038.

Pittman, A. L., Wolfe, D., & Wekerle, C. (1998). Prevention during adolescence: The Youth Relationships Project. In J. R. Lutzker (Ed.), *Handbook of child abuse research and treatment* (pp. 341-356). New York: Plenum.

Reitzel-Jaffe, D., & Wolfe, D. A. (Submitted). *Predictors of relationship abuse among young men.* Manuscript under review.

Rindskopf, D., & Saxe, L. (1998). Zero effects in substance abuse programs: Avoiding false positives and false negatives in the evaluation of community-based programs. *Evaluation Review, 22* (1) 78-94.

Sellers, C., Taylor, T. J., & Esbensen, F. A. (1998). Reality check: Evaluating a school-based gang prevention model. *Evaluation Review, 22* (5) 590-608.

Shapiro, J. P., Baumeister, R. F., & Kessler, J. W. (1991). A three-component model of children's teasing: Aggression, humor, and ambiguity. *Journal of Social and Clinical Psychology, 10,* 459-472.

Smith, J. P., & Williams, J. G. (1992). From abusive household to dating violence. *Journal of Family Violence, 2,* 153-165.

Sroufe, L. A. (1989). Pathways to adaptation and maladaptation: Psychopathology as developmental deviation. In D. Cicchetti (Ed.), *Rochester Symposium on Developmental Psychopathology, Vol I: The emergence of a discipline* (pp. 13-40). Hillsdale, NJ: Erlbaum.

Straus, M. A. (1979). Measuring intrafamily conflict and violence: The Conflict Tactics (CT) scales. *Journal of Marriage and the Family, 41,* 75-88.

Sudermann, M., & Jaffe, P. G. (1993, August). *Dating violence among a sample of 1,567 high school students.* Paper presented at the annual meeting of the American Psychological Association, Toronto.

Tolan, P. H., & Brown, H. (1998). Evaluation research on violence interventions: Issues and strategies for design. In P. K. Trickett & C. Schellenbach (Eds.), *Violence against children in the family and the community* (pp. 439-464). Washington, DC: American Psychological Association.

Tontodonato, P., & Crew, B. K. (1992). Dating violence, social learning theory, and gender: A multivariate analysis. *Violence and Victims, 7,* 3-14.

Walker, L. E. A. (1989). Psychology and violence against women. *American Psychologist, 44,* 695-702.

Wekerle, C., & Wolfe, D. A. (1998a). Windows for preventing child and partner abuse: Early childhood and adolescence. In P. K. Trickett & C. Schellenbach (Eds.), *Violence against children in the family and the community* (pp. 339-370). Washington, DC: American Psychological Association.

Wekerle, C., & Wolfe, D. A. (1998b). The role of child maltreatment and attachment style in adolescent relationship violence. *Development and Psychopathology, 10,* 571-586.

Wekerle, C., & Wolfe, D. A. (1999). Dating violence in mid-adolescence: Theory, significance, and emerging prevention initiatives. *Clinical Psychology Review, 19,* 435-456.

Wolfe, D. A., & McGee, R. (1994). Dimensions of child maltreatment and their relationship to adolescent adjustment. *Development and Psychopathology, 6,* 165-181.

Wolfe, D. A., Wekerle, C., Gough, R., Reitzel-Jaffe, D., Grasley, C., Pittman, A., & Stumpf, J. (1996). *Youth Relationships Manual: A group approach with adolescents for the prevention of woman abuse and the promotion of healthy relationships.* Thousand Oaks, CA: Sage.

Wolfe, D. A., Wekerle, C., Reitzel-Jaffe, D., Grasley, C., Pittman, A., & McEachran, A. (1997). Interrupting the cycle of violence: Empowering youth to promote healthy relationships. In D. Wolfe, R. McMahon, & R. DeV. Peters (Eds.), *Child abuse: New directions in prevention and treatment across the lifespan* (pp. 102-129). Thousand Oaks: Sage.

Wolfe, D. A., Wekerle, C., Reitzel-Jaffe, D., & Lefebvre, L. (1998). Factors associated with abusive relationships among maltreated and non-maltreated youth. *Development and Psychopathology, 10,* 61-85.

Wolfe, D., Wekerle, C., Scott, K., Grasley, C., & Pittman, A. (1998, July). *A self-report measure for adolescent dating violence.* Paper presented at the Program Evaluation and Family Violence Research Conference, Durham, NH.

Wolfe, D. A., Scott, K., Reitzel-Jaffe, D., Wekerle, C., Grasley, C., & Pittman, A. (submitted). *Development and validation of the conflict in adolescent dating relationships inventory.* Manuscript under review.

COLLABORATION
AND ACTIVIST ISSUES

Community Collaboration
to Develop Research Programs
in Partner Violence

L. Kevin Hamberger
Bruce Ambuel

SUMMARY. Effective research and intervention into family violence require interdisciplinary collaboration between professionals in traditional research settings and grass-roots community leaders and advocates. Such interdisciplinary collaboration is frequently difficult. We identify a number of potential barriers to effective collaboration between academic researchers, community agencies and grass roots activists. These include (a) different professional identities, values, world views and motivations for working in the field, (b) social status related to formal degree status vs. lived experience, (c) economic resources,

Address correspondence to: L. Kevin Hamberger, PhD, Racine Family Practice Center, P.O. Box 548, Racine, WI 53401-0548.

[Haworth co-indexing entry note]: "Community Collaboration to Develop Research Programs in Partner Violence." Hamberger, L. Kevin, and Bruce Ambuel. Co-published simultaneously in *Journal of Aggression, Maltreatment & Trauma* (The Haworth Maltreatment & Trauma Press, an imprint of The Haworth Press, Inc.) Vol. 4, No. 1 (#7), 2000, pp. 239-272; and: *Program Evaluation and Family Violence Research* (ed: Sally K. Ward, and David Finkelhor) The Haworth Maltreatment & Trauma Press, an imprint of The Haworth Press, Inc., 2000, pp. 239-272. Single or multiple copies of this article are available for a fee from The Haworth Document Delivery Service [1-800-342-9678, 9:00 a.m. - 5:00 p.m. (EST). E-mail address: getinfo@haworthpressinc.com].

(d) gender, (e) race, (f) ownership of the field and data, and (g) being an unknown quantity. Strategies for overcoming these barriers are described and discussed. Examples of both successful and unsuccessful collaborative efforts illustrate key points. *[Article copies available for a fee from The Haworth Document Delivery Service: 1-800-342-9678. E-mail address: <getinfo@haworthpressinc.com> Website: <http://www.HaworthPress.com>]*

KEYWORDS. Domestic violence, social action research, program evaluation, applied research, community-based research, academic-community partnerships

In concept, it seems as though a natural alliance exists between researchers and community advocates for studying, intervening and evaluating intervention programs to end partner violence. After all, partner violence is by now understood and accepted as a major social problem. Grass-roots advocates and community organizations are actively working to alleviate and prevent partner violence. At the same time researchers are attempting to identify the origins of partner violence as well as the effectiveness of intervention and prevention programs. Researchers disseminate their results so as to facilitate and enable front-line workers to better serve their clientele. In addition, both front-line, community-based workers and researchers often disseminate their work with the goal of informing public policy by educating policymakers and legislators. However, this natural convergence of common interests does not necessarily pave the way for ready collaboration between advocates and researchers.

To begin a discussion of collaboration between researchers and community groups in the area of partner violence, it is necessary to describe the modern historical context in which these collaborative efforts are taking place. The modern elucidation of violence against women as a social problem is credited largely to the emergence of feminism and the women's movement during the 1960s and 1970s. Prior to this time, violence against women in intimate relationships was often discounted, minimized and ignored by the dominant social institutions. As the women's movement identified partner violence as one significant facet of male domination of women in a hierarchical, male dominated and sexist society, feminists began organizing a systematic response to partner violence. The first shelter for battered women in the United States opened its doors in Pasadena, California, in 1964 (Barnett, Miller-Perrin, & Perrin, 1997).

According to Martin (1985), early initiatives to assist battered women and raise the issue to a sociopolitical level of analysis were largely grass-roots, local efforts organized by women to help other women in their local community. Workers in the field were typically women who had experienced violence and oppression themselves. Peer counselors provided help, and support groups were styled on a self-help model. Similar local initiatives occurred throughout the country. A sense of sisterhood pervaded both the larger movement and local battered women's programs. These local efforts were often opposed directly or indirectly by traditional social and political systems, including the criminal justice, social service and health care sectors. In addition, mainline social scientists largely ignored violence against women. Activists rejected poorly developed social science theories of causation and treatment in favor of a feminist analysis of the problem.

Martin (1985) also points out that, in early efforts to reach out to governmental sources of funding, many battered women's programs were very reluctant to develop traditional (and often required) hierarchical organizational structures such as having an executive director and board of directors. Over time, a broad coalition of battered women's programs emerged to form lobbying groups that worked to influence funding, policy and legislation at local, state, and national levels. Because of their political struggle, and because of the ubiquitous nature of violence against women in intimate relationships, and its connection with broader issues of oppression of women in society (Barnett et al., 1997; Martin, 1985), advocates began to change social institutions and public attitudes. At both local and national levels (Attorney General's Task Force on Family Violence, 1984; Soler, 1987), advocates helped develop law enforcement and judicial policies designed to protect battered women and hold perpetrators accountable for the crime of partner assault. During the 1980s the movement to help battered women evolved from a united but marginalized movement to assist battered and oppressed women, to a movement actively involved with policymakers, legislators and key community stakeholders working to change community and societal norms regarding violence against women. During this time, efforts to stop partner violence adopted a community response model that involves many collaborative partners, with the battered women's program at the center. These community partners represent diverse agencies and professional groups, including criminal justice, law enforcement, corrections, social services, legislation, clergy, education, batterer treatment and, more recently, medicine and health care.

Two themes emerge from the literature on coordinated community responses to end partner violence; these collaborative efforts can be problematic (Martin, 1985) but also have great value. For example, Ganley (1987) provided a detailed description of the importance of collaboration between batterer treatment providers, the courts, and corrections to effectively assist perpetrators and enhance safety for battered women. Ganley pointed out the pitfalls and dangers of collaboration, particularly around the issues of setting expectations, establishing professional boundaries, and communicating among disciplines. More recently, Edleson and Tolman (1992) described systems-level interventions for holding abusers accountable and protecting battered women. The goal of such interventions is to ensure that the system, or community, acts in such a way as to protect battered women, not discriminate against them, and behave consistently in responding to prevent and intervene into partner violence.

When researchers began working to understand and address the problem of partner violence, as collaborative partners, they frequently had difficulty fitting in. Reasons for this difficulty have been elucidated by a number of authors. Schechter (1982) pointed out that scientific theories of causes of partner violence frequently provided inconsistent reasons for why men abused their partners, and frequently failed to explain why men seemed to direct their violence only toward their female partners. Martin (1985) pointed out that many theories of partner violence implicitly placed responsibility for the violence with the victim. Barnett et al. (1997) provide a brief summary of how some early research on battered women and partner violence may have actually contributed to misunderstanding about the causes and consequences of partner violence. Examples cited include: (a) the battered woman having a masochistic personality, (b) perpetrators batter because of aberrant personalities, (c) alcohol and drug abuse causes partner violence, (d) partner violence being viewed as rare. Martin (1987) provided a historical analysis of the development of a "male psychology" of violence against women that relegated female reports of early victimization to the status of fantasy, and women's victimization as stemming from masochism. Further, women's behavior and characteristics were objectified and measured in terms of masculine concepts.

Within such models, female victims of male violence were conceptualized as provocateurs.

A series of scholarly presentations at the Third National Family Violence Research Conference, held in 1987, provided a further critique of how the scientific method was being applied to study partner violence. A number of workers criticized traditional scientific models as hierarchical (Fine, 1987a; Hoff, 1987), and possessing an inherent bias, despite claims of objectivity (Hoff, 1987; Yllo, 1987). In addition, Dobash and Dobash (1987, July) provided an analysis that suggested that the way a researcher and "expert" in family violence has been influenced by various sources, including demands of the community and the battered women's movement, will influence how research questions are conceptualized, designed, answered and interpreted. Hence, objectivity is always shaped by the experiences of the researcher and influenced in many ways by subtle and, at times, mechanisms and biases not apparent to the researcher. Fine (1987b) further stated that much so-called objective research disempowers, victimizes and oppresses women. Another problem identified by Fine (1987b) is that researchers have frequently used battered women's programs to collect data, and then left the scene, without ever presenting their findings in such a way that the lives of battered women were made better. In addition, Fine (1987b) recounted case accounts of how data collected by battered women's programs and provided to researchers for analysis was actually taken over by the researchers, with the program disenfranchised from the research, analytic, interpretation, and publication process.

Although the picture appeared bleak for researchers to develop successful collaborations with community groups for research and program evaluation projects, efforts were being made to identify factors that could both obstruct and facilitate collaborative efforts. Sonkin (1988) identified several empirical knowledge gaps in the field of working with male batterers, and recommended that greater effort be made between and by service providers and scientists to identify areas of collaboration to answer them. Contrary to the apparent antagonism between researchers and service providers noted above, Dutton (1988) addressed areas of mutual learning and informing that can occur between the two disciplines. Dutton suggested that such collaboration, while humbling for the researcher, can result in research that is relevant, and not driven by methodology as much as by mutually identified needs. At the same time, researchers can benefit service providers by providing data to support or disconfirm long-held theories, some of which may be erroneous. This overall process of different disciplines learning from each other in a collaborative fashion can lead to a wider variety of testable models.

Gondolf, Yllo, and Campbell (1997) acknowledged that researchers and community workers come from different professional cultures, with different languages and, sometimes, different values and orientations toward the issue of partner violence. They emphasized the importance of developing consensus about research priorities, and ongoing communication related to all aspects of a collaborative project. They described reciprocal and mutual communication between researchers and community collaborative partners that lead to developing scientifically sound, relevant and appropriate research projects.

The purpose of the present paper is to extend the optimism of Gondolf et al. (1997) for the prospects of researchers and grass-roots community activists developing effective collaborative relationships for conducting research on partner violence. We begin by presenting a framework for understanding partner violence research as an example of social action research. We then describe and discuss a number of barriers to collaboration. We have identified these barriers from the literature as well as our own experience conducting partner violence research and program evaluation with community groups for a number of years. For each of the barriers identified, case examples illustrate important points. We then present proactive strategies for enhancing collaboration and overcoming barriers. Case examples illustrate key points of application.

SOCIAL ACTION RESEARCH AS A FRAMEWORK

Collaboration between researchers interested in the design and evaluation of domestic violence interventions and grass-roots advocates in the women's movement is an example of social action research which has a history in psychology dating back to Lewin (1946). Social action research "aims to contribute both to the practical concerns of people in an immediately problematic situation and to the goals of social sciences by joint collaboration within a mutually acceptable ethical framework" (Rappaport, 1985, p. 9). Lewin was a pioneer in establishing an early framework for understanding the process of action research. Action research follows a cyclic process beginning with careful observation, proceeding to theory building, then to program design and informed action, culminating in program evaluation. Information gathered during the evaluation phase provides both new theoretical insights as well as practical guidance to those attempting to solve the social problem of interest. The cycle begins anew with another round of observation and theory building. Action research has unique characteristics, which distinguish it from social science research in general and give it a more narrow focus. The goal of social science research is to enhance our understanding of social and psychological processes by developing and testing theories. Research is often experimental and the desired outcome is often a theoretical understanding that is generalizable to many settings. This goal is achieved through research that describes natural phenomena, states and tests hypotheses, or demonstrates prediction and control. In contrast, the goal of action research is engineering social change by developing theory-based interventions, implementing the interventions, assessing the outcome, and enhancing future change efforts. Action research is often quasi-experimental. Results are used to guide decision-making and policy development in a specific context. For this reason, action researchers often place a higher priority upon the successful, local application of results than upon developing theories that are generalizable in other settings.

Lewin (1946) identified another important distinction between action research and other social science research. Action researchers apply understanding of group dynamics to facilitate an effective partnership between scientist and activist. In other words, in action research both the process of collaboration and the identified content are objects of study. Action researchers apply psychological knowledge and theory to enhance the process of collaboration as well as to understand the intervention.

What is the appropriate partnership between scientist and activist? This remains a fundamental issue in action research today. There are various models of action research (see Table 1). These models differ in:

1. the value placed upon maintaining a separation between researcher and activist vs. asking the researcher to actively participate in the activist's community.
2. the goals of conducting action research.

3. the extent to which the researcher and activist share control over the process of theory building, problem definition and research design.

At one end of this spectrum is the *researcher-centric model* where the researcher views himself or herself as an objective observer of external social phenomena. The researcher controls theory, problem definition and the methods of study. The activist and activist organiza-

TABLE 1. Various Models of Action Research Differ in the Relationship Between Researcher and Activist

Model	Relationship of scientist & activist	Rationale & goals for action research	Process of theory building, problem definition and study design
Researcher-centric	An objective observer of activist and activist's organizational environment	Understand the activist and activist's environment as natural phenomenon	Researcher defines problems of interest and controls design.
Consultation & organizational development	An advisor with expertise in enhancing an organization	Fine-tune the activist and activist organization to function better	Researcher and activist define problems in the context of enhancing the organization's capacity to solve problems.
Community organizing and social advocacy	An advisor with expertise in community change	Change the social and political environment that surround the activist and activist organization	Scientist and activist collaborate in defining problems that lie outside the activist's organization in political society.
Creating new settings	An advisor with expertise in creating new community settings	Create new settings and institutions that prevent the occurrence of the social problem through primary prevention	The creation of sustaining community settings replaces a focus upon problems. Scientist and activist collaborate in creation.
Participatory action research Empowerment research	A fellow human being who forms a partnership with the activist to learn from each other	Create a learning community with the capacity to identify and solve problems, practice primary prevention and celebrate and mobilize strengths and resources	There is a primary focus upon empowering the activist, researcher and citizen by mobilizing strengths and resources. When problems are addressed, all participants share control of problem definition.

tion represents a context or natural experiment that the researcher selects as a focus of study. Our study of battered women's experience with physicians (Hamberger, Ambuel, Marbella, & Donze, 1998) represents one example of the researcher-centric model. In this study, we examined battered women's self-report of past experiences with physicians. Participants were recruited from the women's shelters and other advocacy agencies. In designing the study we developed the key research questions, and the study goal was understanding women's interactions with physicians. Activists who collaborated in this study provided feedback that facilitated the survey design, and recruited participants. There were no direct or proximal benefits for the activists or the activist organizations that assisted us. Instead, benefits were indirect and distal. The results of the study would shed new light upon battered women's experiences in the health care system.

In the *consultation and community development* model, the researcher remains an expert who is external to the phenomenon of study. The activist plays a role in defining the problem and selecting methods of study, while the researcher brings a theoretical framework and research methods from the field of organizational evaluation. We used this model of action research recently when approached by a local social service agency to assist them in evaluating their batterers' treatment program. The agency had specific questions, "How do we document effectiveness to United Way and the county district attorney's office? How do we improve our effectiveness?" Beginning with these questions provided by the agency, we provided a theoretical action-research framework to define the process, and jointly selected or created research measures. Although the resulting research lacked the rigor of a clinical trial, the collaboration met important agency needs including improving data gathering by the agency, creating more uniformity among therapists regarding the goals of treatment, and increasing therapist investment in program enhancement.

In the *community organizing and advocacy model* the scientist continues in the role of an outside expert, but the scientist and activist collaborate in identifying social problems addressing these via new programs, social and political change strategies. Hamberger's series of studies of batterers' treatment programs are an example of the community organizing model. Hamberger initiated his work on batterers' treatment after developing a treatment program in a community that had no existing program. He therefore began his work as a community activist with the goal of creating a new treatment resource to address a pressing social problem. Although working as an activist in creating the program, Hamberger also played a role as a social scientist by designing the treatment program from a theoretical framework and building in scientific measures. Hamberger also recruited two social scientists as scientific collaborators in this work to describe perpetrator characteristics, assess treatment outcome, and predictors of treatment outcome (e.g., Hamberger & Hastings, 1986, 1988, 1990, 1991; Hamberger & Lohr, 1989; Hamberger, Lohr, Bonge, & Tolin, 1996).

The *creating new settings model* focuses the researcher and activist upon the task of building new, positive settings that will prevent the problem(s) of concern. In this model the researcher and activist may collaborate closely in defining, then constructing, new settings that build the strengths and capacities of people. Exemplifying this approach in the area of family violence are studies that employ home visitation and advocacy by nurses on behalf of young, new parents who are "at risk" for family violence. The new setting created in this program is the interpersonal relationship with the nurse-advocate, and the extended social network that results from the nurse-client collaboration (Chalk & King, 1998).

Anchoring the opposite end of this continuum are participatory action research (Brydon-Miller, 1997; Lykes, 1997) and empowerment research (Perkins & Zimmerman, 1995; Zimmerman, 1995). In both the *participatory action research model* and *empowerment research model* the researcher joins and participates with the activist's community. In these models, the researcher and activist collaborate to co-create a learning community that draws upon the unique skills and knowledge of each participant. Both theoretical models explicitly call for shared power so that problem definition, research and intervention methods are selected collaboratively. The process of conducting participatory or empowerment action research, transforms both the researcher and the activist.

Both the domestic violence researcher and activist will want to be cognizant of the diverse models of action research as they seek to develop an effective partnership. These varied approaches each have unique strengths and limitations. Because of the history of partner violence as a social problem discussed previously, collaboration between researcher and activist will often be facilitated by those models that allow for mutuality in defining research goals, theory building and research design. When the researcher adopts a model that is less mutual, for example the researcher-centric model, the researcher bears more responsibility for discussing benefits and disadvantages of the study for the agency and for the participants.

BARRIERS TO COLLABORATION

As can be seen from the above discussion, interdisciplinary and interagency collaboration to conduct partner violence research is a complex, sometimes arduous, undertaking. The researcher will face multiple decisions. This complexity suggests that the researcher apply a systematic approach when developing a collaborative relationship. Attempting consensus to define a research question, develop a scientifically sound methodology that does no harm to research participants, while generating useful and meaningful data for the research and activist community, requires the coordination of multiple agencies with differing agendas. These agencies often represent multiple disciplines and widely divergent experiences with partner violence among individual stakeholders. As such, there are many opportunities for collaborative efforts to be threatened or, in the extreme, to fail. Some of these factors are fairly obvious while others can be quite subtle. We have identified seven factors that can impede and even derail efforts at effective collaboration between researchers and community agencies and workers to study partner violence. These include (a) differing professional identities, (b) differing social status, (c) differing economic status, (d) gender, (e) race, (f) ownership of the field and data, (g) new kid on the block. These barriers do not necessarily operate in isolation. That is, many of these variables, such as gender, race and socioeconomic status, may co-occur. We separate them in this article for purposes of discussion and analysis.

Differing professional identities. The would-be collaborative researcher needs to be sensitive to differences in professional identity between themselves and potential collaborative partners. For example, researchers are trained to think and proceed methodically and dispassionately, even if they have strong feelings about the issue being studied. The dispassionate approach often asks the researcher to set aside her or his own views or opinions on a subject, in favor of observable data trends and statistical differences between groups. This provides a level of objectivity that supposedly reduces the impact of personal values and opinions and requires focus on the data.

Researchers have been chosen for their profession through a long series of highly competitive winnowing exercises such as entrance exam scores, grade point averages, production of intellectual, academic products, ability to analyze and assess data, and ability to design and execute research projects, first under supervision and then independently. Through this winnowing process, researchers are rewarded for their ability to assess current state-of-the-art levels of knowledge in a given area, provide appropriate critiques of current knowledge, and develop recommendations for future directions in research. They are further rewarded for their ability to think and act more quickly than their colleagues in designing and producing the latest, cutting edge research and scholarship. This competitive approach may impede developing effective collaborative relationships.

Another aspect of the professional identity of the researcher is that the researcher is trained in social science research, per se, not necessarily partner violence. Methodology learned for application in one area may be transferable to research in partner violence. For some researchers, investigation of partner violence issues may be part of a heartfelt need to understand a difficult social problem and to make the lives of victims safe, while holding perpetrators accountable. For other researchers, study of partner violence may be their research *de jour* because of funding possibilities. Others, still, may initiate partner violence research as part of a job assignment.

Advocates and other frontline workers in the field of partner violence are often extremely passionate about their work. As we have discussed, the field has evolved from the grass roots level. Such individuals and agencies have often faced and overcome significant community opposition, while receiving little support from traditional community systems. For some activists, fierce community opposition or indifference has come from the very institutions that employ researchers who are now seeking a collaborative partnership. Many programs began and continued on the sheer determination of the few women who believed in the righteousness of their cause. Many workers in battered women's programs are survivors of partner violence themselves. As noted by Martin (1985), the primary training and "credentials" of many women who started shelters and other programs for battered women occurred in the feminist movement and in the home.

This suggests that the knowledge base of advocates and other frontline workers is based more on lived reality, both in one's personal life and in the lives and stories of the myriad victims seen, who have been brutalized by their partners. These women have often experienced re-victimization by the system and professionals that are supposed to help them. Representatives of this system are frequently highly educated individuals, with advanced degrees, as attorneys, clergy persons, physicians, and psychotherapists. Hence, professional status of someone seeking entrée into a battered women's program, or a batterers' treatment program, for that matter, may be viewed as a liability more than as a credential. For those professional researchers who truly wish to collaborate with frontline workers, awareness of these differences in professional identity will be important to consider, if not overtly address.

Social status formal degree vs. lived experience. A related issue to that of professional identity is that of social status conferred by professional degrees. Within our society, possessing an advanced degree such as a PhD or MD often carries considerable prestige, and all the accompanying accoutrements. Examples of such perks include relatively easy access to other professionals and influential stakeholders, such as the district attorney, police chief, and judge or business leaders. Such an individual may also be accustomed to talking to the public, and as a result may be an attractive subject for a media interview, thus increasing their visibility. The professional with the advanced degree probably lives a solid middle-class lifestyle. This individual may never have had personal contact with a battered woman, yet may be widely recognized for the publication of a study on family violence.

In contrast, a formerly battered woman who answers the phone between midnight and 7:00 a.m. for five dollars per hour may have little more than a high school education. Prior to this job, she may have spent years planning escape from a violent relationship. She may have received no help for her efforts from any professional. Her only contact with the police may have been when she called for protection from her abusive partner. No therapist provided her with advocacy services and safety planning. She may never have made a public statement about battering, and may shake with anxiety at the prospect of speaking up at a public forum on the topic. Although her late night efforts to aid battered women in crisis may have made a greater impact on stopping domestic violence in her community than any single research project, she may never receive any recognition for her efforts. On the other hand, other community activists may recognize and value her informal credentials more highly than a researcher's formal degree.

Another facet of social status involves differences between researchers and research participants. Researchers may, minimally, possess a Masters degree and, in many instances, hold a doctoral degree. However, it is not uncommon for research participants in such research to have barely completed high school. A recent example of this from our laboratory is a survey study of battered women's experiences with physicians (Hamberger et al., 1998). The principal investigators hold doctoral degrees. The other investigators hold masters and baccalaureate degrees. In contrast, participant educational status ranged from less than high school (23%) to high school diploma (32%). Thirty-five percent completed some college and only 10% completed college. No participants held an advanced degree. We have observed similar patterns in studies with men who batter their partners, as well (e.g., Hamberger et al., 1996). In the latter study, out of 833 male batterers studied, only 10 identified themselves as college graduates.

One of us (BA) experienced a poignant example of the distinction between formal degree status and lived experience when he met with a focus group of survivors of domestic violence to gain their input in designing a training program for health care professionals (Ambuel, Hamberger, & Lahti, 1997). To begin the meeting the researcher introduced himself by describing his professional credentials much as one would do before an audience of professionals. Each of the women then introduced herself by stating her first name and describing the types of abuse she had experienced. These brief, personal introductions conveyed tremendous power and drew a clear contrast between academic experience and lived experience as distinct ways of knowing about the world.

The implications of these differences relate to informed consent to participate in research projects, as well as methodology. With respect to informed consent, although, ultimately a potential research participant is free to choose whether or not to, say, complete a survey, one must be cognizant of the power and prestige related to differential educational levels as denoted by formal degree status. Individuals with less education, struggling under the oppression of abuse or a coercive court system, may be especially vulnerable to the persuasiveness of a highly-educated researcher to participate in a study. In turn, such participation may provide little or no direct benefit to the participant, and result in immense benefit to the researcher. Community programs are often sensitive to these disparities, and seek to protect their clients from possible exploitation. With respect to methodology, researchers may write survey materials or research protocol instructions that are not sensitive to typical reading levels of prospective research participants. However, research participants may not seek clarification of words or instructions they may not understand, thus adversely affecting validity. In addition, researchers are highly trained to think in terms of theory and methodology. Scientific skepticism and doubt are highly valued within the community of researchers. Such methods of communicating may be foreign to frontline workers, who may see themselves as dealing more in "reality" than in theory. Scientific skepticism, spoken in negative tones, can appear off-putting to a listener untrained in such thought and language.

Economic resources of individuals and organizations. Professional researchers, by virtue of their training, prestige, and professional jobs, typically earn an upper-middle-level income and work for institutions with significant financial resources. In contrast, many frontline workers earn little more than minimum wage. Even the wage scales for administrators in community non-profit agencies are also often significantly below research institutions. These differences are accompanied by a wide range of other differences, including purchasing power for material goods, child care, health care, housing, to name a few. In the work setting, professional researchers may have reasonably well-appointed offices which they share with no one. Shelter settings are often older buildings that have been modified for the purposes they serve. Room is often scarce; several workers may occupy the same, small office. Privacy is valued, but often limited in such settings. Things that a researcher may take for granted, such as little accountability for use of office supplies, telephones, and computers, may be highly controlled due to fiscal restrictions in shelter or other community-based settings.

Even in those cases when a researcher does not have grant support or work for a financially flush institution, there may still be a perception of socioeconomic disparity. Hence, a researcher who requests a shelter program to provide copying and duplication of survey instruments may be viewed as insensitive to the fiscal constraints placed upon the agency. Asking that shelter staff provide data collection services without offering to pay the shelter for the employee time, or make some other type of compensation, may further communicate such insensitivity. Insult may be added to injury through casual and indiscriminate conversation about matters of personal socioeconomic benefit that may not be available to one's community collaborative partners. As one of our doctoral colleagues was kindly, but firmly, told once by an advocate when complaining about pay raises: "Considering the difference in your salary versus mine, don't expect any sympathy here."

Gender. Given the feminist roots of the field of partner violence (Martin, 1985, 1987; Schechter, 1982), and the fact that women are the primary victims of partner violence in heterosexual relationships (Pagelow, 1984), it should not be surprising that male researchers, even those with sincere motivations, may be viewed with suspicion, at least initially. But the issue extends beyond male sex, per se. As argued by Fine (1987a) and others (e.g., Martin, 1985, 1987), academic research, as with most things in Western society, is a hierarchical institution, rooted in the patriarchy. Hence, "objective" research is viewed as biased and failing to account for the richness of the stories and lived realities of battered and oppressed women. As such, traditional research is often viewed as a male phenomenon that, at best, has been and continues to be unhelpful to abused women and, at worst, functions to maintain oppression of abused women. The problem, from this point of view, lies both in the methodology and in the questions asked. For example, objections have been raised to studying violence by women against their male partners. Some scholars have criticized such research as ignoring the context of women's violence, which may include self-defense (Saunders, 1986), or may exaggerate the seriousness of the phenomenon, and ignore the broader, more pervasive problem of violence and oppression of women (Kurz, 1993).

In research on abusive men, study of characteristics of such men has been criticized as "psychopathologizing" and privatizing abuse, diverting attention from the sociopolitical nature of the problem of men's violence toward women (Adams, 1988). Finally, given that the history of the battered women's movement is "women helping women" (Martin, 1985, p. 4), the appearance of male researchers poses several potential threats, including co-opting the field, using the field for personal, professional gain, and lack of commitment to the movement beyond such personal gain.

Race. As with gender, race pervades many aspects of collaborative efforts to conduct partner violence research with community groups. Hart (1987) pointed out that consideration of race and racism in the study of partner violence actually constitutes an ethical imperative. Seiber and Stanley (1988), in their examination of ethical and professional issues in socially sensitive research, point out that research studies that have potential implications for either the research participants or a class of individuals represented by the research pose particularly complex ethical issues for researchers. Particularly, Scarr (1988) states that when investigating variables such as gender or race, researchers bear a responsibility to consider the most likely, proximal uses of the results. Researchers, in such a situation, are also expected to explain their stance on the major issues related to their research, and to spell out their interpretation of the results. In this regard, race, like gender, is an important issue in partner violence research. First, members of minority groups have experienced oppression and discrimination. Research that does not take these factors into account may further harm members of such groups. Researchers have not always been sensitive to how their research questions, methodologies and results may affect and reinforce racial stereotypes and oppression. For example, Williams and Becker (1994) point out that research on batterer treatment outcome studies fairly consistently shows that white participants tend to have more successful outcomes than black participants. Without sensitivity to issues of race in such studies, one could conclude, erroneously, that black perpetrators should not be offered treatment options. For those men in the criminal justice system, this could result in a higher rate of incarceration among black men who have assaulted a partner in comparison with white counterparts. Hamberger and Hastings (1989) observed that black partner abusers showed higher attrition rates than their white counterparts. After examining the findings in light of the broader literature on racial factors in treatment attrition, the authors observed that programs that exhibited large imbalances of racial groups typically exhibited disproportionate dropout among the less-represented group, regardless of race. Subsequently, the abuse abatement treatment program worked deliberately to achieve greater racial balance in the composition of treatment groups.

Another treatment attrition study conducted several years later (Hamberger, Lohr, & Gottlieb, in press) found no differences in treatment dropout related to participant racial identity.

In a review of the literature on demographic characteristics of violent perpetrators, Hastings and Hamberger (1997) cautioned that while race often emerges as a correlate of violent behavior, it is often confounded with other variables such as socioeconomic status, age and education level. In a related area, the literature on personality pathology consistently shows that black respondents exhibit profiles indicative of psychopathology, cynicism, alienation and lack of trust (e.g., Gynther, 1981; Ingram, Marchioni, Hill, Caraveo-Ramos, & McNeil, 1985). Likewise, Hamberger and Hastings (1992) observed similar racial differences among men participating in spouse abuse abatement counseling. An uninformed interpretation of such findings could be that black men exhibit greater personality pathology than white men. However, an appropriate interpretation of such findings takes into consideration the adaptive nature of cynicism and cynicism among individuals who have experienced oppression by the dominant society. As a result of such issues, Hastings and Hamberger (1997) recommended conducting careful, multivariate analyses to control for potential confounds so as to minimize or avoid misleading and harmful results. These examples point to the need for researchers to take extra care, when investigating sensitive issues, to utilize sound and valid methodology that takes into account the many contextual issues of race and ethnicity. Furthermore, researchers need to develop theoretical frameworks that define what race means as a scientific construct, and explain why race is a significant variable in a specific study (Phinney, 1996; Seiber & Stanley, 1988).

Another aspect of race is the need for more minority researchers to conduct partner violence research. Campbell (1998) asserted that minority researchers need to be involved in family violence research to ask and guide the asking of appropriate research questions that both avoid disempowering and alienating the minority community, and provide relevant, empowering information for violence prevention within the minority community. Williams and Becker (1994) recommended, specifically, that batterer treatment programs take steps to provide culturally competent environments to facilitate success of minority program participants. Specific recommendations include developing active networking with minority communities, working with minority consultants to evaluate programs and provide feedback and recommendations, becoming informed about minority issues and, where necessary, employing bilingual associates. Though these recommendations were made for developing culturally competent treatment programs, failure of researchers to adopt similar strategies could adversely affect collaborative opportunities.

We followed several of these recommendations in a study of battered women's experiences with physicians (Hamberger et al., 1998) when we observed a small number of unexpected differences between African American and white women in the desirability ratings of specific physician behaviors. The pattern of findings appeared to suggest that African American women rated certain negative physician behaviors as much less undesirable than did white women. To further explore this result, we shared the findings with an African American domestic violence caseworker for help in interpreting the data. The outcome of the consultation suggested a number of possibilities, such as racial differences in where medical treatment was sought (e.g., emergency room versus private physician), differential expectations based on where treatment was sought, and responses to a history of institutional racism. The consultation also resulted in acknowledgment of the need to continue and extend such research to determine the replicability of the findings, and to control for a number of potential confounds prior to presenting the findings as "fact."

"Ownership" of the field and data. Although some researchers have been active in the field for a long time (e.g., Straus, 1979; Straus, Gelles, & Steinmetz, 1980), the field of partner violence intervention has arguably been developed primarily by grass roots organizers, activists and advocates. The urgency of the movement was sufficiently severe that the demand for services outstripped the ability of research to provide answers. As noted previously, programs for victims and perpetrators frequently were begun and maintained on shoestring budgets, against considerable community opposition or, at least, benign neglect, and on the dedication and passion of those willing to do the work. Researchers were often perceived as outsiders with limited passion and, at times, knowledge of the field, interested only in collecting data for their studies and publications, and providing nothing back to the programs and people they studied. As one shelter director recently described: "This graduate student called and said she was needing to collect some survey from battered women. She never offered to come

over and talk to us about her research. She just wanted to send us her surveys and have us hand them out to our clients, and then mail them back to her. Needless to say, we weren't interested in working with her."

Many programs have developed their own system of data collection, sometimes gathering rather large amounts of data. Sometimes researchers have accessed this data for program evaluation and other research. Fine (1987b) reported on instances of academic researchers conducting studies of such databases, and failing to include the program as a collaborative partner in the publication process. Such co-opting of the research process provides benefits to the researcher in terms of prestige and positioning for possible future funding. The community program, on the other hand, receives nothing, despite having collected the data and shared it. Experiences such as this paint all researchers with the same, broad brush, creating barriers to collaboration.

Being an unknown quantity, e.g., the "new kid on the block." In some communities, a researcher with interest in domestic violence may be relatively new to the scene. This is a particularly difficult position to be in, because being new means being an unknown quantity to community workers, many of whom may have been working in the same agency for many years. As such, the travails of being an unknown, untested individual can include many or all of the barriers described thus far, since community workers in this case have nothing to go by except their own previous experience. In the early 1980s, one of us (LKH) endeavored to begin a treatment program for men who batter their partners. An early meeting with a representative of the District Attorney went something like a deposition in a legal proceeding. The representative asked in a rather suspicious voice: "Why should we believe you're not just another fly-by-night operation like so many other therapists who promised something, didn't deliver, and left town in six months?" Later in the meeting, the official agreed to make some referrals as a test case, saying: "We'll send you a couple of referrals, and watch closely to see how you handle them." The official explained further: "You have to understand that the D. A. is elected to his job by the people of the community. Therefore, if you screw up, and one of these men hurts someone, little might happen to you, but the D. A. could lose his job. So, until we know what you can do, we're going to be very careful."

Although the case illustration above related primarily to developing contacts and collaborative partners for development of a clinical program, researchers new to a community or agency might expect similar initial treatment. In the case above, the community official was assertive and clear about their reservations. For present purposes, it allows us to see that unknown individuals are initially evaluated on the basis of the agency's prior experiences with others perceived to be similar. While unfortunate, and perhaps unfair, this does reflect a realistic picture of what a researcher new to the field or to an area could expect. Second, parameters may be established by the agency as a kind of preliminary test. The researcher is then faced with the decision of whether to accept or reject the period of enhanced scrutiny.

STRATEGIES TO OVERCOME BARRIERS

It may seem that, from the above discussion of barriers to researcher-community agency collaboration, achieving such relationships to conduct meaningful and scientifically sound research is all but impossible. On the contrary, we are optimistic that the barriers discussed above can be successfully addressed and overcome. In this section, we describe strategies for doing so. These strategy recommendations are drawn from social science research on negotiation and our own experiences working with community activists as partners in action research.

Fisher and Ury (1981) provide a theoretically based and empirically validated model of negotiation that can be applied to the process of collaboration. Their method is based upon four general principles of successful negotiation. First, separate people and problems. The skillful action researcher recognizes that collaborating agencies are run by activists who are people first. People value human relationships, and relationships are the medium through which collaborative work is accomplished. Every collaborative effort therefore involves these two dimensions, the work to be done (program design and evaluation), and the human relationships which develop and sustain the collaboration. Both the work and the relationships require intentional effort.

Second, focus upon interests, not positions. Successful action research collaboration involves many choices. In almost every case, a specific collaborative goal can be achieved by many methods. When differences of opinion arise, focus upon identifying and understanding each partner's interests rather than arguing over positions. This discussion often reveals that each partner has multiple interests, some of which are compatible and some of which are in conflict.

Third, invent options for mutual gain. Partners often approach collaboration acutely aware of what they have to lose, for example, scarce resources for a financially strapped community agency, and precious time for a researcher under pressure to rapidly complete and publish studies. To be stable, collaborative efforts must be based upon mutual gain. Therefore, the wise action researcher will look for ways to expand the pie before dividing it (Fisher & Ury, 1981). This can and must be discussed directly but with creativity and a spirit of mutual exploration.

Fourth, identify objective criteria for decision making. Collaborative partners make many mutual decisions and choices. Does an experimental intervention need to be revised to improve services for the agency's clients? What are the important outcomes that define a program's success from the researcher's perspective, and from the activist's perspective? Ultimately, should a collaboration continue? Each of these decisions can potentially lead to conflict. The wise action researcher will talk directly with their partner about the criteria for making decisions before attempting to make the decision.

These principles of negotiation can be applied throughout the collaborative process. Below we describe nine specific tasks that the action researcher can focus upon to develop a productive collaboration. These nine tasks are divided into three stages of collaboration: establishing preconditions, negotiating a collaborative agreement, and sustaining collaboration.

Establishing Preconditions

Task 1: Develop personal relationships. Although science is often described as an objective process, the successful pursuit of science through community collaboration is social process (Lewin, 1946). Given that many of the barriers to successful collaboration described above involve perceptions and relationships with others, it appears that one way to begin breaking down such barriers is to develop at least some type of familiarity with potential collaborative partners. During the early stages of developing a research program with domestically violent men, one of us (LKH) met regularly with the local shelter director. These meetings were typically during breakfast or lunch, during which time many issues were discussed, in addition to research with abusers. These included family issues, child rearing, buying first-time homes, career development, evolution of thought about partner violence and related issues, and so on. This self-disclosure and personal sharing allowed both parties to see each other from perspectives other than simply what we did for a living. An outgrowth of this process was the development of trust to share ideas, seek and provide mutual input and critique, and negotiate the development of research, clinical and educational programs that were viewed as both scientifically appropriate and useful to the community, which the shelter program could support.

Moreover, in these informal meetings, even those ideas that were viewed by one or the other parties as inappropriate or ill-timed, were not automatically and permanently shelved. Rather, they frequently remained on the agenda for periodic discussion and updating. An example of this process is a recent study on the experiences of battered women with their physicians while seeking abuse-related medical services. The original study protocol called for the survey to be administered by shelter personnel. The shelter director objected, noting the need for on-site debriefing by a trained investigator. Due to funding and personnel shortages, project startup was delayed until the condition of providing an on-site research assistant could be provided. The duration of the delay was about seven years. It is possible that this and other projects could have been completed more quickly or at least at the same pace without the researcher and shelter director having developed a personal relationship. We believe, however, that the mutual trust developed through nurturing personal relationships facilitated ongoing discussions that resulted in finding a way to complete the study, as well as to develop other projects that may not have otherwise taken place.

Negotiating a Collaborative Agreement

Task 2: Discuss scope and limitations. In seeking collaborative relationships with community groups to conduct research, it is important for researchers to acknowledge and discuss the scope of their proposed work, as well as any possible limitations of that work. This should be done openly, honestly, and at the very outset of any discussion of a proposed project. For example, we recently consulted with a batterer treatment program to conduct a treatment outcome evaluation.

In evaluating both extant resources, as well as possibilities for random assignment to a treatment and no treatment control condition, it was determined that such a level of sophistication would not be possible in this case. Detailed discussion of the strengths and limitations of a nonrandomized trial approach to program evaluation ensued. Alternative strategies for conducting program evaluation, as well as their limitations and strengths, were discussed. The program administrator understood the limitations of the research to be conducted on the treatment program.

This level of candor and honesty can prepare both the researcher and collaborative partner for the possibility that actual research outcomes may not be as predicted by theory or previous research in other settings. Providing prospective collaborative partners with information about such possibilities at the beginning of collaboration can enable preparation for less than ideal outcomes, and provide a kind of informed consent to proceed with the project, given known and anticipated limitations, as well as the possibility of unanticipated risks.

After discussing the scope and limitations of a collaborative effort, it can often be helpful to draft a letter of agreement to serve as a written reminder of the discussion. Drafting such a letter calls upon the partners to identify their expectations. This letter can then become a helpful reference for later meetings to discuss how the collaboration is working. If there is financial support to fund the collaborative effort, then this letter of agreement may also serve as a contract.

Task 3: Establish common goals. Collaborative efforts can sometimes bog down in differences over procedure, and other issues. Moreover, sometimes the prospect of overcoming some of the other barriers described and discussed above can seem daunting. One can become easily discouraged and decide that a particular collaborative effort is not going to work out. In such cases, one is faced with a difficult choice–jettison a promising project or somehow muddle ahead in a project that is beset with conflict and dissatisfaction. An alternative option is to explore with the potential collaborative partner areas of common ground and common goals. These areas may range from common goals of ending domestic violence to providing excellent services for victims and perpetrators of partner violence. Other areas of common interest may include specific problems identified at the community or programmatic level that need to be addressed. As in any endeavor, discoveries by seemingly disparate groups that significant goals are shared can lead to dialogue and negotiation. In addition, possession of common values and goals can help overcome stereotypes of how the other "must" be. Further, discussion proceeding from a position of common goals can lead to identification of appropriate roles for each collaborative partner, leading to a team concept for addressing pressing problems. In this way, the researchers can bring their special skills to bear within a particular niche, while at the same time develop appreciation of the bigger picture through collaborative participation in community projects.

Task 4: Design the collaboration for mutual gain. As noted above in the section on barriers to collaboration, researchers often derive substantial professional benefit from a collaborative partnership without benefiting their community partners or acknowledging their efforts. As described above, community-based partners often expend a great deal of time and energy in helping develop surveys, recruiting participants and gathering data. Community partners also frequently provide insights that add greatly to problem conceptualization or data interpretation. Therefore, researchers should give their collaborative partners appropriate credit for their contribution to a project. Such credit may include academic acknowledgements ranging from a footnote acknowledgement to co-authorship on publications and professional presentations. Such public acknowledgment can enhance a sense of pride in partnership, even if it does not have immediate financial benefits to the organization.

Because researcher and activist are working in different professional cultures, activists and researchers often value different types of benefits. For example, activists and their organizations may be interested in practical support ranging from letters of support for grant applications to assistance in fund-raising, consultation in designing new programs and service upon a board of directors. Supporting the activist agency by assisting in these areas validates and affirms the value of the community partner's involvement in a project.

Task 5: Anticipate and discuss differences honestly. In any collaborative relationship, there are going to be inevitable differences of opinion in approaches to problem-solving and priorities. In developing collaborative relationships with community agencies, the wise action researchers anticipate and openly discuss possible differences between their goals and objectives, and those of their collaborative partner. Failure to address such potential differences at the outset can lead to frustration and disappointment with the collaborative process. In the extreme, differences that are not acknowledged or addressed can lead to project failure. For example, a shelter may value development of a research program that provides direct application to service provision. On the other hand, the researcher may believe that the state of knowledge in the area of interest requires more preliminary, foundational research prior to undertaking studies of an applied nature. These differences in priority need to be discussed during the early stages of negotiation, together with realistic strategies for resolving them.

Not all differences can be anticipated. It is therefore important to have a plan in place to address concerns that arise in the normal course of the collaboration. One approach that we have found helpful is to predict that the two agencies will encounter some unanticipated bumps in the road. "When this occurs, will you please contact me so that we can discuss possible solutions?"

As with discussion of scope and limitations of a research project, proactively addressing potential and real differences enhances trust and credibility of both collaborative partners. Though not an exhaustive list of possible areas of conflict, our experience has taught that the following issues can be anticipated to pose problems, even among partners who wish to collaborate:

1. theoretical framework
2. definition of the problem
3. specific data to be collected
4. methods of data collection
5. who will collect the data
6. interpretation of data
7. uses of the data
8. time commitment to the research project
9. participant recruitment and debriefing
10. type of research to be done, e.g., applied versus basic
11. write-up and dissemination of the research report.

Sustaining the Collaboration

Task 6: Solve problems based upon mutual respect by focusing on interests, not positions. One of the primary challenges for researchers collaborating with frontline, community agencies and workers is how to resolve the inevitable conflicts that arise. As noted previously, advocates and other frontline workers frequently face and overcome significant obstacles to carry out their missions. In the process, they develop strong feelings and opinions about a variety of issues, and learn to defend their position vigorously. Likewise, researchers also frequently develop strong opinions based on their study and experience in a particular area, and are trained to debate their positions vigorously.

While there is a place for vigorous and spirited discussion and debate of issues, it is wise to approach these discussions about problems in the collaborative relationship from a perspective of mutual respect with a focus upon understanding of interests rather than debating positions. The researchers must remember that while they may be armed with data and theory, their community collaborative partner has a wellspring of experience and knowledge of the local setting, and how certain projects or approaches to research might affect both his/her clients and the field in general. Furthermore, the wise researcher will remember that historically social scientists have participated in minimizing violence against women.

The tactful and diplomatic action researchers who encounter conflict with their community partner will work hard to first understand their partner's perspective. What interests are at stake for the activist-partner and the collaborating institution? Wise researchers will then work hard to communicate their interests in the situation, inviting their partner to help identify solutions for mutual gain. These inevitable conflicts represent an opportunity to learn valuable lessons from one's community partner. The lessons learned will often improve the quality of the study, resulting in a win-win outcome.

An example of this occurred in the early stages of development of the survey of battered women's experiences with physicians, discussed previously (Hamberger et al., 1998). It was disappointing to hear the shelter director say that she could not allow the survey to be administered without the presence of a research assistant. It seemed to be a straightforward task that did not require a trained assistant to handle. The director explained, however, that the survey instrument contained items that described egregious physician behavior, and since the participants likely would not be health care professionals, there was a chance that, without proper debriefing, they could inadvertently misinterpret such items to describe acceptable physician behaviors. The recruitment and training of a research assistant actually increased rate of participation in the project. She displayed great enthusiasm for the project, which was infectious. In addition, many potential participants who had difficulty reading were supported by the assistant. Hence, by listening and cooperating with the shelter director's concerns, the project actually was more successful than anticipated. A diplomatic failure would have resulted in no project at all.

Task 7: Seek feedback. Another strategy for enhancing prospects of successful collaboration is used when the researcher seeks feedback from frontline workers for key aspects of a project. As with so much of what has been discussed so far, seeking input and feedback from frontline workers can improve a project by providing a real world perspective. This, in turn, can lend ecological validity to the project. The survey of battered women's experiences with physicians (Hamberger et al., 1998) serves as an example of the value of seeking input and feedback to enhance a project. Items for the survey instrument, which was developed for the project, were garnered from a series of interviews and discussions with battered women and physicians. Items were then written in a manner thought to be appropriate for survey administration. The early draft of the survey was then submitted to groups of battered women and advocates to be evaluated for readability and comprehensiveness. We then further modified the survey, based on that input, and resubmitted the revised product to another group of battered women for further review and feedback. We then submitted the "finished" survey instrument to an inner city-based, urban battered women's shelter for further review. We received feedback that, while the instrument was appropriately comprehensive, it was written in a manner more suitable for white, middle-class suburban readers. Shelter personnel provided help developing a version of the instrument that reflected the language of inner city residents. The result was a satisfying collaborative relationship with a number of shelter workers who helped in the data collection process and with interpretation of several aspects of the findings.

Task 8. Walk the walk. It is important to remember that building collaborative relationships requires sincerity, respect and a deep commitment to serve the needs of battered victims. This commitment must remain central to all collaborative efforts. There are various ways to live out this commitment. For example, a women's shelter that helped us provide on-site educational experiences to medical residents and students later requested help in recruiting physicians who would meet with shelter residents to discuss women's and children's health. We responded promptly by helping the shelter recruit 12 community physicians who were interested in making weekly visits on a rotating basis. Any request for help is an opportunity to cement the relationship and learn something new about one's partner.

Community service demonstrates personal and institutional commitment to collaboration. Such work also keeps the researcher in touch with community needs and can provide a type of pay-back to community agencies for their assistance. We have performed a variety of such services, including participating as members of boards of directors and special *ad hoc* committees, volunteering time and expertise facilitating support groups, and providing consultation on such issues as burnout prevention and stress management for agency staff. In addition, we have found that community agencies also appreciate receiving donations of goods and money to help them fulfill their missions.

In assessing these types of activities, the reader might think that such involvement is inappropriate, possibly leading to loss of objectivity. We believe that, contrary to such expectations, community involvement enhances researcher credibility and opens the door to richer dialogue about issues, problems and ideas of interest to both the researcher and the collaborative partner. Spending time in the actual community setting in roles other than that of researcher facilitates a broader, more in-depth perspective on possible research questions. It also provides a visibility that fosters ongoing professional relationships, thus increasing opportunities for new collaborative projects. An example of this is early research one of us (LKH) has conducted on motivations for partner violence among male and female perpetrators. While actively involved in the field as a treatment provider and researcher with male perpetrators, state statutory changes resulted in sudden and dramatic increases in arrests of female perpetrators, and subsequent referral for services. Active collaboration with both university-based researchers (e.g., Hamberger & Hastings, 1989, 1992; Hamberger et al., 1996), as well as the local women's shelter (e.g., Hamberger & Arnold, 1990) created added opportunity to assess motivations for perpetrating partner violence among male and female perpetrators. That research, conducted using a researcher-centric model, indicated that, on average, male perpetrators report using violence to dominate and control their partners, while female perpetrators reported using violence to defend themselves or retaliate against prior partner assaults (Hamberger, Lohr, & Bonge, 1994; Hamberger, Lohr, Bonge, & Tolin, 1997). In turn, collaborative discussion of such findings between key community stakeholders and the clinician-researcher, using a participatory action research model at regular community response meetings, resulted in development of a model for conceptualizing and treating female partner violence victims (Hamberger & Potente, 1994). Without the development of prior close working relationships with key community stakeholders, together with ongoing relationships with experts in methodology for studying the phenomenon, such work would have been delayed.

Task 9: Recognize irreconcilable differences gracefully: Maintain the relationship. Sometimes, despite sincere efforts of both potential partners, it may be impossible to collaborate on a given project. Elliott and Kassekert (1994) described scenarios in which researchers and advocates may not be able to jointly develop a research project. Primary barriers include no case sharing, no maintenance of written records for compilation of data bases, inability to agree on how data will be collected, recorded and stored. In addition, other barriers identified by Elliott and Kassekert that could lead to irreconcilable differences include respective world outlooks of advocates and researchers. For example, advocates may view their primary purpose as changing society and benefiting all women, whereas researchers may be interested primarily in understanding a phenomenon, based on a sample. In some cases, these and other barriers described above may be sufficiently different as to make collaboration impossible, despite intentions and motivations of respective parties.

In those instances where collaboration is not currently possible, it is best to view it as situation or project-specific. As such, continued contacts and dialogue can lead to further understanding of barriers, as well as strategies for overcoming them. We have regular, ongoing dialogues with a number of community agencies, often with no specific projects or ideas under consideration. We have found that, sometimes, after months of discussion and contact, new ideas for collaboration arise with the very people and agencies with which a previous idea was not tenable.

CONCLUSION

Collaboration between researchers and community workers to develop and conduct research projects comprises a complex process of negotiating philosophical, professional, personal and cultural differences. Successful collaboration entails clear and honest acknowledgment of potential barriers. It also involves working with such differences through focusing on common goals and values. In addition, researchers can bring to bear a number of specific strategies for facilitating the collaborative process. These strategies include anticipating differences and discussing them openly and honestly, clarity about the scope and limitations of any given project, as well as responsible study design that takes into account the sensitive nature of the research being conducted. Further, seeking feedback about project content, methodology and conceptualization enhance collaboration. Finally, working actively with community agencies, providing something back to them for their efforts, and including acknowledgment of contributions to projects are also valuable collaboration strategies. In the end, it appears to us that successful collaboration between researchers and community workers basically entails developing relationship-building skills and showing respect for those with whom one wishes to collaborate. Nevertheless, despite best efforts and intentions, sometimes collaborations do not succeed. In such situations, it is important to analyze why collaboration failed, but also to keep such failure in perspective. Any given failure is frequently situation- or project-specific, and not necessarily permanent.

REFERENCES

Adams, D. (1988). Counseling men who batter: A profeminist analysis of five treatment models. In M. Bograd & K. Yllo (Eds.), *Feminist perspectives on wife abuse* (pp. 176-199). Beverly Hills, CA: Sage.

Ambuel, B., Hamberger, L. K., & Lahti, J. (1997). The Family Peace Project: A model for training health care professionals to identify, treat and prevent partner violence. In L. K. Hamberger, S. Burge, A. Graham, & A. Costa (Eds.), *Violence issues for health care educators and providers* (pp. 58-82). Binghamton, NY: The Haworth Press, Inc.

Attorney General's Task Force on Family Violence (1984). *Final report*. Washington, DC: U.S. Department of Justice.

Barnett, O. W., Miller-Perrin, C. L., & Perrin, R. D. (1997). *Family violence across the lifespan*. Thousand Oaks, CA: Sage.

Brydon-Miller, M. (1997). Participatory action research: Psychology and social change. *Journal of Social Issues, 53* (4), 657-666.

Campbell, J. (1998, July). *Discussant comments for methodological issues in research concerning family violence when collaborating with community agencies.* Symposium presented at Program Evaluation and Family Violence Research: An International Conference. Durham, NH.

Chalk, R., & King, P. A. (Eds). (1998). *Violence in families: Assessing prevention and treatment programs.* Washington, DC: National Academy Press.

Dobash, R. E., & Dobash, R. P. (1987, July). *Research, "experts" and policy on wife abuse in Britain and the United States.* Paper presented at the Third National Family Violence Research Conference. Durham, NH.

Dutton, D. G. (1988). Profiling wife assaulters: Preliminary evidence for a trimodal analysis. *Violence and Victims, 3,* 5-29.

Edleson, J. L., & Tolman, R. M. (1992). *Intervention for men who batter: An ecological approach.* Newbury Park, CA: Sage.

Elliott, B. A., & Kassekert, R. (1994, November). *Domestic violence partnerships: Pitfalls and potentials.* Paper presented at the Second Society of Teachers of Family Medicine Violence Education Conference. Albuquerque, NM.

Fine, M. (1987a, July). *The politics and paradoxes of interviewing female victims of male violence.* Paper presented at the Third National Family Violence Research Conference. Durham, NH.

Fine, M. (1987b, July). *Overview of intervention/treatment research evaluating programs for women who have been abused: Empowerment in the sharing of voice.* Paper presented at the Family Violence Research Conference for Practitioners and Policymakers. Durham, NH.

Fisher, R., & Ury, W. (1981). *Getting to yes: Negotiating agreement without giving in.* Boston, MA: Houghton-Mifflin Company.

Ganley, A. (1987). Perpetrators of domestic violence: An overview of counseling the court-mandated client. In D. J. Sonkin (Ed.), *Domestic violence on trial: Psychological and legal dimensions of family violence* (pp. 155-173). New York: Springer.

Gondolf, E. W., Yllo, K., & Campbell, J. (1997). Collaboration between researchers and advocates. In G. Kaufman-Kantor & J. Jasinski (Eds.), *Out of the darkness: Contemporary perspectives on family violence* (pp. 255-267). Thousand Oaks, CA: Sage.

Gynther, M. D. (1981). Is the MMPI an appropriate assessment device for Blacks? *The Journal of Black Psychology, 7,* 67-75.

Hamberger, L. K., Ambuel, B., Marbella, A., & Donze, J. (1998). Physician interaction with battered women: The women's perspective. *Archives of Family Medicine, 8,* 575-582.

Hamberger, L. K., & Arnold, J. (1990). The impact of mandatory arrest on domestic violence perpetrator counseling services. *Family Violence Bulletin, 6,* 10-12.

Hamberger, L. K., & Hastings, J. E. (1986). Personality correlates of men who abuse their partners: A cross-validation study. *Journal of Family Violence, 1,* 323-341.

Hamberger, L. K., & Hastings, J. E. (1988). Skills training for treatment of spouse abusers: An outcome study. *Journal of Family Violence, 3,* 121-130.

Hamberger, L. K., & Hastings, J. E. (1989). Counseling male spouse abusers:

Characteristics of treatment completers and dropouts. *Violence and Victims, 4,* 275-286.

Hamberger, L. K., & Hastings, J. E. (1990). Recidivism following spouse abuse abatement counseling: Treatment program implications. *Violence and Victims, 5,* 157-170.

Hamberger, L. K., & Hastings, J. E. (1991). Personality correlates of men who batter and nonviolent men: Some continuities and discontinuities. *Journal of Family Violence, 6,* 131-148.

Hamberger, L. K., & Hastings, J. E. (1992). Racial differences on the MCMI in an outpatient clinical sample. *Journal of Personality Assessment, 58,* 90-95.

Hamberger, L. K., & Lohr, J. M. (1989). Proximal causes of spouse abuse: Cognitive and behavioral factors. In P. L. Caesar & L. K. Hamberger (Eds.), *Treating men who batter: Theory, practice, and programs* (pp. 53-76). New York: Springer.

Hamberger, L. K., Lohr, J. M., & Bonge, D. (1994). The intended function of domestic violence is different for arrested male and female perpetrators. *Family Violence and Sexual Assault Bulletin, 10,* 40-44.

Hamberger, L. K., Lohr, J. M., Bonge, D., & Tolin, D. (1996). A large sample empirical typology of male spouse abusers and its relationship to dimensions of abuse. *Violence and Victims, 11,* 277-292.

Hamberger, L. K., Lohr, J. M., Bonge, D., & Tolin, D. (1997). An empirical classification of motivations for domestic violence. *Violence Against Women, 3,* 401-423.

Hamberger, L. K., Lohr, J. M., & Gottlieb, M. (in press). Predictors of treatment dropout from a spouse abuse abatement program. *Behavior Modification.*

Hamberger, L. K., & Potente, T. (1994). Counseling women arrested for domestic violence: Implications for theory and practice. *Violence and Victims, 9,* 125-137.

Hart, B. (1987, July). Ethical considerations in research on family violence. Paper presented at the Third National Family Violence Research Conference. Durham, NH.

Hastings, J. E., & Hamberger, L. K. (1997). Sociodemographic predictors of violence. *The Psychiatric Clinics of North America, 20,* 323-335.

Hoff, L. A. (1987, July). *The politics of collaborative research: The interface between academics and activists.* Paper presented at the Third National Family Violence Research Conference. Durham, NH.

Ingram, J. D., Marchioni, P., Hill, G., Caraveo-Ramos, E., & McNeil, B. (1985). Recidivism, perceived problem-solving abilities, MMPI characteristics and violence: A study of black and white incarcerated male adult offenders. *Journal of Clinical Psychology, 41,* 425-432.

Kurz, D. (1993). Physical assaults by husbands: A major social problem. In R. J. Gelles & D. R. Loseke (Eds.), *Current controversies in family violence* (pp. 88-103). Newbury Park, CA: Sage.

Lewin, K. (1946). Action research and minority problems. *Journal of Social Issues, 2*(4), 34-46.

Lykes, M. B. (1997). Activist participatory research among the Maya of Guatemala: Constructing meaning from situated knowledge. *Journal of Social Issues, 53*(4), 725-746.

Martin, D. (1985). Domestic violence: A sociological perspective. In D. Sonkin, D.

Martin, & L. Walker, *The male batterer: A treatment approach* (pp. 1-32). New York: Springer.

Martin, D. (1987). The historical roots of domestic violence. In D. J. Sonkin (Ed.), *Domestic violence on trial: Psychological and legal dimensions of family violence* (pp. 3-20). New York: Springer.

Pagelow, M. (1984). *Family violence.* New York: Praeger.

Perkins, D. D., & Zimmerman, M. A. (1995). Empowerment theory, research and application. *American Journal of Community Psychology, 23*(5), 569-581.

Phinney, J. S. (1996). When we talk about American ethnic groups, what do we mean? *American Psychologist, 51,* 918-927.

Rappaport, R. N. (1985). Research in action. In R. N. Rappaport (Ed.), *Children, youth and families: The action-research relationship* (pp. 1-25). Cambridge, MA: Cambridge University Press.

Saunders, D. G. (1986). When battered women use violence: Husband abuse or self defense? *Violence and Victims, 1,* 47-60.

Scarr, S. (1988). Race and gender as psychological variables: Social and ethical issues. *American Psychologist, 43,* 56-59.

Schechter, S. (1982). *Women and male violence: The visions and struggles of the battered women's movement.* Boston: South End Press.

Seiber, J. E., & Stanley, B. (1988). Ethical and professional dimensions of socially sensitive research. *American Psychologist, 43,* 49-55.

Soler, E. (1987). Domestic violence is a crime: A case study–San Francisco Family Violence Project. In D. J. Sonkin (Ed.), *Domestic violence on trial: Legal and psychological dimensions of family violence* (pp. 21-35). New York: Springer.

Sonkin, D. J. (1988). The male batterer: Clinical and research issues. *Violence and Victims, 3,* 65-79.

Straus, M. A. (1979). Measuring intrafamily conflict and aggression: The Conflict Tactics (CT) Scale. *Journal of Marriage and the Family, 41,* 75-88.

Straus, M. A., Gelles, R. J., & Steinmetz, S. (1980). *Behind closed doors: Violence in the American family.* Garden City, NY: Doubleday.

Williams, O. J., & Becker, R. L. (1994). Domestic partner abuse treatment programs and cultural competence: The results of a national survey. *Violence and Victims, 9,* 287-296.

Yllo, K. (1987, July). *Issues of bias and objectivity in wife abuse research.* Paper presented at the Third National Family Violence Research Conference. Durham, NH.

Zimmerman, M. A. (1995). Psychological empowerment: Issues and illustrations. *American Journal of Community Psychology, 23*(5), 581-600.

ETHICAL ISSUES IN EVALUATING INTERVENTIONS

Human Subject Issues in Batterer Program Evaluation

Edward W. Gondolf

SUMMARY. Batterer program evaluations raise several human subject issues that have yet to be uniformly addressed in evaluation guidelines

The author wishes to thank Edmund Ricci of the Graduate School of Public Health, University of Pittsburgh, and Susan Schechter of the School of Social Work, University of Iowa, for their helpful comments and advice. Research Assistants Mimi Prada and Gayle Moyer, and Project Coordinators Jewel Lee Doherty and Crystal Deemer, helped to develop and implement the discussed procedures. The research was made possible through a grant from the Centers for Disease Control and Prevention (CDC), U.S. Department of Health and Human Services (Grant No. R49/CCR310525-02), but does not necessarily represent the official view of the CDC. Information from this paper was presented at the Program Evaluation and Family Violence Research Conference at the University of New Hampshire, July 26-29, 1998.

Address correspondence to: Edward W. Gondolf, EdD, MPH, Mid-Atlantic Addiction Training Institute, 1098 Oakland Avenue, Indiana University of Pennsylvania, Indiana, PA 15705 (E-mail: EGondolf@Grove.IUP.edu).

[Haworth co-indexing entry note]: "Human Subject Issues in Batterer Program Evaluation." Gondolf, Edward W. Co-published simultaneously in *Journal of Aggression, Maltreatment & Trauma* (The Haworth Maltreatment & Trauma Press, an imprint of The Haworth Press, Inc.) Vol. 4, No. 1 (#7), 2000, pp. 273-297; and: *Program Evaluation and Family Violence Research* (ed: Sally K. Ward, and David Finkelhor) The Haworth Maltreatment & Trauma Press, an imprint of The Haworth Press, Inc., 2000, pp. 273-297. Single or multiple copies of this article are available for a fee from The Haworth Document Delivery Service [1-800-342-9678, 9:00 a.m. - 5:00 p.m. (EST). E-mail address: getinfo@haworthpressinc.com].

or institutional review boards. Experience conducting a multi-site evaluation of batterer programs, human subject procedures developed for research with violent psychiatric patients, and protocol developed for clinicians assessing domestic violence cases are used to illustrate and address these issues. The major issues include (1) obtaining informed consent from resistant batterers, "volunteered" female partners, and new female partners; (2) maintaining victim safety in conducting follow-up interviews and in response to information gained in these interviews; and (3) tracking female partners in a way that violates privacy and may recreate a sense of being stalked. A tested protocol for identifying and addressing imminent violence, suicidality, and child abuse is presented as one way to help address victim safety. Feedback from the multi-site evaluation suggests few subjects refused consent, faced safety problems, or were bothered by tracking; and high response rates and disclosure of information were associated with efforts to address the human subject issues. *[Article copies available for a fee from The Haworth Document Delivery Service: 1-800-342-9678. E-mail address: <getinfo@ haworthpressinc.com> Website: <http://www.HaworthPress.com>]*

KEYWORDS. Informed consent, research ethics, domestic violence, battered women

INTRODUCTION

The dramatic increase in program evaluation of batterer interventions intensifies the many difficult "human subjects" issues in the domestic violence field. The main issue is how to avoid endangering battered women who are asked to report on their partner's abusive behavior. Their abusive partners may attack or threaten them in retaliation for the women's being interviewed. It is not uncommon for researchers to encounter outright opposition to batterer program evaluation because of the potential for endangering battered women and the lack of safety precautions in research designs. The familiar ethical matters of confidentiality and voluntary participation are also magnified in batterer follow-up studies that expose criminal activity (i.e., assault, drug use, child abuse) and include resistant and suspicious men as subjects.

Unfortunately, no uniform guidelines or protocol exist to address human subject issues in the domestic violence field. Institutional review boards (IRBs), charged with monitoring human subject issues, often do not have experience in the domestic violence field or precedent from previous batterer program evaluations to appropriately assess the unique human subject issues. IRBs tend, therefore, to be either overly cautious or naively lenient about proposals for batterer program evaluation. Similarly, grant review panels face uncertainty about sufficient protective measures in proposals for funding, and reviewers of journal submissions seldom have sufficient information to assess the ethics of reported evaluations. In sum, there is an urgent need to explicitly identify the human subject issues associated with batterer program evaluation and develop systematic responses to these issues.

We compile here the major human subject issues raised in our multi-site evaluation of batterer interventions in four cities (Gondolf, 1997, 1999, in press), and discuss the procedures that we developed to address them. Informed consent, confidentiality, voluntary participation, and minimizing risks set forth in the federal guidelines, of course, apply to batterer program evaluations (USDHHS, 1991). We encountered several additional complications, however: obtaining informed consent from resistant batterers and unexpecting battered women, maintaining victim safety and responding to danger, and conducting intrusive tracking with transient and protective subjects. Some other issues that emerged include gaining informed consent from new partners and responding to apparent needs for additional intervention or services.

Our response to the human subject issues was forged from several sources and experience. One, prior experience with research on violent psychiatric patients (Gondolf, 1990) offered some precedent for tracking and studying batterers. This research with psychiatric patients was particularly relevant since it involved involuntary treatment and interviews with family members similar to batterer program evaluations. One of the primary contributions of our multi-site evaluation may be a tested and refined protocol for identifying and addressing imminent violence, suicidality, and child abuse based largely on procedures developed for researching violent psychiatric patients (Monahan, Appelbaum, Mulvey, Robbins, & Lidz, 1993).

A second source was batterer program staff, battered women advocates, and institutional review board (IRB) members who raised questions and made suggestions during the design of the multi-site evaluation. The evaluation included co-investigators from different institutions which meant that several different IRBs reviewed our research. We were consequently in the position to weigh diverse requirements or recommendations across the IRBs and negotiate compromises, as well as identify some emerging consensus.

We also drew on a group of policy consultants and on the program staff at the sites involved in the evaluation. They had experiences, especially with gaining informed consent and contacting battered women, that were crucial to developing appropriate procedures.

Our discussion of issues and procedures is substantiated with feedback from male and female subjects about the impact of interviewing on their confidentiality, safety, and privacy. Research assistants administered a separate questionnaire about the impact of the follow-up interviews at the end of the 15-month follow-up. This information offers documentation of the extent of the human subject issues in our evaluation and a test of the procedures used to address them. It offers a basis for additional discussion on the issues and a precedent for assessing the ethics of further and more extensive batterer program evaluations.

Our multi-site evaluation of four batterer programs is based on a sample of 840 male batterers and their initial female victims and any identified new partners. The men and women were interviewed at program intake and every three months for a cumulative period of 15 months. The follow-up was resumed at 30 months to be continued for a full four years from intake. A comparison of different program formats (e.g., program duration, counseling approaches, additional services) was achieved by comparing different research sites, rather than through a randomized experimental design at one site. Programs varied from three to nine months in length, in didactic and process counseling, and in additional alcohol treatment and victim case management. An evaluation of this scope and complexity managed to intensify expected human subject issues and surface new ones, and therefore provides a useful place to identify, refine, and assess human subject issues.

INFORMED CONSENT

Recruiting Batterers as Subjects

The most fundamental human subject obligation in social science research is establishing informed consent. Subjects in program evaluations must routinely be advised of the nature of the research, any possible risks or consequences to the research, and that participation is voluntary (i.e., they can withdraw at any time without consequence). In our study, we also had to advise the men that we would access their program and police records and periodically contact their partners. We, of course, also needed to inform the female partners about our intent to interview them, the potential risks in participating in the research, and their rights as research participants. Both the men and their female partners needed to formally agree to participate in the research after being "informed" in this way.

Obtaining informed consent is, however, more than a perfunctory task of administering and signing permission forms (Lidz, 1984). The prospect of being sent back to court for program non-compliance or violating probation may subtly coerce court-ordered batterers to participate in the research. They may, additionally, agree to participate in order to please or impress batterer program staff. At the same time, suspicious and resistant batterers are not likely to readily participate in research without some persuasion and reassurances. Without some tacit coercion, the recruitment rate of subjects in our multi-site evaluation would have been much lower than it was.

In one of our initial research sites, potential male subjects were told to stay after the program intake session if they were interested in participating in a program evaluation. Less than a third of the men remained and about 10% of these men did not complete the forms indicating informed consent. This amount of avoidance and refusal is not uncommon with these sort of subjects, especially in experimental or clinical trial designs. The site was, nevertheless, replaced because of difficulties in recruiting a sufficient quota of subjects.

Other sites included an explanation of the study and informed consent forms as part of the program intake. They adopted the research questionnaires and tests as part of their clinical intake protocol, and they already had a provision that provided for follow-up contact. The informed consent forms for our study basically asked permission (1) to have the clinical records shared with the external researchers and (2) to replace the program's follow-up contact with our periodic and paid phone interviews.

Participation in the research under this system appeared to be less imposing to the potential subjects. The refusal rates fell to 10% during a pilot period, and later to 5% as the researchers became more methodical at addressing questions. For instance, the researchers reminded reluctant subjects that they could drop out of the study later without penalty or consequence, and that they would be paid for each completed interview. The final refusal rate is the equivalent to the refusal rate of violent patients recruited in a psychiatric emergency room, and is generally considered a sufficiently low refusal rate for research reliability (Gondolf, 1990).

As the research progressed, it became apparent that some men were complying in part because they associated our research with the court. Male subjects occasionally would say that they wanted to withdraw from the research because their probation was over, or they would ask interviewers to give messages to the program staff or court officials. These comments occurred even though the initial informed consent procedures and the follow-up interviews indicated that our interviewers were independent from both the batterer program and the court.

One additional issue related to subject recruitment and informed consent is payment for interviews. Interview payment in follow-up interviews has become conventional practice in order to compensate individuals for their time and contribution to the research, but also to offer an incentive to participate in the research. If the payment is too high, it can be construed as a form of coercion; if it is too low, the subjects may be viewed as exploited (Lidz, 1984). Some battered women's advocates rightly question whether batterers should receive any payment for participating in the program evaluations. The payment might appear as a kind of reward for their criminal behavior. We offered both the male subjects and their female partners a compromise amount of $10 for each completed interview and gave an extra $10 for the 12-month and 15-month interviews to encourage participation over the long term. Each phone interview generally lasted between 20-30 minutes, with a few lasting an hour or more.

In sum, our nearly 70% response rate with the men over the 15-month follow-up may have been attributable to some tacit coercion at program intake and to interview payments. According to commentary about informed consent with psychiatric patients, a certain amount of tacit coercion is inevitable (Appelbaum, Lidz, & Meisel, 1987; Lidz, 1984). In our multi-site evaluation, the payment of $10 to $20 for a phone interview appeared a sufficient compromise of ethical and practical concerns. Our use of program intake to recruit subjects blurred the boundaries between program obligations and voluntary research, but in the process established a recruitment rate that substantially strengthened the research.

Recruiting Female Partners

Initial Victims. Recruiting the female partners of batterers raises even more complications regarding informed consent. The female partners of the male subjects in our multi-site evaluation were in a very different situation from women in shelter samples with high recruitment and response rates (Rumptz, Sullivan, Davidson, & Basta, 1991). The shelter women have sought services for themselves, are in a more protective environment, and are more likely to be separated from the batterers. There is much less risk and more reason, therefore, for them to participant in an evaluation. The female partners of batterer program participants, on the other hand, may be frightened that their research participation could bring retaliation from their battering partner. The women may not have initiated the batterer's arrest and may be skeptical of the intervention in general. Some may simply want to "get on with their lives" and not complicate it with research interviews.

In our batterer program evaluation, female interviewers initially called the women to explain the program evaluation and read an informed consent statement at that time. We opted for this procedure rather than send letters that were more likely to be intercepted by their partners or ignored by the women. Our interviewers signed a form to verify their reading the informed consent statement to the women and the women's response to the statement. (This alternative procedure conforms to the appeals for appropriate and tailored informed consent [Hansson, 1998]). We did manage to recruit 77% of the men's initial partners across the four research sites. Only 3% of the women refused to participate, and 20% could not be reached.

An additional issue arose over the extent of the women's consent. We initially proposed to accept a man as a subject only if his female partner consented to have the man included in the research. Battered women's advocates suggested that some women might view their batterer's research participation as a risk and intrusion and should therefore have a say in their partner's participation. An institutional review board, however, indicated that the men had a right to decide for themselves whether they wanted to participate in the research, irrespective of their female partner's consent. As it turns out, none of the women we contacted raised objection to their partner's participation.

New Partners. Our evaluation presented another set of issues with the inclusion of new partners. "New partners" refers to women with whom the male subjects have an intimate relationship (more than two weeks) after the battering incident that brought the man to the batterer program. New partners are of special interest for two main reasons. First, over half of the male subjects were not living with their partners at the program intake, and approximately 25% did not have contact with their initial partner for at least a three-month period during the 15-month follow-up. Second, advocates have observed that many batterers continue their battering with new partners. We attempted, therefore, to recruit new partners of the batterers at each three-month follow-up.

Each male subject was asked if he had a different intimate partner from the woman involved in the incident that led to his entering the program. If he answered "yes," the interviewers asked permission to contact the woman and include her in the study. Nearly 18% of the male respondents identified new partners at intake or during the 15-month follow-up, and 88% of these women were reached for an interview. We suggested that the men tell their new partner about their past participation in the batterer program and that we would be calling her. Our questions about domestic abuse would then not be a surprise to the new partners, and would be less likely to raise suspicions and concerns. We also explained that discussing his past now would be preferable to the new partner eventually finding out about it through someone else.

Rapport. Our interviewers overwhelmingly added another dimension to the recruitment and continued participation of the female subjects. In the questions about the impact of the interviews, the researchers asked what motivated the women to participate in the interviews. The vast majority of the women indicated they responded to the interviewer, which they characterized as "not judgmental," "caring," and "considerate." As one woman explained, "It is nice to hear your voice on the other end of the phone asking me how I'm doing. It's nice to have someone to talk to who really cares and understands my situation." Another woman was even more explicit about rapport: "I talked with you as a result of rapport. Talking with the same person all the time makes you feel more at ease. You don't feel that you want to hold anything back. You don't feel restrained or inhibited. If it was a different person each time, you would lose something." Something beyond just training was evidently involved as several women noted: "You guys have a gift. This is personal information and it's sometimes hard talking about it, but you made it easier. You guys kept me here."

SAFETY ISSUES

Risks Associated with the Interviews

Risks in General. The greatest ethical and human subject concern in the field is the safety of victims being interviewed to verify batterer behavior. Some battered women's advocates believe the risks of endangering battered women are sufficiently high that follow-up interviewing for batterer programs should not be done at all. Admittedly, we do not have substantial documentation to refute this concern, but precautions can be taken to reduce it. Research on violent psychiatric patients, for instance, has developed protocols to minimize risks to interviewed family members (Monahan et al., 1993), and battered women's advocates have formulated safety procedures for clinical interviews (Gondolf, 1998). There is, however, no definitive protocol for dealing with safety issues in batterer program evaluation and one clearly needs to be developed.

There are actually two kinds of risks to be addressed. The first kind of risk is related to the actual interview. What precautions are needed to minimize the risk of harassment, threats, or retaliation for a woman telling interviewers about her partner's abusive behavior? Also, what might be done, as well, to reduce the imposition, confusion, or intrusion that interviews about abuse may cause? The second kind of risk is the abuse, threats, or danger that battered women may experience independent of any research interviews. How are potentially dangerous situations to be identified and what actions should be taken in response? Additionally, potential harm to oneself, in the form of attempted suicide, and potential child abuse need to be identified and addressed.

Phoning and Interview Protocol. There are at least three aspects of interviewing that can help minimize the risk associated with interviews themselves: establishing privacy in the interview, using "funnel questioning" in the interview, and debriefing the interviewee at the end of the interview. First, we attempted to establish as much privacy around the interviews as possible in order to reduce the chance of the batterer's punishing a woman for the interview or influencing a woman's responses. The female subjects in our multi-site evaluation were (1) asked if it was a safe time to speak, (2) instructed to hang up if their partner arrived or could overhear them, (3) told to identify our calls to inquiring partners as "a cosmetic survey," and (4) given an "800" number to call back at a more convenient and private time. As mentioned previously, a substantial portion of the women were not living with their battering partners. They had a great deal of privacy by virtue of their living circumstances. Other women, in order to gain privacy, chose to be interviewed from their workplace, a car phone, a neighbor's house, or a phone booth over our toll-free line. The women were also asked in subsequent interviews whether their partners pressured, hassled, or threatened them in any way about the previous interviews. This questioning helped us monitor the risks of the interviews, and determine if interviewing should be discontinued with any particular woman.

PHONING PROTOCOL

Precautions for Interviewee
- checking that person is *alone*
- ask for *a time* when would be alone
- give a *toll-free number* of a more convenient return call
- offer *code words* to interrupt a call that is overheard
- explain *"contact" persons* and update information

Leaving Messages
- messages identified with *interviewer's name only*
- identify only as *"program evaluation,"* if pressed by answerer
- a maximum of *five messages* at different times
- attempt contact over *a 2 week period*, then forward case

A second and less obvious way to decrease risks associated with interviewing battered women lies in the interview itself. Administering a battery of tests or series of close-ended questions can leave interviewees feeling confused, used, or "put upon." This approach may replicate the interrogation or "drilling" that the women's batterers have used on them as part of their control and abuse. For men, this kind of questioning may be reminiscent of their encounter with police and the courts and thus add to their suspicion and resistance. An interview that allows subjects to tell their own story and "be heard" is more likely to promote disclosure, cooperation, and continued participation. Battered women advocates have long argued that interviewing needs to "validate the women's experience" for these reasons (Yllo, 1988). Furthermore, the interview should not be overly structured, asking the same battery of questions to all interviewees, as we found in the development of our questionnaire. Some questions might be skipped or additional ones asked, depending on the woman's relationship to the man. Women who have no contact with the batterer or women who are new partners with the batterer, for instance, warrant different questions about current safety and past abuse.

To address these issues, we used a form of "funnel questioning" that begins with broad open-ended questions which allow the subjects to convey their experience, and respond with increasingly specific questions (Mulvey & Lidz, 1993). For instance, the interviewing about re-assault begins with a broad open-ended question, "Tell me how your relationship has been going," followed by more specific questions, such as "Describe any hassles, communication problems, or conflicts," and ending with an inventory of abusive and assaultive behaviors (e.g., Did your partner push or shove you?). The questioning appears to increase disclosure, as well as put specific behaviors in a context. As one woman pointed out, "You allowed me to speak freely. This was not just a list of questions for quick answers. I felt comfortable enough to be able to bring up any concern." Several of the women commented that the interview structure also led them through their experience and helped them to assess their situation. One woman explained, "I liked the questions. They gave me room to open up and say how I felt. The fact that you were willing to let me go further and talk was kind of therapeutic. You were willing to listen. It all helped me evaluate my feelings and the whole thing." Another woman added, "The questions helped me listen to myself. They made me stop rationalizing the abuse and realize what I was going through."

A third precaution attempts to limit the impact that the interview might have on an individual. The interview questions about abuse and violence could cause uncomfortable feelings, traumatic recollections, and even flashbacks of incidents. At the end of each interview, the male subjects and their female partners were debriefed in order to identify and ease potential emotional disturbance as a result of the interview. The interviewers routinely ask a series of questions: How are you feeling at this point? What depression, anxiety, or fear are you aware of right now? What recollections or thoughts about abuse or conflict has the interview raised? Using probing and reflective listening, the interviewers encourage subjects to elaborate on their responses. They ask subjects who did raise feelings of depression, anxiety, or fear to talk further with a batterers' or women's program counselor in their local area, and provide them with the telephone numbers of such counselors. They also suggest that the subject call back the interviewer or directly contact a batterers' or women's program, if they later encounter anxiety, anger, depression, or "flashbacks" and nightmares. As discussed further in the next section, "Risks Independent of Interviews," clinical consultants experienced with domestic violence need to be on call to consult in cases of potential suicide, violence, or child abuse.

INTERVIEW DEBRIEFING

Questions for the end of an interview:
- How are you *feeling* at this point?
- What *depression, anxiety, anger, or fear* are you aware of right now?
- What recollections or thoughts *about abuse* has the interview raised?
- What are you likely *to do* about the feelings or thoughts?

Recommended responses:
- Encourage subject to *elaborate* on the feelings and thoughts with reflective listening
- *Refer* subject to batterer program or women's center staff
- Follow *procedures* for potential suicide, violence, or child abuse, if appropriate
- Offer a *call back* if subject's feelings or thoughts continue
- Give *referral numbers* in case feelings or thoughts recur or new ones develop

---

Reported Risks. In a set of additional questions administered following the final 15-month interviews (n = 465), we asked the women about the lack of privacy and its impact. A fifth of the women (20%) admitted that their partner was "present or listening" during at least one of the three-month interviews during the 15-month follow-up. However, over half (59%) of these women insisted that they were not affected at all, and another 31% said they felt at most "uncomfortable." Only 11% (n = 9) of those with a partner present (or 2% of the entire sample) said they had "changed an answer" or "did not tell everything" as a result of their partner's presence. Although privacy was not achieved in all the interviews, the lack of privacy did not appear to substantially affect the interviews. Most of the women with a partner present decided to go ahead with the interview because they perceived little consequence for doing so.

The female subjects were also asked if they were hassled, intimidated, threatened, or abused in any way in response to participating in the interviews. Ten percent (10%, n = 47) of those who completed the questioning said "yes," but this was primarily in the form of being "questioned about the interview" (5% of the sample, n = 22). Two women reported threats (1% of the sample), but no one reported physical abuse in response to the interviews. Nearly all (97%) of the female subjects said they were willing to continue to be interviewed if an extended follow-up were conducted. These findings seem to suggest that the risks from the interviews were relatively low.

Risks Independent of Interviews

Training and Approach. Human subject guidelines generally require that imminent violence be addressed, including harm to one's self, and that child abuse, in particular, be reported. Our interviewers were, therefore, trained to identify the need for intervention in these areas and help facilitate appropriate steps in that direction. Our approach was threefold: (1) the interviewers were extensively trained in the dynamics and dangers of abusive relationships and how to identify cues associated with imminent violence, suicidality, and child abuse; (2) a procedure for responding to the cues was developed and implemented; and (3) cases with past severe violence or threats were routinely reviewed at weekly staff meetings. In general, the interviewers were instructed not to intervene directly with the male subjects or female partners, or act as counselors. That was not their job or expertise. As part of our obligation to maintain confidentiality, the interviewers were also not to act on criminal behavior or alcohol use that happened in the past, except for child abuse.

The interviewers were trained to identify imminent danger through articles, case studies, and discussion. First, the interviewers studied three articles regarding the assessment of danger in clinical and research settings (Monahan et al., 1993; Saunders, 1995; Sonkin, 1987). Second, they were instructed in a list of criteria derived from these articles. With the help of the battered women's advocates serving as consultants, we operationalized these criteria into specific cues. Third, the interviewers analyzed a series of case studies to practice applying the criteria. Fourth, the project coordinator debriefed the interviewers in our weekly meeting about potentially dangerous cases in order to keep the assistants alert to subtle cues.

Cues and Probes. Several of the questions of the follow-up interviews asked about recent and current emotional states, abuse and threats, and child discipline and abuse. In the course of these questions, imminent suicide, violence, or child abuse was occasionally disclosed or implied. Our interviewers were to respond to a series of "cues," or wording suggesting a problem, with probes and a series of contingent actions. There are, of course, limits to this sort of procedure. Cues can be missed or withheld, probes can solicit denial or rebuff, and predictions can be false or imposing. The main objective, however, is not to assess risk as a counselor, but to respond to obvious crises disclosed in the course of research.

More specifically, the interviewers were to respond to the following kind of cues: (1) suicide thoughts in the form of despair and hopelessness, problems sleeping or eating, plans or fantasies about taking one's life; (2) imminent violence in the form of threats or plans of attack, extreme blame or projection (e.g., "she is really asking for it this time"), feelings of rage or "losing control"; and (3) child abuse in the form of harsh physical discipline, "red marks" on or injury to a child's body, or reports of a child's fear, sleeplessness, or extreme withdrawal. When interviewers identify cues for these behaviors, they are to probe for more specific information about severity, duration, intent, and service contact.

CUES AND PROBES FOR POTENTIAL SUICIDE, VIOLENCE, OR CHILD ABUSE

Cues (examples)
- suicide:
    "I don't care any more,"
    "I'm feeling really down,"
    "I'm not eating or sleeping"

- violence:
    "I'm going to get her,"
    "she's asking for it,"
    "I'm nearing my limit"

- child abuse:
    discipline with spanking,
    "red marks on body"
    "child is frightened"

Probes
- How *long* has this been happening? How *often* has it happened?
- What *thoughts*, plans, threats or intents are there to do it again?
- What *access* is there to the victim, weapons, and drugs or alcohol?
- What is the *likelihood* that it will happen again?
- What have you or others done in *response* to this behavior?
- What persons, agencies, or services have you *told* about it?

The interviewers responded immediately to ongoing crises and potential emergencies, and reported other cases to the project coordinator to determine the appropriate response. Our interviewers have only occasionally identified an ongoing or "imminent crisis," that is, suicide, violence, or child abuse which is highly likely to occur within the next 24 hours. Two examples emerged in our study. At the time of an interview, a woman's partner had just left the house angry and was threatening to come back later to "get her." In another case, a male subject had been drinking heavily and talked of ending his own life. If there is such an "emergency," the interviewers asked the interviewee to contact the appropriate service agency or police and gave her or him the phone numbers to do so. The research assistant is to report the details of the case promptly to the project coordinator, and the project coordinator reviews the case with the investigators and clinical consultants to determine further actions or intervention. The research assistant calls back the subject to see if he or she has contacted the referral and resolved the crisis, and offers any additional advice or directions developed from the project coordinator's consultations.

Nearly all of the instances of potential suicide, violence, or child abuse were not "emergencies" in the immediate sense described above. In these cases, the interviewers collected as much detail as they could on the intent, duration, frequency, and future plans regarding the behavior. They also helped the subject identify responses, assistance, or intervention acceptable to the subject. The interviewers then reported the information to the project coordinator for further consultation. One of four responses was selected depending on the severity, likelihood, and imminence of the violence or suicidality and the actions already taken by the subject being interviewed. The possible responses were: (1) the interviewer calls back and suggests the subject contact a batterer program and/or women's center staff for further assistance, (2) the interviewer asks the subject to contact an appropriate agency or social service and gives the referral phone numbers to do so, (3) the interviewer directly contacts and warns an identified intended victim, or (4) the interviewer contacts police, child protective services, psychiatric, or hospital staff directly. (The local battered women's and batterers' programs had been consulted about our evaluation and asked for permission to refer women in need of help.)

Subjects who were asked to contact a program for assistance were called again within a day to ensure that they complied and that the contact was sufficient. We asked when they called the program or service and the name of the contacted person, in order to verify that action had been taken. If a subject was still reluctant to call or contact a referral source, the interviewers asked if she or he could arrange to have program staff call the woman or man. The specific cues, details of the problem, recommended actions, and actions taken were described in a short narrative report kept in the interviewed person's file, and the case was reviewed in a weekly staff meeting.

In our weekly staff meetings, the principal investigator and project coordinator convened with the interviewers. Besides reviewing tracking procedures and problems, the interviewers presented cases with any human subject issues. The cases were discussed for two reasons. One reason was to raise other actions or interpretations that were not previously considered. Another reason was to help sensitize and alert staff to problem cases and how to respond to them.

INTERVIEWER RESPONSE TO POTENTIAL SUICIDE, VIOLENCE, AND CHILD ABUSE

Emergency*
1) make *immediate referral* to appropriate agencies or services

2) *report behavior* and action to project director

3) *call back* subject within 3 hours to verify subject's action

4) *write report* listing behavior, response, and action for files

5) review case at weekly *staff meeting*

* "Emergency" is defined as imminent (i.e., within next 24 hours) or ongoing behavior

Imminent Risk**
1) ask subject to *contact a batterer program or women's center* for assistance and further referral***

2) ask subject to *contact appropriate service* and give referral number to do so***

3) *directly contact* and warn an identified or intended *victim*

4) *directly contact police*, child protective services, psychiatric or hospital staff.

** Response depends on the severity, likelihood, and imminence determined by project coordinator and clinical consultants

*** *Call back* subject within 24 hours to verify contact:
   ask when subject called referral and whom subject contacted
   if no contact made, ask if interviewer can have program or agency call the subject.

Child Abuse. The most difficult problem to address was that of potential child abuse. The informed consent statement in our study indicated that we may have to report child abuse to child protection services. This possibility raises fear in some battered women of having their children removed from them, or bringing interventions that might further antagonize their battering partner. It may contribute, moreover, to disclosure of potential child abuse in less than 5% of the cases in our study. Our response to any cues of child abuse was to encourage the women to contact the local battered women's services for advice and counsel. The women's centers at our research sites had a child specialist on staff with training in mandatory reporting laws and familiarity with local children services. The battered women's services also had programming for children and classes in parenting that could be used as well.

There remains some debate, however, over how best to handle child abuse cases reported by battered women (Schechter & Edleson, 1994). Our referral to battered women's services could be construed as deferring our responsibility to report and deal with a difficult case. A women's center, furthermore, may not have the expertise to assess and address child abuse, or it may experience a conflict between a battered woman's concerns and the child's interest. Additionally, there are some battered women's advocates who question the mandatory reporting for child abuse when there are not appropriate, sufficient, or effective services for abused children of battered women.

Batterer Threats. The most difficult issue with the male subjects was their reporting anger toward their female partners and expressing intentions of "getting her." The interviewers obtained details on how long a man felt this way, what plans or actions he has taken in this regard, how much he currently used drugs and alcohol, and what access the man had to the victim and weapons. The interviewers then mentioned some of the consequences and alternatives to his feelings and intents. They encouraged the man to contact the batterer program to discuss his feelings and intents further. This would ultimately be in his best interest. If the man refused or did not comply, the interviewers explained that they were required to report threats of violence to the police or the potential victim. Then we initiated some intervention. We either had batterer program staff attempt to contact the man, or warned police and the victim directly. We did not encounter any cases where intervention of this latter sort was needed.

An unanticipated issue of violence did arise with the men. Three women reported partner violence or depression that they thought should be reported to the batterer program. For instance, one man had completed the batterer program and was training to be an assistant group leader, but he was still very abusive toward his female partner. The woman felt the abuse would escalate if she reported it to the program directly. She feared that if she told the program about his behavior, he would be dismissed from the training and would blame the dismissal on her. Our resolution was to discuss the issue of abusive trainees in general with the program director and to urge the program to further examine the behavior of all the trainees. As a result, the man's abusive behavior was exposed, he was dismissed from the training, and re-enrolled as a program participant. The woman contacted a battered women's center for help in separating from the man.

Identified Risks. The number of women cases with identified risks was relatively low overall. We completed nearly 4,000 interviews with 654 women during the 15-month follow-up, and only 25 cases warranted review under the above criteria. About 15 of the cases had information that suggested possible child abuse, four cases involved severe depression and suicide ideation, and six cases involved severe, escalating violence. All but five of the potential child abuse cases were resolved with further information. The women in these cases were urged to contact the battered women's services in their area and all of them complied. All the other types of cases contacted battered women's services in order to address the identified risks, except for two cases in which a women's center was contacted and asked to intervene. In one of those cases, the woman was in the midst of severe depression and threatening to end her life. In the other case, the woman was experiencing severe, escalating violence and was too discouraged to take action. In both cases, the women were told that a program was being contacted on her behalf and would attempt to reach her. There were no cases that required our direct contact with a potential victim, police, or child protection services. In general, women felt safe; nearly three-fourths of the interviewed women indicated that they felt "very safe" during the previous follow-up period, and only 3% indicated they felt in danger (i.e., "not safe at all").

One concern about addressing risk is that it may contaminate the research. Also, the interview itself could become an intervention and effect the program outcome. Thirty-nine percent (39%) of the women did indicate that the interviews had changed their response to abuse or views of abuse. However, only 13% of our interviewed sample said that the interviews contributed to their "getting additional assistance or help," and 2% said that the interviews helped them "resolve to get out of the relationship." Approximately half (56%) of the women who did get additional services received some counseling and about a third (37%) simply obtained advice or information. Only a few (n = 6) sought legal action. The vast majority of the women explained that the interview effect was to help them "realize the extent of the abuse" or "clarify their feelings about the abuse," and those who did obtain services did so primarily in response to continuing abuse.

INTRUSIVE TRACKING

Tracking Needs. One additional area of human subject concern arises around the aggressive tracking procedures involved in program evaluation. Achieving a respectable response rate of approximately 70% requires repeated waves of interviewing (e.g., every three months). The repeated interviews decrease recall time and increase disclosure, as well as help keep contact with a very transient population (Mulvey & Lidz, 1993). These follow-up interviews, conducted by phone in our evaluation, required numerous and persistent calls in order to track the batterers and their female partners. This is especially the case with the partners of batterer program participants, because many are separated and living temporarily with relatives or friends, living by themselves, or in hiding. Moreover, the dramatic increase of answering machines, caller identification, beepers, cell phones, and unlisted numbers makes it more difficult to reach potential interviewees in general. (Tracking results and response rates are discussed in Gondolf, 1997, in press.)

Ethical Problems of Tracking. The ethical problem is how to persistently call a variety of phone numbers and designated contacts (i.e., neighbors, relatives, employers, etc.) without violating a person's right to privacy, without replicating the stalking of many batterers, and without endangering a woman (e.g., her battering partner intercepts the phone messages). The problem escalates considerably when professional locators are used to track missing subjects, as is customary in most survey follow-up research. Locators generally use computerized databases (e.g., automobile license information, telephone records, charge card invoices, credit records, etc.) to find the current address and phone number of previously unreachable subjects. They also may contact residents living near the previous address of the subjects and ask those residents where the subject has gone. The "locating" usually involves calling potential phone numbers of the subjects to confirm that the correct person has been found. All these procedures are typically done without the permission or knowledge of the subject. For many battered women, this tracking and locating may not only be intrusive, but also "scary." Having someone pursue them with such thoroughness may recreate the sense of being stalked by their batterer. A woman may have no way of knowing whether an interviewer or locator is trying to reach her rather than her abusive partner.

The increased concern over intrusive phone practices in general is evident in the recently developed workshops for phone privacy. State coalitions of battered women's services have begun training advocates about phone privacy issues and techniques. The workshops inform advocates how to teach battered women to protect themselves against increasing phone intrusions and tracking technology. The main objective of the workshops is to help protect battered women against abuse and pursuit from battering partners whom they have left. However, the training also helps to block researchers who may be tracking women for follow-up interviews.

Tracking Protocol. There are a few steps that can alleviate the human subject issues associated with tracking and locating efforts. Women need to be informed about the tracking and locating when recruited for research and reminded at each wave of interviewing. They should be asked to designate contact persons who are acceptable to them, and given a toll-free number to call if they want to cancel access to these persons or the follow-up in general. As mentioned previously, a phoning protocol needs to limit the number of tracking calls and their scope (i.e., who they are made to). After two weeks of no response from a maximum of five messages to any one person, we moved the case forward to the next interview period. After two consecutive interview periods with no response, we dropped the case. (We have recovered over 5% of the sample by attempting to call a previously unreachable subject at a subsequent follow-up wave.) Finally, we asked permission at each interview to send reminders of future interviews (i.e., letters when we could not reach them by phone), the best address for mailing interview payments, and an up-date on persons who might best know how to reach the woman in the future. Women who felt that their partner might intercept mailings or future calls to their home were asked for an address where they could be contacted without any such threat (e.g., friends, relatives, or work address).

Locating Protocol. At the 30-month interview of our extended fol-low-up, we reverted to locator procedures for unreachable cases. This was done because of the 15-month lapse from the end of the initial 15-month follow-up evaluation to the 30-month follow-up. It was more difficult to contact subjects without the periodic three-month interviews used throughout the 15-month interviews. We first sent a sample of 50 unreachable cases to a professional locator to explore the effectiveness of its database search. (Researchers should obtain and review the confidentiality policy of any locators employed to find subjects, and inform them of domestic violence issues and tracking protocols.) The number of women who were relocated in this way was fairly low; the locator found information for only two thirds of the eligible cases, but most of this information was either incomplete or dated. Consequently, we were able to reach only about 10% of these "located" subjects. We have since begun to conduct the locator proce-dures ourselves with a better "location rate" than the professional locators. Our locating efforts have also enabled us to cross reference information with our own records and thus eliminate addresses and phone numbers that are outdated. Our interviewers, with the training and sensitivity discussed above, are the ones making the decisions about which subjects to pursue and to what extent.

The following steps, moreover, were taken to avoid frightening or offending subjects. We reviewed previously unreachable cases for any prior evidence of "danger" in terms of reported threats, stalking, re-assaults, severe violence, re-arrests or drunkenness, and did not track such cases. This information by itself indicates outcome "fail-ures," as well as signaled cases where intensified tracking could be detrimental. Women who had previously refused to participate in the research also were not pursued. In addition, we restricted the locating attempts to only public database information and contacted persons designated by the women in advance.

CONCLUSION

Human Subject Procedures. We have reviewed the major human subject issues that face batterer program evaluation and illustrated some possible ways to address them. The conventional issues of informed consent, minimal risks, and privacy rights are increased in batterer program evaluations. These evaluations tend to have resistant and suspicious male subjects, use female victims to help verify outcomes, and track respondents who are relatively transient and cautious. Obtaining informed consent from resistant or suspicious batterers may require some tacit coercion in linking the evaluation with program intake and providing payment for interviews. Confidentiality, privacy, and voluntary participation, however, need to be weighed throughout subject recruitment and follow-up.

Informed consent from the batterers' partners is particularly difficult when these women are recruited by phone, and are not necessarily voluntary recipients of program services themselves (as battered women in an evaluation of a shelter might be). It seems especially important to develop rapport with the women in order to enlist and sustain their participation in the evaluation. Contacting and obtaining the consent of new partners of the batterers required additional consideration. We asked the men to identify new partners, asked their permission to contact them, and suggested the men brief the women on the reasons for the evaluation.

There are two separate areas of risks that emerged in our multi-site evaluation of batterer programs. One, the risks associated with interviewing itself can at least be reduced with an interview structure that allows subjects to convey their experience, a protocol that ensures the women's privacy during an interview, and debriefing subjects at the end of each interview. Two, risks that arise independent of the interviews (e.g., imminent violence, suicidality, and child abuse) require specialized training to identify these risks, procedure to respond to cases at risk, and regular case reviews to improve response and maintain alertness to risks.

We identified only a few cases where threat or harm was caused by the interviews themselves, but several women reported potential child abuse, imminent danger, or suicide tendencies. Only a few of these possible risks warranted direct intervention. The relatively low level of risk might be a result of the human subject procedures employed in our multi-site evaluation, a fact of batterer program follow-ups in general, or an artifact of the interview feedback and risk cues we employed. At least, the results suggest that follow-up with our human subject procedures raises only minimal risks, and increases support and referral for the majority of women subjects. We believe that the procedures are useful in another important way. They appear to contribute to the high response rate of approximately 70%. The sense of safety, concern, and respect that human subject procedures convey helped make our subjects more cooperative and informative.

Finally, aggressive tracking impinges on privacy and may be threatening to battered women. Researchers might take the following precautions in this regard: (1) have women indicate acceptable contact persons, times, and procedures, (2) limit the number of pursuing calls and the duration of repeated calling, (3) identify and drop cases at risk, and (4) selectively use and monitor locator services. The contribution of aggressive tracking to response rates and sample reliability, however, warrants further examination, and the impact of such tracking on subjects remains unclear.

Collaboration. The human subject procedures recommended here require a close collaboration with battered women's advocates and services, as well as with batterer counselors and programs. The collaboration is needed to develop and refine protocol that deals with subject recruitment and risks associated with the evaluation. Collaboration is also needed in assessing and responding to "high-risk" cases. There needs to be an agreement and procedure with both battered women's services and batterer programs for the referral of men or women in need of intervention, protection, or care. Establishing this kind of collaboration is not necessarily an automatic or easy task; a certain level of trust, familiarity, and cooperation is often a prerequisite. Moreover, no clear map or plan for collaboration exists even though it has become a highly touted necessity in evaluation research. We have attempted to provide an overview of some of the issues, objectives, and models of collaboration in a separate report (Gondolf, Yllo, & Campbell, 1997).

Our discussion of human subject issues also raises cautions about delegating the follow-up interviews to independent survey offices or companies. Our experience suggests the importance of investigators, project coordinators, and program staff actively monitoring cases and maintaining sensitivity to the human subject issues accentuated in batterer program evaluations. Interviewers with training in domestic violence, clinical support, and ongoing supervision are essential to implementing many of the procedures indicated here. We have found, furthermore, that having the same female interviewers call the same female subjects in subsequent follow-up interviews contributes to rapport, disclosure, and cooperation.

We have found that the information compiled here has been helpful in easing IRB resistance and in developing IRB expectations for domestic violence research. It has also helped in establishing support and cooperation from battered women's services and batterer programs. We have presented the IRBs and programs involved with our study with (1) the precedent from other fields studying interpersonal violence (e.g., violent psychiatric patients, violent prisoners), (2) some documentation on the extent and nature of risks experienced by victims in other follow-up studies or pilot studies, and (3) a specific set of procedures to anticipate and address risks. In our experience this sort of information helped shift discussions from an absolutist position to a more situational consideration–that is, from categorical objections to a realistic assessment of the potential risks and means to offset them. While victim safety is definitely an issue, we have not been able to find much evidence that cautious interviewing has contributed to abuse or violence of the interviewees and most of the interviewees were very positive about their interview experience.

The recommendations we pose from our experience are, admittedly, not sufficient in themselves. Ultimately, a protocol for recruiting, protecting, and tracking subjects in violent relationships needs to be developed with the guidance of battered women's advocates and support from agencies funding domestic violence research. This sort of protocol is especially needed given the call for longitudinal follow-ups that increase the reliability of self-reports and provide a more dynamic view of batterer and victim behaviors.

REFERENCES

Appelbaum, P., Lidz, C., & Meisel, A. (1987). *Informed consent: Legal theory and clinical practice.* New York: Oxford University Press.

Gondolf, E. (in press). Reassault at 30-months after batterer program intake. *International Journal of Offender Therapy and Comparative Criminology.*

Gondolf, E. (1990). *Psychiatric response to family violence: Identifying and confronting neglected danger.* Lexington, MA: Lexington Books.

Gondolf, E. (1997). Patterns of reassault in batterer programs. *Violence and Victims, 12*, 373-387.

Gondolf, E. (1998). *Assessing women battering in mental health services.* Thousand Oaks, CA: Sage.

Gondolf, E. (1999). A comparison of reassault rates in four batterer programs: Do court referral, program length and services matter? *Journal of Interpersonal Violence, 14*, 41-61.

Gondolf, E., Yllo, K., & Campbell, J. (1997). Collaboration between researchers and advocates. In G. K. Kaufman & J. Jasinski (Eds.), *Out of the darkness: Contemporary research perspectives on family violence* (pp. 255-261). Thousand Oaks, CA; Sage.

Hansson, M. (1998). Balancing the quality of consent. *Journal of Medical Ethics, 24*, 182-188.

Lidz, C. (1984). *Informed consent: A study of decision-making in psychiatry.* New York: Guilford Press.

Monahan, J., Appelbaum, P., Mulvey, E., Robbins, P., & Lidz, C. (1993). Ethical and legal duties in conducting research on violence: Lessons from the MacArthur Risk Assessment Study. *Violence and Victims, 8*, 387-396.

Mulvey, E. P., & Lidz, C. W. (1993). Measuring patient violence in dangerousness research. *Law and Human Behavior, 17*, 277-278.

Rumptz, M., Sullivan, C., Davidson, W., & Basta, J. (1991). An ecological approach to tracking battered women over time. *Violence and Victims, 6*, 237-244.

Saunders, D. (1995). Prediction of wife assault. In J. Campbell (Ed.), *Assessing the risk of dangerousness: Potential for further violence of sexual offenders, batterers, and child abusers* (pp. 68-95). Thousand Oaks, CA: Sage.

Schechter, S., & Edleson, J. (1994). *In the best interest of women and children: A call for collaboration between child welfare and domestic violence constituencies.* Report to the Ford Foundation, New York City, NY.

Sonkin, D. J. (1987). The assessment of court-mandated male batterers. In D. J. Sonkin (Ed.), *Domestic violence on trial* (pp. 174-196). New York: Springer.

U.S. Department of Health and Human Services (1991). Protection of human subjects. *Code of Federal Regulations (45 CFR 46).*

Yllo, K. (1988). Political and methodological debates in wife abuse research. In K. Yllo & M. Bograd (Eds.), *Feminist perspectives on wife abuse* (pp. 28-50). Thousand Oaks, CA: Sage.

Index

Aboriginal (Canadian Native) children
  adoption by non-aboriginal parents,
    173
  child welfare services for, 175
  ethno-cultural-based placements of,
    172,185
Abuse Dimensions Inventory, 157
Abuse histories, confidentiality and
    privacy of, 46
Academic status, of researchers,
    251-253
Action social research
  cyclic process of, 244-245
  goal of, 244,245
  models of, 245-249
Adjustment disorders, in children of
    abused women, 197
Administrators
  lack of involvement in evaluation
    research, 40
  outcome assessment use by, 178,
    179-180
  salaries of, 253
Adolescents
  criminal behavior of, 183
  dating violence by
    patterns of, 218
    predictors of, 219-220
    prevalence of, 219
  dating violence prevention
    programs for, 217-238
    assessment strategies in,
      223-224
    follow-up in, 225
    multiple informants in,
      224-225,234
    operational definitions in,
      220-222
    pre-post intervention design of,
      225

randomized design of, 225
recruitment of participants for,
  222-223
videotaping use in, 223,232
as physical violence victims, 144
pregnancy prevention programs for,
  34
psychotherapy for, 152-153
suicide by, 74-76
Adoption
  as child welfare indicator, 184
  ethno-cultural factors in, 173,185
Adoption and Safe Families Act,
  171-172,173
Adoption Assistance and Child
  Welfare Act, 13
Advocacy
  for family violence interventions,
    30
  for protection of women and
    children, 30
  in social problem research, 2
  for victims of partner violence,
    203,208,241
AFDC (Aid to Families with
  Dependent Children), 126
African-American children
  adoptive placement of, 173
  out-of-home placement of, 8
African-American men, participation
  in batterer treatment
  programs, 255-256
African-American women, physicians'
  behavior toward, 257
Aggression
  by abused children, 144, 155
  by children of battered women,
    violence prevention
    interventions for, 202,203,
    207-208

*For Product Safety Concerns and Information please contact
our EU representative GPSR@taylorandfrancis.com Taylor & Francis
Verlag GmbH, Kaufingerstraße 24, 80331 München, Germany*

T - #0032 - 090625 - C0 - 212/152/18 - PB - 9780789011855 - Gloss Lamination